Philosophy of Min~ ~ ~ ~ition

For Bella and Caroline

Philosophy of Mind and Cognition

*David Braddon-Mitchell and
Frank Jackson*

Blackwell
Publishing

350 Main Street, Malden, MA 02148-5020, USA
108 Cowley Road, Oxford OX4 1JF, UK
550 Swanston Street, Carlton, Victoria 3053, Australia

The right of David Braddon-Mitchell and Frank Jackson to be identified as the Authors of this Work has been asserted in accordance with the UK Copyright, Designs, and Patents Act 1988.

First published 1996 by Blackwell Publishing Ltd
Reprinted 1997, 1998, 1999, 2000, 2001, 2002, 2003, 2004

Library of Congress Cataloging-in-Publication Data

Braddon-Mitchell, David
  The philosophy of mind and cognition / David Braddon-Mitchell and Frank Jackson.
     p. cm.
  Includes bibliographical references and index.
  ISBN 0–631–19167–4 (hardback)—ISBN 0–631–19168–2 (paperback)
  1. Philosophy of mind. I. Jackson, Frank. II. Title.
  BD418.3B72   1996   95–53332
  128'.2—dc20   CIP

A catalogue record for this title is available from the British Library.

Set in 10 on 12 pt Imprint
by Graphicraft Typesetters Ltd, Hong Kong
Printed and bound in the United Kingdom
by TJ International Ltd, Padstow, Cornwall

For further information on
Blackwell Publishing, visit our website:
http://www.blackwellpublishing.com

Contents

Preface

We have two aims in this book. The first is to provide a good coverage of issues in the philosophy of mind for those who are approaching the subject for the first, or near to the first, time – though not at the cost of shirking hard questions. The second, and more ambitious, aim is to change a few minds among those who have been thinking about philosophy of mind for almost as long as they can recall.

We think these aims are complementary. Combining them avoids the twin pitfalls that can beset philosophy books that aim for a general coverage of an area. The scrupulously even-handed book which is full of extensive quotation from the literature – whose primary concern is to explain the views of various authors – is an admirable project, but it is not ours. For it can be hard to extract a coherent picture of the intellectual terrain from such a book. No matter what general perspective the authors may take, much of the literature will have to be racked to fit the picture. The other pitfall is associated with books that give the appearance of exegetical purity, even though the organization and perspective implicitly colour everything that is said. Better, we thought, to discuss a broad range of positions in our own words and from our own perspective, while being explicit about where we stand on the issues. Then readers can judge for themselves, engage with our arguments, and have a reference point from which to assess competing views.

So where do we stand? In different places on different issues, of course. But one unifying theme emerges clearly. We think that, for all its difficulties, a certain kind of functionalism is the best candidate for a philosophical theory of the mind. That kind of functionalism is common-sense functionalism, or analytical functionalism. It is the view, explained and defended in chapter 3, which is realist in holding that mental states are internal states of beings, which are part of a causal network of internal states. Certain aspects of the particular role of a state in the network, and of its role in producing the behaviour we associate with having a mind, determine the kind of mental state it is. The aspects that matter are an implicit or explicit part of common sense about the mind.

This is a view that lies between two popular current directions in the philosophy of mind. Its realism distances it from instrumentalist or interpretationist views that do not think of mental states as internal, causally efficacious states. However, unlike many realists in the philosophy of mind influenced by cognitive science, we do not think that the details of the internal workings – a fascinating and important topic in cognitive science – tell us about the *essence* of the mental. We think that beings with very different cognitive architectures might still have mental states of the same general kind as ours.

This perspective has an important consequence for the content of the book. You will not find any diagrams of connectionist networks or descriptions of dynamical systems, or even descriptions of the architecture of classical artificial intelligence (AI) systems in it. In our view, they are of concern only at the level of implementation, and, important as they are, are best treated separately. We argue for this view in chapter 5, and consider the many different ways in which you might come (mistakenly in our view) to regard certain facts about implementation as revealing the essence of the mind.

Although we aim for a reasonably comprehensive coverage – we try to say something helpful about all the major topics in the current debate and to fill in the needed background – there are few quotations, and relatively few mentions of individual authors. Sometimes it is best, for explicatory reasons, to discuss the strongest and clearest version of some position before criticizing it, and what we take to be the strongest and clearest version is not always a published one: so, rather than laboriously explain how the version we address varies from those actually found in the literature, we typically present our own version in our own words. This also saves the reader from having to adjust continually from one writing style to another, and enables us to impose some uniformity in technical terminology. Also, very often (and very properly), published views are hedged with qualifications, and presented in a style suited to fellow professionals. In a book with the present aims, we thought it best to address the core, central claims and avoid as much as possible the more recondite qualifications.

For these reasons, references to the literature are rarely made in the text. At the end of each chapter there is a section of annotated reading. The relevant references can be found there, along with comments about the relationship between what we say in the chapter and what the authors cited say. Readers will then be in a position to judge for themselves if we have been arguing against straw philosophers. We also trust that this approach of ours will enable those who are new to the philosophy of mind to make best use of the excellent collections of articles that are available. Approached cold, as they often are in higher-level courses in the philosophy of mind, they can be daunting. Indeed, what first prompted us to plan this book were requests by even the best of our students for help in getting the most out of these collections. There is a consolidated bibliography with publication details at the end of the book.

The book is in four parts. The first builds to a discussion of common-sense functionalism (chapter 3) via chapters criticizing dualism and behaviourism. We include in this part a detailed discussion of the relationship between various particular views of the mind and a general physicalism or materialism about the mind. Physicalism is current orthodoxy, and though we are sympathetic to it, it seems to us that explicating what exactly it comes to and why it is plausible is more important and more difficult than is often realized. Also in this part we include a discussion of supervenience and the possible worlds methodology.

The next part deals with rivals and objections to common-sense functionalism, and has six chapters. Some of the most important rivals are inspired by recent discussions of reference – of how terms pick out things in the world. Chapter 4 gives the background in the philosophy of language needed to come to grips with these rivals. Then, in chapter 5, we give details of the rivals and defend common-sense functionalism. A discussion of the identity theory of mind follows in chapter 6. The type–type version of this theory is generally thought of as a precursor to functionalism which was displaced by it. We argue, however, that there is a type–type identity theory which is not only consistent with, but is in fact also strongly supported by, common-sense functionalism. This theory is important in solving problems we address later in the book. The two chapters that follow are concerned with some well-known and important objections to common-sense functionalism. This part of the book finishes with a chapter concerned with the anti-realist rivals to it: namely, instrumentalism and interpretationism.

The third part deals with the question of mental representation and content. We begin with a consideration of two general approaches to representation: the language of thought or internal sentence approach, and the map-system theory. We argue that it is an empirical issue to be settled by future neuroscience which of these is the best description of the mechanics of human representation; what we know as of now is neutral on the choice between them. We expound the internal sentence approach in some detail, partly because it is so influential, but also because an understanding of it is required when we go on to consider internal sentence-based theories of content. In chapter 11 we address directly the issue of content, comparing the distinctive approaches of the internal sentence and the map-system theories. We spend a little time on defending the map-system approach against certain criticisms that have been very influential and on advertising its strengths. We also discuss in some detail theories of content set in the internal sentence framework, including informational, bio-functional and teleological theories.

The final chapter in this third part, chapter 12, concerns the debate over broad and narrow content. We argue that there is room for both kinds of content but take a view of broad content which, we should warn the reader, will be found too deflationary by many.

The last part – the shortest – is concerned with the place of common-sense psychology in science and in philosophy. Chapter 13 discusses eliminativism about the propositional attitudes – the view that certain mental states are explanatory posits that have turned out not to exist – and concludes (unsurprisingly, since we have written so much by then about beliefs and desires!) that they and their ilk indeed exist. The final chapter concerns the distinctive explanatory role they have – in short, the point of psychological explanations.

Readers will notice that some headings have asterisks appended to them. This indicates that the material that follows, up to the next heading without an asterisk, is rather more demanding, and is not essential for what follows. One other point concerning organization: the first instance of most technical or semi-technical terms (and sometimes the first instance in a section that might well be read out of sequence) is set in bold face type. These terms are explained in a glossary at the end of the book.

Many people have contributed to this project. Students in philosophy of psychology courses at the Australian National University have seen the material in various forms, and it is much the better for their feedback. Friends and colleagues who have discussed the issues with us or commented on parts of the manuscript include Michael Devitt, Brian Garrett, Alan Hajek, Richard Holton, Lloyd Humberstone, Peter Menzies, Karen Neander, John O'Leary-Hawthorne, Graham Oppy, Philip Pettit, Huw Price and Kim Sterelny. We have also benefited from the comments of the publisher's readers. Finally, we owe special debts to David Lewis and Denis Robinson.

Enough of preliminaries. We hope you will enjoy reading the book as much as we enjoyed writing it.

Part I

From Dualism to Common-sense Functionalism

1

The Flight from Dualism

The issue between dualism and materialism

It is natural to distinguish what we might call the material, physical or bodily nature of a person from the mental, psychological or sentient nature of a person. On the material or physical side are such features as how much a person weighs, how many hairs they have on their head, their genetic make-up, how their brain operates, and generally those facts about a person studied in the physical and biological sciences. On the mental or psychological side are such features as how a person is feeling (hot, cold, dizzy), what they are thinking, what they are seeing, and how intelligent they are. These are rough lists, but they serve to pose in a preliminary way the fundamental issue between **dualism** and **materialism**. According to dualists the ingredients we need in order to understand and account for the items on the mental list are different in kind from those we need in order to understand and account for the items on the physical list. According to materialists the ingredients are essentially the same, and the basic ones are those we need in order to account for the material or physical side of our natures. The mental side of us is an enormously complex construction and arrangement of the very same ingredients that make up our material natures. The classical Greek philosopher Democritus famously said that there exist just atoms and the void. He did not mean by this to deny the manifest diversity of the world around us: trees are different from apples or the sun. He meant to express the idea that the diversity is to be explained in terms of a limited number of basic ingredients differently arranged. Fundamental physics tells modern materialists that the really basic ingredients cannot be atoms, but modern materialists agree with Democritus that everything, the mental included, is fully explicable

Preliminary characterization of the difference between dualism and materialism

in terms of whatever it is that we need in order to understand material nature.

Idealism   An inverse of materialism is **idealism**. Idealists agree with materialists, and against dualists, that material nature and mental nature should ultimately be understood in the same terms. But instead of seeking to understand mental nature in terms of material nature, they seek to understand material nature in terms of mental nature. Materialists and idealists are alike in being monists – both material and mental nature should ultimately be understood in the same terms – but differ over where to find the ultimate ingredients. Idealism is a historically important doctrine, but has very few adherents today, and we will not be concerned with it further.

Materialism is orthodoxy nowadays. Indeed, dualism is almost as unpopular as idealism. To many, dualism is as discredited as vitalism. According to vitalism, the chemistry of the animate is different in fundamental nature from that of the inanimate; the matter in living organisms contains a vital force as an essential extra ingredient different in kind from anything found in inanimate nature. This doctrine did not survive the rise of modern chemistry towards the end of the eighteenth century. The unity of chemistry is now a commonplace of modern science. Inanimate ingredients rightly combined can make something animate. In the same way, runs the anti-dualist orthodoxy, inanimate ingredients rightly combined can make something sentient. The purpose of this chapter is to explain why dualism is so unpopular, but first we need to note a distinction among dualisms.

Two kinds of dualism

Substance
dualism and
attribute
dualism   The idea that there is a fundamental difference in kind between the mental and the material can be spelled out in two broadly different ways. One way leaves the material world as such unaffected. The special nature of the mental is entirely a matter of the nature of a special substance. Our bodies themselves are fully described by the physical sciences. What is missing from the material story about us is mention of the nature of something distinct from our bodies, a special substance whose nature determines our mental nature. If you are in pain or are thinking about tigers, that is where your pain or your thinking is, strictly speaking, taking place. The sensation and the thinking both inhere in the substance. This

style of dualism is called, for obvious reasons, **substance dualism**. Typically, substance dualism goes along with the view that the identity of a person over time is constituted by the identity over time of this substance, and in versions of the doctrine that countenance life after death, it is the survival of this substance, often called the 'soul', perhaps along with certain memory and psychological continuities, that constitutes the survival of the person.

The alternative approach holds that the physical story about our bodies is incomplete even as an account of those bodies. Along with the kinds of properties to be found instantiated in the material world in general, the bodies of persons and certain higher animals instantiate special properties. Given the central role that the brain and central nervous system are known to play in the possession of mental natures – things without brains neither think nor feel – these special properties are most likely attributes of certain states of the brain. This style of dualism is called, again for obvious reasons, **attribute dualism**.

Attribute dualism has a significant advantage over substance dualism. It avoids the awkward question of what happens to mental substance when we are not thinking. If the nature of your mental substance at any given moment is entirely a matter of what you are thinking or feeling at that moment, if all there is to say about the nature of your mental substance when you are, say, thinking about tigers is that it is in the thinking-about-tigers mode, then when you are not thinking or feeling or undergoing some sort of mental activity, it does not exist. Nothing can exist without having a nature. There is no difference between 'existing' without a nature and not existing at all. But then what happens to you when you are not thinking or feeling? Do you, strictly speaking, go out of existence during sleep each and every time you are not dreaming? The only alternatives seem to be to insist, implausibly, that you *never* stop thinking or feeling in some sense or other, or else that mental substance's nature at a time is not exhausted by the nature of the mental state the subject is undergoing at the time. But then we face the mystery of saying what the additional nature might be. For this reason and others, contemporary dualists are typically attribute dualists, and the presentation that follows of the major problem for dualism will be framed in terms of attribute dualism. It will, though, be obvious that the objection could be modified easily enough so as to apply to substance dualism.

A famous problem for substance dualism

The principal reason for the unpopularity of dualism is what we will call the causal problem.

The causal problem for dualism

There is a causal link between mental states and behaviour

Sometimes our desires are satisfied. Not as often as we would like, but sometimes. When they are satisfied, typically what happens is that the desire plays a significant causal role in the changes in the world around us that are required for the desire to be satisfied. You desire coffee. This desire leads your body to move in such a way that you end up with coffee inside you. Likewise, the intention to get married, the belief that it is opening time, itching, and so on and so forth, often cause changes in the way our bodies move that lead to signing marriage registers, being inside pubs, scratching, and so on. The question for dualists is what role is played in the causation of bodily movements by the special attributes which they hold to be distinctive of the mental.

Suppose they say that these attributes play no causal role, that the special, mental properties of their theory are epiphenomenal, so embracing a version of **epiphenomenalism**: the doctrine according to which mental properties (and substances if it comes to that) are causally impotent – they make no difference to what happens. They may themselves have causes, but they do not cause anything. If dualists are committed to epiphenomenalism, then they are committed to saying that the very feature that makes something a desire for coffee is causally irrelevant to movement towards coffee. Similarly, the very feature that makes something an intention to get married or an itch is irrelevant to signing marriage papers or scratching. This is hard to believe. Indeed, it seems more than a merely empirical matter that the itchiness of an itch tends to produce scratching. It seems part of our very concept of itchiness that it tends to produce scratching, in somewhat the way that it is part of our concept of a poison that it tends to make people sick when it is ingested. The same goes for the intention to get married. Although the intention to get married need not be followed by getting married – people change their minds – someone who thinks that it is an accidental fact that intending to get married often leads to getting married does not know what it is to intend to get married. It is of the essence of intending to get married that it tends to bring about getting married.

The evolutionary objection to epiphenomenalism

Moreover, it is hard to make good evolutionary sense of the special attributes the dualist believes in if they play no causal role. Mentality was not a feature of the world from the beginning. It evolved. We have mental lives; amoebae do not. But then Darwinian considerations suggest that having a mind should in some way or other contribute to survival. But having a mental life can hardly do that if it is constituted by the instantiation of attributes that do not in any way affect behaviour. Perhaps, it is sometimes suggested, the special attributes are epiphenomenal by-products of complex physical structures in the brain that evolved by virtue of being conducive to survival. The structures are fitness-enhancing by virtue of the behaviour they lead to, and the special properties are inevitable concomitants of them, but they themselves make no contribution to the process whereby states of the brain cause certain behaviours. This is a consistent position, but hardly an attractive one.

Finally, it is hard to see how we can be justified in believing in these epiphenomenal properties. Epiphenomenal properties can leave no traces in the world. They are not involved in the production of the claims we hear from others – or from ourselves, if it comes to that – to the effect that they, or we, are in pain, hoping for rain, or expecting Mary to come to the party. Further, it is hard to see how epiphenomenal properties could in strictness be remembered. To remember something is to have some kind of trace of it, caused however indirectly by the thing we are remembering. If you remember your holiday on the Great Barrier Reef, it is because things you saw and heard there had a causal impact on you, leaving the traces which are your memories by virtue of the way they sustain your beliefs about your holiday. Epiphenomenal properties, by definition, have no causal powers whatsoever, so they can leave no traces and so, runs the objection, cannot be remembered.

The epistemological objection to epiphenomenalism

For taxonomic completeness we will mention parallelism, another position that dualists have held. Perhaps, they thought, there are distinct mental and physical substances or attributes, but there is no causal path to or from the mental and the physical. Physical states have no causal impact on mental states, and mental states have no impact on physical states. On this account, if our beliefs are to be any guide to how the physical world is, or if our desires are ever to be satisfied, it would require a miracle, since there is no causal connection between beliefs and desires and the physical world. Parallelists have usually believed in just such a miracle: in the late seventeenth century Leibniz held that God had set up the world in such a way as to ensure that there was a pre-established harmony between its physical and mental sides. The idea was that physical and mental events moved on in parallel, never affecting

Parallelism

one another, but always harmonious enough that beliefs about the world are often enough true, and desires are often enough satisfied (though only in a strange sense, for our desires about how the physical world should be never contribute to the process that satisfies them!). There are, as far as we know, no parallelists left. So we will pass over this implausible view.

Dualist interactionism

Dualists, it then seems, must hold that the special, non-physical properties they believe in causally affect behaviour. They must embrace a dualist species of **interactionism** according to which the instantiation of the special properties they believe in is both caused by physical happenings – presumably especially physical happenings in the brain – and also causes behavioural responses – presumably by affecting what happens in the brain in a way that in turn causally influences behaviour. They must accept that there is a two-way causal interaction between the special mental properties they believe in and the physical world. But this means that they must deny that the physical world is **causally closed**. They must hold that although the movement of matter typically has a purely physical aetiology, the movement of the matter in a person's arms and legs, for instance, does not always have a purely physical aetiology.

The physical world is causally closed

This is hard to believe. The search for physical causes of the physical has been one of science's great success stories. Once we explained lightning in terms of Thor's anger; now we explain it in terms of electrical discharge across a potential difference. Once we explained the operation of pumps in terms of abhorrence of a vacuum; now we explain it in terms of air pressure. Once we explained the growth of plants in terms of vital spirit; now we explain it in terms of cell division. It is hard to believe that as we trace back through the causal antecedents of the arm bending that was caused by your desire for beer, we will find evidence of something from 'outside' affecting what happens. It is implausible that we will find that the rate of muscle contraction is just that little bit faster than can be accounted for in terms of the chemical changes in the muscle fibres, or that the signal from the brain that activates those changes cannot be accounted for in terms of prior states of the brain as described physically, or that certain causal interactions in the brain or the way certain stimuli from outside us affect the central nervous system are in principle beyond the reach of neuroscience to explain.

The point is not that we can, given the current state of scientific knowledge, explain in full in physical terms the causation of bodily movements. We cannot. The point is that we have gone far enough down the track to make it very likely that the job can be done in principle – particularly when we bear in mind the good track record of the search for physical causes of the physical – and if that is right there is no causal place for the special properties the dualist believes in.

The problem arose in a particularly acute form for Descartes. He was a substance dualist rather than an attribute dualist, and thought that the mind was something from outside the physical world that acted on the physical world by affecting what happened in the pineal gland, which in turn affected behaviour. The pineal gland was in his view the locus of the interaction between an other-worldly mind and the body. We now know that it could not possibly be the pineal gland (what happens there is simply not important enough to mental activity), but, what is more, and with the wisdom of hindsight, we can say that Descartes's mistake was a much more radical one. All the evidence suggests that there is nothing non-physical, of an attribute or substance kind that steps in and somehow regulates the physical world's goings-on.

The causal problem can now be stated very simply. Dualists must hold that the special properties they believe in affect behaviour. But to affect behaviour is to affect something physical, and the evidence in favour of the view that the physical world is causally closed rules out these special properties affecting behaviour.

Some responses for the dualist

It is sometimes suggested that the dualist can evade the causal problem by insisting on the distinction between behaviour (in the sense of bodily movement) and **action**. Your arm's rising is behaviour; your signalling a taxi is action. Mental properties are typically invoked to explain actions rather than behaviour. Mary's arm goes up: she is signalling a taxi. Why did she signal a taxi? Because she wanted to get to the airport. By contrast, we might explain her arm going up in terms of certain muscles being stimulated by various messages from the brain. Dualists sometimes argue that although there may be a physical explanation of the arm going up, the action – the signalling of the taxi – requires a non-physical explanation. However, although the precise relation between actions and their associated bodily movements (in the case of those actions that do involve bodily movement – mental

Action is different from behaviour

arithmetic is also something we do) is a controversial matter, it is hard to see how invoking the distinction is going to help with the fundamental, causal problem for dualism.

When you signal a taxi, you move your body in a way that you think will increase your chances of getting a taxi. This is why you, say, raise your arm or whistle, rather than hiding in a doorway. But then it is true that your thought caused one bodily movement, an arm going up or an expulsion of air through the lips, as the case may be, rather than the movements or lack of movements that lead to being unnoticed in a doorway. The crucial point is that however precisely we should distinguish between bodily movement and action, it is obvious that a great many actions essentially involve the body moving in one or another way, and if mental states causally explain the actions, they had better causally explain the movements also. Someone who cannot control the movement of their body cannot act in the world, so the dualist is still stuck with the problem of explaining mental causation of physical movements.

Over-determination   A second possible way out for the attribute dualist is to appeal to the possibility that mental properties and physical properties separately overdetermine causally the physical changes that typically lead to behaviour. **Overdetermination** is roughly the idea that there can be two or more distinct causes of an effect, each sufficient by itself for bringing about that effect. Suppose that Jane and Mary are both persuading Bill of the merits of socialism. He is persuaded, but we know that Jane and Mary are both such good arguers that either of them alone could have done the job. We say that Bill's being persuaded was overdetermined. Again, the death of someone who has major heart failure while falling from the top of a skyscraper will typically be overdetermined.

Perhaps, runs the response, we could allow that everything in the physical world has a sufficient physical cause, consistently with allowing that the special attributes the dualists believe in cause behaviour, by treating the situation as an instance of over-determination. The physical causes by themselves are enough for the behaviour, but this does not exclude a causal input from special mental properties; it simply means that we have a case of overdetermination.

Causal explanations tend to exclude each other   We should be suspicious of this response to the causal problem. Distinct explanations of the very same phenomenon typically *exclude* each other. When science came up with the explanation of the operation of pumps in terms of air pressure, this was taken to exclude the older explanation of their operation in terms of nature's abhorrence of a vacuum. Likewise, the explanation of lightning in terms of electrical discharges displaced the explanation in terms of Thor's thunderbolts, and the explanation of plant growth in terms of the chemistry of cell division displaced the explanation in terms of a vital spirit. In none of these cases did scientists say, 'How nice. We now have two explanations, where before we had only one.' However, in order to discuss the response in proper detail, it is necessary to distinguish various kinds of overdetermination. We will see that none is a comfort to the interactionist dualist.

X fires at Jones. Y fires at Jones. X's bullet is deflected by Y's bullet, and sails harmlessly by, but Y's bullet goes on to kill Jones. X's bullet would have killed Jones except for the deflection caused by Y's bullet. This is not a case of X's and Y's bullets together causing Jones's death, for X's bullet sailed harmlessly by. All that is true is that it *would* have done some killing but for the impact of Y's bullet. X's bullet is, we say, pre-empted by Y's bullet. This case of **pre-emptive overdetermination** is of no use to the dualist. If mental properties are pre-empted by physical properties, they do no causing. All that is true is that they might have done some causing. *Pre-emptive over-determination*

Suppose that, instead of clashing in mid-air, the two bullets enter Jones's body at different points but each ends up in his heart in such a way that, by itself, it would have killed Jones. The case still need not be a genuine case of overdetermination. Perhaps one bullet has already killed Jones by the time the other gets to his heart, in which case we again have a case of pre-emption. To get a case of overdetermination proper, the bullets will have to arrive pretty much together, and typically the case will not be one of full overdetermination, but rather of **partial overdetermination**. Perhaps each bullet by itself would kill Jones, but together they do the job more quickly. Then the death is overdetermined, but the timing of the death is not; or perhaps the time of death would be just the same, but the damage to the surrounding organs would have been different, in which case the death is overdetermined, but the damage to the surrounding organs is not; and so on and so forth. *Partial over-determination*

The point is that **full overdetermination** of everything that happens by distinct factors is very hard to come by. The very fact that there are two bullets means that some things – the paths to the heart, the magnitude of the entry hole or holes, the exit wound or whatever – would have been different had there been just one bullet. But it is full overdetermination that dualists need to believe in if they are to reconcile the causal efficacy of mental attributes *Impossibility of full over-determination* with the causally closed nature of the physical world. If we had only partial overdetermination, there would be *some* trace of the causal efficacy of the mental. But then there would be physically inexplicable phenomena, something about how things are physically that cannot be explained physically, and it is precisely that which it is so hard to believe.

Sequential over-determination

Also, **sequential overdetermination** is of no use to the dualist. *C* may be overdetermined in the sense that it is fully determined by an earlier state of affairs *B*, where *B* in turn is fully determined by a still earlier state of affairs *A*. Indeed, this situation is the normal one. What you do today is no doubt determined by what happened yesterday; but since that in turn is determined by the state of the world the day before, it is also true to say that what you do today is determined by the state of the world the day before yesterday. Thus, the fact that behaviour is fully explained in physical terms as far as what happens, say, from brain to bodily movement is concerned, is consistent with non-physical factors being required to explain how the brain gets to be the way it is. But, of course, that would still involve a violation of the principle that everything in the physical world has a sufficient physical cause. It is just that the violation would occur earlier.

Over-determination by the non-distinct

The final kind of overdetermination we will consider, **overdetermination by the non-distinct**, is of equally little use to the dualist. A particle's acceleration due north might be fully explained by a force of magnitude ten due north and one of magnitude seven due south. It might equally be explained by the resultant force due north. Again, Fred's death might be explained by a failure of one of his major organs, or by the failure of his heart, if that was indeed the major organ in question. In both these cases we have, in some sense, two different explanations of one and the same event, but clearly they are not cases of overdetermination proper. The different explanations are not in terms of genuinely distinct factors: the resultant force due north is constituted by the component forces; the failure of the major organ *is* the heart's failure. These kinds of example do not, in consequence, help the dualist. There is no problem about giving mental properties a causal role in explaining behaviour in the face of the full story being givable in principle in entirely physical terms *if* the mental properties invoked are not really distinct from the physical ones. The trouble for dualism is that, according to it, the mental properties *are* quite distinct from the physical ones.

Indeterminism

Finally, we should note that **indeterminism** is not of any help to the dualist in responding to the causal problem. The physical story that explains each and every physical happening may very well have irreducibly probabilistic elements. That follows from the best current understandings of quantum mechanics. This might seem to give the dualist's mental properties a role to play in causing behaviour. Perhaps the physical antecedents make it probable to such-and-such a value that something will happen in the brain that will then cause behaviour that leads to Fred's getting married. What the intention to get married does, it might be suggested, is to make it more probable than it otherwise would be that the right thing happens in the brain. But then there would be 'outside' interference with the probabilistic laws governing certain physical interactions in the brain. Certain things would happen more often than could be explained physically, and this is incompatible with the causally closed nature of the physical world. The crucial point is that the plausible contention that the physical world is causally closed need not be understood deterministically. Although for some physical events there may very well be no prior condition that fully determines that they will come about (but only a prior condition that determines their *chance* of coming about), all the evidence suggests that this prior condition is a purely physical one: the chance of each and every physical event is physically determined.

Refining the definition of materialism

We drew the contrast between materialism and dualism in terms of the contrast between views that hold, and views that deny, that the ingredients that we need to account for the physical or material side of us and our world – the physical ingredients – are in principle enough to account for our mental side as well. Views of the first kind are materialistic, those of the second kind are dualistic. It is time to try for a little more precision. We need to say more about what a *physical* ingredient is, and more about what it means to claim that the physical story about our world is *enough* to account for the mental side as well. We need to be more precise about (a) what ingredients count as physical ones, ones that the materialist allows, and about (b) what it means to say that these ingredients are enough.

By a physical ingredient, we mean the kinds of entities, proper- *Defining the*
ties and relations posited in the physical and biological sciences *physical*
(for short, the physical sciences). We cannot count psychology,

and the social sciences in general, as physical sciences for the purpose of *explaining* the notion of a physical property, for then the contrast between materialism and dualism would be lost. Every theory would automatically count as a version of materialism, because the psychological states referred to in the social sciences would, by definition, be physical. Now, of course, the physical sciences are far from complete. Physics especially is far from complete. To that extent, we do not yet know exactly what the physical properties, entities and relations are according to our definition. But the hope is that the problems in current physical science are not going to call for the acknowledgement of properties, entities and relations different in kind from those now on the scene. The incompleteness of current physical theory does not imply incompleteness in the *kinds* of ingredients that will be needed to complete the job. Thus, our definition serves to identify the kind of property, entity and relation we have in mind.

Moreover, should this optimism prove ill-placed, we can fall back on the fact that the major conceptual problems lie in basic physics and physical chemistry. It is in those domains that it is possible that we will need to make adjustments in the very categories and frameworks we use, and in ways that are currently inconceivable, and so may need to expand and revise our views about the kinds of properties needed. We can be confident that as far as the physical sciences that most directly serve to explain behaviour – medicine, biology, molecular chemistry, neuroscience and the like, the relatively high-level physical sciences in the sense of being directed to the explanation of the behaviour of reasonably large bits of the physical world – are concerned, we have a pretty complete list of the kinds of entities, properties and relations that are needed, while of course being very much in the dark in many places concerning how to put these ingredients together aright. And that is enough to make the contrast between materialism and dualism. The materialist affirms, and the dualist denies, that a full story about the mental side of us and our world can be told in the terms of these relatively high-level physical properties.

Supervenience

Introduction to supervenience   Given this account of what a physical property (relation, entity, etc. – from now on we will mainly talk in terms of properties) is, what does it mean to say that a *full* story about the mental side of us and our world can be told in terms of these properties? Or, conversely, what are dualists saying when they say that the story about the world in physical terms is *incomplete*, that it leaves out the mind by leaving out the special mental properties? What is the materialist affirming that the dualist denies? Or take a simple example. Believing that snow is white is a mental property of a great many of us: we believe that snow is white. But it is not a property that appears *as such* in the physical sciences. It appears in psychology but not, for instance, in neuroscience or genetics, or at least not in the sense of being one of the properties out of which neuroscientists or geneticists build their theories. The materialist must hold, accordingly, that it appears in some indirect way in the physical story about our world – the story contains it though not under the name 'believing that snow is white'. What does this claim amount to? What is being claimed, correctly or incorrectly, when it is said that believing that snow is white appears or is included in the physical story about us?

What the materialist has to say is that mental nature, the psychological way things are, including *inter alia* our believing that snow is white, *supervenes* on physical properties. But what is this notion of supervenience? How does it bear on questions of completeness and inclusion, and in particular on whether the physical story includes the mental story? We will approach these questions via a simple example, that of baldness.

Supervenience and completeness

What kind of fact makes it true that someone is bald? The answer lies in facts about hair distribution. It is the way a person's hair is distributed (which includes where the gaps are!), along with the way the hair of others is distributed (there is an element of comparison in ascriptions of baldness), that makes it true, if it is true, that a person is bald. This making true is not a causal making true. Suppose that you have not a hair on your head. Then this fact about you is certainly enough to make it true that you are bald. But it does not cause you to be bald. You did not become bald a moment later than you became hairless, and no energy transfer was involved. It constitutes your baldness. The relation between hair distribution and baldness is one of logical determination.

A way of capturing this idea is to say, surely plausibly, that exact similarity in regard to matters of hair distribution ensures exact similarity in regard to baldness: two people exactly alike in hair distribution *must* be exactly alike in whether or not they are ·bald. We say that baldness supervenes on hair distribution. Why is this a way of expressing the idea that hair distribution logically determines whether or not someone is bald? Roughly – and we will see how to put the point more exactly shortly – the supervenience of baldness on hair distribution means that what settles without remainder whether or not you are bald must be facts to do with hair distribution; otherwise, two people could be alike in hair distribution, but unlike in regard to baldness by differing in the other relevant facts. The supervenience of baldness on hair distribution means that there are no relevant facts for being or not being bald other than how your hair is distributed, and so your hair distribution determines whether you are bald or not. Incidentally, the relation between baldness and hair distribution is asymmetric. Alikeness in hair distribution ensures alikeness in baldness, but alikeness in baldness does not ensure alikeness in hair distribution: two bald people may (and typically do) have what hair they have in different places on their skulls.

How does supervenience connect with questions of completeness and inclusion? The idea is that because baldness supervenes on hair distribution, facts about baldness are included in facts about hair distribution: baldness is nothing over and above the way hair is distributed. Or consider the view that motion is entirely a matter of – is nothing over and above – change of position over time, the so-called at–at theory of motion. *If* this theory is true, motion supervenes on facts about change of position over time. Two objects exactly alike in the way they change position over time must be exactly alike in their motion. Conversely, if two objects exactly alike in how they change position over time can differ in their motion properties – if the supervenience of motion on change in position fails – then motion must be more than a matter of change of position over time: for they are not alike in the one regard, though they are alike in the other. In sum, supervenience theses can be used as a way of expressing (and testing to the extent that some supervenience thesis is or is not appealing) claims about what makes it true that things are some way or other, about what is included in what. Thus the materialists' claim that the psychological can be fully accounted for in physical terms can be expressed in terms of a supervenience thesis: the psychological supervenes on the physical. Exact similarity in physical respects ensures exact similarity in psychological respects.

We can say all this with greater precision by setting it within the **possible worlds** framework. We will take the opportunity to say rather more than is immediately needed about this framework, as the possible worlds way of looking at various issues will be important at a number of places in this work and has been enormously fruitful in sharpening many issues in the philosophy of mind. At the same time, we will steer clear of some of the more recondite issues concerning possible worlds.

Supervenience and possible worlds

Possible worlds: an introduction

Possible worlds are complete ways things might be. One possible world is the way things actually are in every detail, past, present and future, down to the last subatomic particle. It is our world (but not our Earth – 'world' here means 'universe'). But things did not have to be exactly the way they actually are. You decide to have red wine with dinner, let us say. That then is the way things actually are, or rather it is the way things actually are in that particular respect (it is a very far from complete way things actually are). But you might have decided to have white wine with dinner. That then is a way things might have been, though it is not how things actually are.

Possible worlds as complete ways things might be

The apparatus of possible worlds is a very familiar one. We routinely think and talk in terms of possibilities, calling them: possible scenarios, available options, possible combinations and so on. We survey the possibilities before we act, ranking some more highly than others, and use the ranking to determine what we ought to do. Chess masters are characterized by their ability to follow out the possible consequences of various possible moves to a much greater depth than we mere mortals. Debate about the merits and likelihoods of various possible scenarios is commonplace. We calculate the probability of drawing an ace by summing the probabilities of drawing the ace of spades, the ace of hearts, the ace of diamonds and the ace of clubs. This is summing over probabilities of the various possibilities that count as drawing an ace. You might learn that someone has withdrawn their candidature for a job you have applied for, and say 'Well, that is one less possibility I need to worry about'. A doctor reviewing your medical history

Possible worlds in everyday talk

lists the possible conditions you might have, and tells you that only one of them is bad. Travel agents specialize in knowing all the possible ways of getting to London.

The philosopher's apparatus of possible worlds is simply an extension of this familiar practice in two directions. First, as we have already remarked, a possible world is a *complete* way things might be. In any possible world, every detail is settled one way or the other. This is the most general notion: for we can think of a possibility in which all sorts of matters are left unresolved as a subset of the possible worlds in which each of the matters left unresolved varies as we go from one member to at least one other of the subset, while the resolved matters are uniform throughout all the worlds in the subset. Second, we count as a possible world any complete way things might be that is possible in the widest, most inclusive sense of possibility, the sense sometimes called **logical possibility** and sometimes called **metaphysical possibility**. (And sometimes a sharp distinction is drawn between these two senses of 'possible' – we return to this later in chapter 4.) In no world does two plus two make five, and in no world is the part greater than the whole, but in some worlds light is not a first signal. Although it is a law of nature (assuming the special theory of relativity) that no signal travels faster than light, it is not impossible in the widest sense for a signal to travel faster than light. Similarly, in some worlds the moon is made of cheese, though not in any that are at all like ours. Again, this is the most general notion. For we can think of what is possible in some narrower sense as a subset of what is possible in the widest sense: the **nomologically possible** worlds, for instance, are the subset of the (logically) possible worlds which are consistent with the actual laws of nature. In all these worlds no signal would travel faster than light, even if in some of them (strange worlds indeed) there are moons made of green cheese – just so long as no actual law of nature was violated in their making.

In terms of this apparatus of possible worlds we can give simple and perspicuous representations of a number of central notions which we will be referring to later in the book and which are of central importance in the philosophy of mind.

Explications in terms of possible worlds

Necessary truth   Some sentences make claims about how things are. Sentences like 'Mururoa is where the French test nuclear devices' and 'Mary is

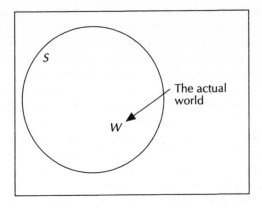

Figure 1   The worlds inside the circle are the worlds at which S is true. If the actual world is inside the circle (as depicted), S is true. If the region which is outside the circle and inside the square is empty, S is necessarily true. If the region inside the circle is empty, S is impossible.

taller than Arthur' are such sentences, and they are either true or false. Not all sentences get to be true or false. Arguably, it does not make sense to ask if questions (like 'Is Paris the capital of France?') or commands ('Shut the door!') are true or false. Sentences which are true or false are often called 'statements'. In this book, the sentences with which we are concerned are statements.

For each sentence (in this sense of statement) there is a set of possible worlds where (or at which) the sentence is true. We can think of this set of worlds as the set of all the conditions under which the sentence is true – its truth conditions, or the conditions under which the sentence's capacity for truth is realized. A sentence is true if among the worlds where it is true is the actual world (this world, the world we are actually in). A **necessarily true** sentence is one that is true come what may, or true under all conditions, or true at all possible worlds. A possible, or **possibly true**, sentence is one that is true at one or more worlds. A **necessarily false** sentence is false at all worlds, or equivalently, is impossible. The set of worlds at which a necessarily false sentence is true is of course the empty set; for there are no such worlds. A **contingent** sentence is one that is neither necessarily true nor necessarily false; that is, it is one that is true at some worlds and false at some worlds. In figure 1 the worlds inside the circle are the worlds where S is true. The square is the set of all possible worlds. The worlds inside the square but outside the circle are the worlds where S is false. If the actual world is inside the circle (as in fact we have drawn matters), S is true. If the region outside the circle and inside the square is empty, S is necessarily true. If the region inside the circle is empty, S is impossible. If the regions inside and outside the circle are both non-empty, S is contingent. If the region inside the circle is non-empty, S is possible.

Propositions   It is useful to have a term for the set of worlds where a sentence is true, and we will follow the tradition of calling it the **proposition** expressed by the sentence. Any sentence that is truth-valued expresses a proposition, that proposition being the set of possible worlds where it is true. We can think of the proposition expressed by a sentence as the way the sentence represents things as being. The proposition expressed by a sentence is *not* on this usage the same as the meaning of a sentence in at least one everyday sense of 'meaning'. 'There are wives' is true at exactly the same worlds as 'There are husbands', and so they express the same proposition, but arguably they do not mean the same. You should bear in mind in your reading that many philosophers use the term 'proposition expressed by a sentence' for a notion more closely related to meaning. In their usage the proposition expressed by 'There are wives' is distinct from the proposition expressed by 'There are husbands'.

Just as we defined the logical modalities – necessity, possibility and so on – for sentences in terms of truth at worlds, so we can define them for propositions. Thus a possible proposition is one that is true at one or more worlds, which is one and the same thing as saying that it is non-empty. There is, of course, only one necessary proposition: namely, the set of all possible worlds or universal set; and there is only one impossible proposition: namely, the null or empty set, for an (the) impossible proposition has no worlds where it is true.

Entailment   We can also define (logical) **entailment** or **implication** between sentences. Intuitively, S entails or implies S' if and only if *it is necessary* that if S is true, then so is S'. We capture this in terms of possible worlds thus: S entails or implies S' iff (if and only if) every (logically possible) world where S is true is a world where S' is true; or, equivalently, the proposition expressed by S is a subset of the proposition expressed by S', as shown in figure 2.

Essential and accidental properties   Finally, we can contrast the properties, or characteristics, an individual or particular thing has – that is, has in the actual world – with those it has in various possible worlds. The properties an individual might have had but does not in fact have are the properties

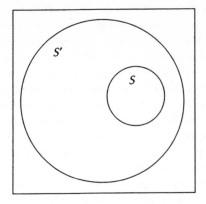

Figure 2 S entails S': every world at which S is true is a world at which S' is true.

the individual does have in possible worlds that are not actual. We are often interested in how things would have been for some individual or other, as well as in how things in fact are for that individual. Investors who failed to bail out before the stock-market crash of October 1987 regret the failure precisely because they know that they would have been wealthier than they in fact are had they bailed out in time. In this world they are poor. In the possible world that would have been actual had they bailed out in time, they are wealthy. Someone caught in the rain without an umbrella gets wet, but would have remained dry had they not forgotten it. In the possible, but regrettably non-actual, world where they remember their umbrella, they are dry. A property that an individual has in the actual world but not in other worlds is an **accidental** property of that individual (not to be confused with the everyday sense of an accidental property which is a property that is in some sense a fluke). A property that an individual has in every possible world in which it exists is an **essential** property of that individual. It is a property that the individual could not fail to have. To suppose that it lacks the property in some possible world is tantamount to supposing that it does not exist in that possible world.

A vexed question is the ontological or metaphysical status of the possible worlds that figure in these elucidations. Some say that each and every possible world is as real as our world, the actual world. This view is called (extreme) **modal realism**. It is a minority view. Few can believe that accepting that it is possible that everyone might have been bald means accepting that there is *literally* a world where the pates are all *literally* shiny. Others say that the non-actual worlds are abstract or transcendent entities outside space-time, like numbers, or that they are structured universals, or are certain combinations of the things and properties in the actual world, or are maximal, consistent sets of interpreted sentences, or. . . . We will not be entering into that debate in analytic ontology. What is important for us is the great heuristic value of the possible worlds way of thinking about modality and a great many topics that are important in the philosophy of mind, as will become apparent as we proceed. For now, we will be concerned with the way the apparatus of possible worlds helps us make precise the significance of supervenience theses.

*Supervenience and possible worlds

We said that baldness supervenes on hair distribution, and that this is a matter of exact similarity in regard to hair distribution implying exact similarity in regard to baldness. How can we express the central idea in terms of possible worlds? Well, if baldness is entirely a matter of how hair is distributed, then any two worlds exactly alike in hair distribution must be exactly alike in who and what is bald. For suppose that they differed in who or what is bald, then something other than hair distribution must matter – for only in matters other than hair distribution do they differ – contrary to our hypothesis. Thus, we can express the supervenience of baldness on hair distribution as follows:

> For all w and w', if w and w' are exactly alike in hair distribution, then w and w' are exactly alike in who or what is bald.

This is known as a **global supervenience** thesis, for it concerns similarities *between worlds*. It says that what makes a person bald in a world, if they are, is how hair is distributed in that world (including especially, but not exclusively, how their own hair is distributed). It is the kind of supervenience thesis that tells us what makes what true, that expresses claims we naturally express in terms of determination. For it tells us that if we fix the way hair is distributed, we necessarily fix, and so settle without remainder, the way baldness is distributed.

*Materialism and supervenience

Materialists need a global supervenience thesis to capture what they hold about the mental, for their view is that the total physical way things are makes true all of the mental way things are. But what global supervenience thesis precisely? Not the simplest, namely:

Finding the right supervenience thesis for materialism

(I)   Any two possible worlds that are physical duplicates (physical property, particular and relation for physical property, particular and relation identical) are psychological duplicates.

(I) does not capture what the materialists have in mind. Materialism is a claim about *our* world, the actual world, to the effect that its physical nature exhausts all its nature, or at any rate all its mental nature, whereas (I) is a claim about worlds in general. It is quite consistent with materialism to hold that there are possible worlds that are physically exactly alike but in which there are psychological differences due to *non*-physical facts about them, provided none of these worlds is ours. In those worlds non-physical facts do some determining of psychological nature, but provided those worlds are not our world, this is no skin off the materialist's nose.

A more restricted supervenience thesis in which our world is explicitly mentioned is:

(II)   Any world that is a physical duplicate of our world is a psychological duplicate of our world.

However, materialists can surely grant that there is a possible world physically exactly like ours but which contains as an *addition* a lot of mental life sustained in non-physical stuff, as long as they insist that this world is not our world. Some theists hold that materialism is the correct account of earthly existence, but that it leaves out of account the afterlife. When we die, our purely material psychology is reinstated in purely non-physical (and fortunately, longer-lasting) stuff. Surely materialists can grant that these theists are right about some world, some way things might be, as long as they insist that it is *not* our world, not the way things actually are. Hence, materialists are not committed to (II). (For more argument that materialists should deny (II), see the discussion of multiple realizability in chapter 3.)

The trouble with (II) is that it represents materialists' claims as more wide-ranging than they in fact are. What we need is something like (II) but which limits itself to worlds more nearly like ours, or at least more nearly like ours on the materialists' conception of what our world is like. We suggest:

> (III)   Any world that is a *minimal* physical duplicate of our world is a psychological duplicate of our world.

What is a minimal physical duplicate? Think of a recipe for making scones. It tells you what to do, but not what *not* to do. It tells you to add butter to the flour but does not tell you not to add bats' wings to the flour. Why doesn't it? Part of the reason is that no one would think to add them unless explicitly told to. But part of the reason is logical. It is impossible to list all the things *not* to do. There are indefinitely many of them. Of necessity the writers of recipes rely on an intuitive understanding of an implicitly included 'stop' clause in their recipes. A minimal physical duplicate of our world is what you would get if you used the physical nature of our world (including of course its physical laws) as a recipe in this sense for making a world. In short, a minimal physical duplicate of our world contains nothing more than it *must* in order to be a physical duplicate.

We arrived at (III) by eliminating alternatives. But we can give a positive argument for the conclusion that the materialist is committed to (III). Suppose that (III) is false. Then there is a difference in nature between our world and some minimal physical duplicate of it. But what could constitute the difference? By definition the minimal physical duplicate does not contain any particulars or instantiate any properties or relations that do not appear in our world. So does our world contain some particulars or instantiate some properties or relations that the minimal physical duplicate does not? But then these particulars or properties and relations would have to be non-physical, as our world and the minimal physical duplicate are physically identical, and materialism would be false. Hence, if (III) is false, materialism is false – that is to say, materialism is committed to (III). Equally, (III) commits us to materialism; for if materialism is false, then there is a non-material nature to our world which we could leave out in a minimal physical duplicate of our world. Thus the minimal physical duplicate would not be a duplicate *simpliciter*, so (III) would be false. So if (III) is true, materialism must be true.

*Making true and the varieties of materialism

We said that a global supervenience thesis makes a claim about what makes what true. Thus, (III) says that the physical way our world is makes true the mental way it is, and the answer to our earlier question of what a materialist should say about a property like believing that snow is white is that it appears in the physical story about the world, not by being one of the properties *explicitly* mentioned in the physical sciences but by supervening on the properties (and relations) explicitly mentioned. Consider an analogy. Does the fact that Smith is taller than Jones appear in a story in which we are told that Smith's height is six foot and Jones's height is five foot ten? Not explicitly, but implicitly in the following sense: Smith being the taller supervenes on the particular heights they have. All worlds where they have those particular heights are worlds where Smith is the taller.

We can say the same thing in terms of entailment. The physical makes true the psychological just if a certain entailment holds. Let ϕ be the sentence which tells the rich, complex, detailed physical story that is true at the actual world and all and only the minimal physical duplicates of the actual world, and false elsewhere. ϕ will not be a sentence of any actual language but rather of some ideal language of the future suited to describe fully the physical way our world is. (Alternatively, we might think of ϕ as the *proposition* true at our world and at all its minimal physical duplicates.) Let ψ be any true sentence about the psychological nature of our world: ψ is true at our world, and every world at which ψ is false differs in some psychological way from our world. If (III) is true, every world at which ϕ is true is a psychological duplicate of our world. But then every world at which ϕ is true is a world at which ψ is true – that is, ϕ entails ψ. The same is true, of course, in the heights example. Smith's being taller than Jones is entailed by Smith being six foot and Jones being five foot ten (but not conversely, of course).

The general point is that global supervenience theses generate entailment theses. So we have another way of expressing the 'making true' idea that underlies supervenience theses. If the mental supervenes on the physical, the physical way things are makes true the psychological way things are in the sense that a certain sentence (or proposition) about the physical way things are entails each and every sentence (or proposition) about the psychological way things are.

Materialism, then, is the doctrine that the physical way things are makes true the psychological way things are. Physical nature entails psychological nature. But, of course, not any old bit of the physical story about our world bears on its psychological nature. There are protons outside the Earth's light cone, but they have nothing to do with what you or President Clinton are thinking about or feeling. There is, that is, the major task of describing *which* physical matters matter for psychology. Different answers to this question give us different materialistic theories of mind. They are united by being theories that have the physical way things are making true the psychological way things are, but differ sharply about which aspects of the physical way things are constitute the important ones, and why. Some say behaviour is crucial, some say neural nature, some say functional organization, some say evolutionary history. Others say the crucial factor is one or another combination of these. There is also a lively debate about whether the crucial factors are intrinsic physical properties of the creatures that have the mental states, or in part physical properties of the environments the creatures inhabit. We will be concerned with these matters in chapters to come.

*Two warnings

Intra-world supervenience theses

Global supervenience theses, the ones we have been concerned with, tell us about what makes what true. They should not be confused with **intra-world supervenience** theses, and unfortunately it is not always clear which kind of supervenience thesis a particular writer has in mind. An intra-world supervenience thesis is a thesis of the following kind: for all worlds w, if x and y are exactly alike in respect A in w, then x and y are exactly alike in respect B in w. It concerns relations of things *within* worlds, not relations between worlds. An intra-world supervenience thesis gives very limited information about what makes what true. Here is a simple example to make the point. For all worlds, if persons x and y are exactly alike in height (both six feet tall, say), they are exactly alike in whether they are among the tallest 5 per cent of persons in their world. But it is not true that one's individual height exhausts what makes it true that one is or is not among the tallest 5 per cent. How one's height relates to that of others is crucial.

The meanings of 'physical property'

Our official definition of a physical property (item, relation, etc.) is that physical properties are ones that appear in the physical sciences, broadly construed, or anyway are of the same general kind as required to give a complete account of inanimate nature. Materialism is then the doctrine that psychology supervenes on the physical so defined. But it is common, and no harm is done thereby, to allow an extended use of 'physical' to mean physical either according to the official definition (or some near relative) or that which supervenes on what is physical according to the official definition. Thus, on this extended usage, if materialism succeeds in showing that believing that snow is white supervenes on physical nature, it may be said to have shown that it *is* a physical property. But it is important that in the argument for the conclusion that it supervenes on physical nature, 'physical' is given its official sense, otherwise the argument would be begged in favour of materialism.

A materialism that can be defined in terms of the notion of the physical is often called **physicalism**, and we will usually follow this usage. But in the literature 'physicalism' is sometimes used for a doctrine that is more radical in two ways from the view we will be concerned with. Our physicalism is a doctrine about psychology to the effect that the mental is not an extra feature of reality over and above material nature. It is simply materialism given a name that highlights the role of the notions of a physical property, relation and law in specifying it – via (III) above, for instance. But sometimes 'physicalism' is used for the doctrine that everything, not just everything mental, is physical; it denies, for instance, that there are sets or numbers conceived as entities outside space-time. We will not be concerned with this more far-reaching doctrine.

Also, 'physicalism' is sometimes used for a doctrine specified in terms of an official definition of 'physical property (relation and particular)' tied not to the physical sciences broadly conceived, but to physics in particular. Physicalism in this sense is sometimes called physics-alism. We will not be concerned with this stronger doctrine. It seems to us a natural extension of physicalism in the sense that will concern us, but the issue is irrelevant to the particular concerns in the philosophy of mind that we engage with in this book.

Physicalism and physics-alism

In the next chapter, we turn to a consideration of one of the earliest theories of mind designed to be compatible with physicalism.

Annotated Reading

Most textbooks in the philosophy of mind have an early chapter or two outlining dualism's problems. Among the most accessible are Keith

Campbell, *Body and Mind*; P. Smith and O. Jones, *Philosophy of Mind*; and Paul Churchland, *Matter and Consciousness*. Although Campbell gives a good account of dualism's problems, he ends up defending an epiphenomenalist style of attribute dualism. Smith and Jones, and Churchland (especially), come down on the materialist side. D. M. Armstrong, *A Materialist Theory of the Mind* is not a textbook. It is an early classic defence of physicalism, but it starts with a very clear account of some of dualism's problems. A recent, maverick attack on the very terms in which we, and the authors of the books just mentioned, approach the issue between dualism and physicalism is John Searle, *The Rediscovery of the Mind*.

Although the nature of the supervenience, if any, of the psychological on the physical, and the possible worlds methodology figure prominently in recent journal and monograph discussions in the philosophy of mind, there is a dearth of textbook-style presentations of the issues. For possible worlds it is probably best to look at David Lewis, *On the Plurality of Worlds*, and John Bigelow and Robert Pargetter, *Science and Necessity*. The first is the classic defence of extreme modal realism; the second favours a version of the structured universals approach. Both contain clear discussions of various alternatives to the view they favour, and despite being research monographs are reasonably accessible to keen tyros. Both contain many references to the literature. For supervenience and physicalism, one place to start would be the first chapter of David Papineau, *Philosophical Naturalism*. Terence Horgan, 'From Supervenience to Superdupervenience: Meeting the Demands of a Material World', is an excellent survey article on supervenience that includes sections on the history of the notion and its role in elucidating physicalism. It also contains a good bibliography. You will find that we disagree with much of what these two authors say.

There are a number of collections which contain articles of interest for many issues discussed in this book. Three excellent collections are W. G. Lycan, ed., *Mind and Cognition: A Reader*; Ned Block's two-volume collection *Readings in the Philosophy of Psychology*; and David Rosenthal, ed., *The Nature of Mind*.

2

Behaviourism and Beyond

Behaviourism is the doctrine that mental states are behavioural dispositions. In the hands of philosophers it is typically advanced as a conceptual claim: it is a conceptual truth that mental states are behavioural dispositions in much the same way that it is a conceptual truth that fragility is the disposition to break on dropping. Just as the concept of fragility is the concept of that which is apt to break on dropping, so the concept of any particular mental state is the concept of a behavioural disposition of the appropriate kind. Behaviourism of this ilk is called **analytical behaviourism**, or sometimes philosophical behaviourism. The way to show that it is true, insist its supporters, is by doing proper conceptual analysis of the mental language.

Analytical behaviourism

Behaviourists do not have to be physicalists. Their doctrine is consistent with mental states being dispositions of certain non-physical stuff of some kind; behaviourists could consistently believe in angels and allow them mental states. But clearly by far the most plausible version of behaviourism holds that mental states are dispositions of purely physical bodies – our bodies and the bodies of the higher animals – and the principal motivation for behaviourism came from physicalism. Behaviourism was an obvious way of explaining the mental without countenancing strange, occult mental substances or properties.

Behaviourism and physicalism

We saw in chapter 1 that physicalism is the doctrine that physical nature fully determines psychological nature. Behaviourism of the (usual) physicalist kind offers an account of which part of physical nature fully determines psychological nature: it is the highly sophisticated behavioural dispositions of certain purely physical bodies that determine psychology; psychology supervenes on certain behavioural dispositions of purely physical bodies.

The case for behaviourism

Someone who says that they intend to get married but somehow never gets round to it, lays themselves open to the charge that they never really intended to get married in the first place. As we noted in the discussion of dualism, intending is an example of a mental state that is conceptually linked to behaviour. This is why there is something absurd about saying, 'I intend to have a cup of coffee, but I won't have one'. But intending is not an isolated example. Consider perception. Surely it is part and parcel of perception that it enables certain behaviours. Why did Ahab offer a reward for sighting the white whale? Because of the role such sightings can play in capturing whales. Or consider what happens when you first realize that you have presbyopia – a kind of visual disorder. The connection between the fuzzy look of the letters on the page and your inability to make them out is not an interesting empirical discovery: the behavioural incapacity is part of what it is for the letters to look fuzzy. Again, it seems to be of the essence of desire that it points towards behaviour that typically leads to its satisfaction. Someone who thought that desire for beer and beer-seeking behaviour were only contingently connected would not understand what desire for beer is. Of course, desire for beer only leads to beer-seeking behaviour in the sense of behaviour that moves the subject in the direction she thinks the beer is. That is, what has the flavour of tautology is not strictly that desire leads to behaviour that satisfies it, but that a person will typically behave in such a way that if their beliefs are true, their desires will be satisfied. This is the central contention of what is called **belief–desire psychology**, and is one of the principal motivations for being a behaviourist.

It might be objected that we can imagine an extremely secretive person who values above all that their beliefs and desires be unknown, and that such a person's beliefs and desires will not be manifest in their behaviour. But what does such a person desire above all else? That their beliefs and desires be a secret! How does such a person believe that this overriding desire will be realized? By lying low. But then this person's behaviour does satisfy the axiom of belief–desire psychology: it is such as to realize their overriding desire if what they believe is true. And the unexpressed desires are not idle; they tell us what the person would do if they ever lost the desire to be secretive.

In sum, it is of the essence of mental states to show up in behaviour in the appropriate circumstances: a person in pain is disposed to move in such a way that the pain is relieved; intelligent people are better at solving problems than unintelligent people; there is behaviour typical of someone who intends to get married; anyone who has felt nauseous does not need to be told what behaviour that disposes towards. What is more, acknowledging these connections is part of understanding what it is to be in a mental state. Someone who does not realize that if Helena is better at chess than Mario, then Helena typically beats Mario when they play against each other, does not properly understand the concept of being good at chess.

One obvious way to accommodate these conceptual connections between behaviour and mind is to hold that our concept of a mental state is such that we can identify each mental state with the relevant behavioural disposition. Thus we arrive at analytical or philosophical behaviourism: just as fragility is the disposition to break on dropping – and that is not an interesting discovery about fragility, but an analytical truth about it; it reflects what we mean by 'fragility', our concept of fragility – so desire for beer is the disposition to behave in what we believe is a beer-getting manner, and this is a reflection of our very concept of desire for beer.

A terminological note: sometimes behaviourism is described as the doctrine that there are no mental states, though mental language is fine because it does not refer to such non-existent mental states, but instead refers to tendencies to behave. Other times behaviourism is described, as here, as the doctrine that there *are* mental states; they just *are* these tendencies to behave. The disagreement is more verbal than real. On both ways of describing behaviourism, it is agreed that (a) mental states are not inner, **categorical** states of persons, and (b) what makes psychological claims true are subjects' behavioural dispositions. We will stick to the second way of characterizing behaviourism, but nothing of importance hangs on this choice.

Behaviourism and the existence of mental states

There is a simple way of encapsulating the essential case for behaviourism in terms of supervenience. Suppose that Smith and Jones differ in their mental states. It is plausible that *somehow or other* the difference could be revealed in their behaviour. Suppose that Smith's itch is that little bit worse than Jones's. Won't he scratch with a little bit more vigour? Or perhaps the social conventions in place prevent that difference from showing up – not all societies permit scratching where it itches. In that case won't Smith

The supervenience argument for behaviourism

nevertheless be that little bit more distracted, and won't that show up in the speed with which he answers the telephone? Or suppose that you want to be President of the United States. In most situations that actually arise, wanting to be President makes no difference to behaviour because being President is such a remote possibility. No action that is available to one significantly increases one's chances. Yet, it makes a difference in counterfactual situations. Should, against all the odds, the opportunity to run for President with a real chance arise, you will act appropriately (and if you don't, that shows you did not really want the job, you were just amusing yourself with the thought). For any difference in mental states, it is plausible that there is a difference in actual or potential behaviour which can be found somewhere, somehow. Difference in psychological state implies difference in behavioural disposition. So *sameness* in totality of behavioural dispositions must imply *sameness* in psychological state: that is to say, psychological states supervene on behavioural dispositions. But then, it seems, what makes it true that a subject is in some psychological state are his or her dispositions to behave. What is more, the claim that led us to this conclusion – that psychological difference implies behavioural difference somewhere – seems to be a conceptual one. So the behaviourism it leads us to is analytical behaviourism.

We will see in later chapters that there are major problems for the claim that psychological nature supervenes on behavioural dispositions (especially in the discussion of Blockhead in chapter 7), but the supervenience claim is certainly initially appealing.

Methodological and revisionary behaviourism

The analytical behaviourists were able to reinforce their case by appeal to the success of behaviourism as a methodological doctrine in empirical psychology. **Methodological behaviourism** is the doctrine that the way to study the mind is through behaviour and capacities for behaviour: don't study colour-blindness by asking subjects to introspect; study it by asking them to *discriminate* between one colour and another. Adopting methodological behaviourism in preference to the method of introspection (a method which involved psychologists writing about their own inner lives) transformed scientific psychology for the better. This was a considerable embarrassment for dualism. It is hard to see why the study of properties allegedly different in kind from those studied in the physical sciences should have been so greatly aided by the study of behavioural capacities. On the other hand, if mental states are analysable as behavioural dispositions, there is no mystery about the success of methodological behaviourism. And in fact most methodological behaviourists were either analytical behaviourists or held a view that might be called **revisionary behaviourism**. Revisionary behaviourists grant that our ordinary mental concepts are not analysable without remainder in terms of behavioural dispositions, and, they say, so much the worse for our ordinary concepts. They think that the success of methodological behaviourism shows that even if our mental concepts are not entirely behaviouristic, we should revise them so that they are.

Problems for behaviourism

Despite the appeal of analytical behaviourism, it faces some very serious problems. The objection that immediately occurs to almost everyone is that it is much more appealing from the third-person perspective than from the first-person perspective. Some people cannot feel pain (and accordingly have to be carefully checked at regular intervals in case they have incurred serious bodily damage, without noticing it). They, runs the objection, might well think of pain – the pain of *others*, that is, as they never feel pain themselves – as a behavioural disposition to cry out, to move away from the cause of the damage and the like, perhaps combined with the very useful ability to say when knocking against something has caused serious damage, without recourse to medical expertise. But their conception of pain is seriously incomplete; something they will realize quickly enough if they ever come to experience pain themselves.

The first-person objection

There are in fact two different objections here. The weaker of these is the one contained in the joke about two behaviourists meeting on the street. One says to the other, 'You feel fine, how do I feel?' The joke assumes that behaviourists think that we have better access to the mental states of others than we do to our own. It is a weak objection, because the behaviourist can admit that people typically know more about their own dispositions to behave than they do about someone else's. You know more than most others do about how you will answer the question, 'Red wine or white wine?' The behaviourist just has to analyse this knowledge about dispositions as itself dispositional.

The more serious objection arises from the most natural explanation of the fact that we typically know more about our own mental states than we do about the mental states of others. We have, it seems, some kind of direct access to our own mental states. We can **introspect** them, and when we do, we seem to be aware or conscious of something internal and occurrent – which is not a mere behavioural disposition. The problem of what we are aware of in introspection, and its connection with being conscious, is a notoriously contentious one in the philosophy of mind. We will return to it later in chapter 8 on phenomenal qualities and consciousness. It is so difficult that it can perhaps be described as a problem for everyone. Nevertheless, it would be too quick to infer that it is thus not a problem for *anyone in particular*: behaviourism seems *peculiarly* unable to say anything sensible about it, whereas, as we will see, certain versions of functionalism can at least make a start on the problem.

The analyses are never delivered   A further objection to analytical behaviourism is that it has never delivered on its analytical claim. It holds that psychological statements can be analysed in terms of behavioural dispositions. The models for this were successful analyses of properties like fragility and solubility. We can give fairly decent, if rough, analyses of these concepts. To be fragile is to be disposed to break if dropped or otherwise impacted. To be water-soluble is to have the disposition to dissolve when placed in water. But no one has even gone close to giving a plausible analysis of a single psychological state in terms of behaviour and dispositions to behaviour. We will see in the course of our discussion of the final objection below that this failure is no accident. There is a principled reason why the task of analysing individual mental states in terms of straightforward behavioural dispositions is an impossible one.

The causal objection   The causal objection to behaviourism is that it denies a causal role to mental states with respect to behaviour. When you believe that it will rain, your belief might, for example, be responsible for your being such that were you to go out, you would take an umbrella. When you open your eyes and see a tiger, your perception of the tiger makes you sweat and start to run. When you cry out in pain, it is your pain that produces the cry. Being intelligent is what is causally responsible for Jones's ability to solve hard problems, and on the occasions when she exercises this ability, will be a cause of the production of correct solutions. The behaviourists must deny these truisms. If your itch *is* your behavioural disposition to scratch, then it is not causally responsible for the disposition, because something cannot cause itself. Nor can it be causally responsible for the scratching on the occasions when the disposition to scratch manifests itself. The disposition to scratch – the itch, on the behaviourists' view – does not cause its manifestation. What causes the scratching is the underlying nature of the subject that is responsible for the subject's disposition to scratch. The disposition itself is the very fact that the subject would be caused to scratch in certain circumstances, not what would do the causing.

How did behaviourists get themselves into the position of denying the truism that mental states are causally responsible for behaviour and dispositions to behaviour? Two factors played a role. One was hostility to the positing of unobservables in science. Behaviourists noted that evidence for the mental states a person is in ultimately comes back to the behaviour, including verbal behaviour, of the person in various situations. It is your choosing red wine that leads people to think that you prefer red wine. And they held that to go beyond our evidence was to traffic in mysteries and violate the maxims of good scientific practice. Also, they were influenced by **verificationism**: the doctrine that the meaning of a sentence is the method you should use to determine if it is true. They concluded from this that sentences about mental states could only mean something about behaviour, since it is by others' behaviour that we attempt to verify claims about their mental states. But in fact we all, scientists and non-scientists alike, go beyond what is directly observed all the time. We might explain a noise next door in terms of a party we are not at. A doctor diagnoses cancer in terms of outward signs. Astronomers deduced the existence of Pluto from perturbations in the orbit of Neptune before they were in a position to directly observe Pluto. Electrons were posited as the best explanations of cloud tracks in Wilson cloud chambers. And so on and so forth. It is good scientific and good everyday practice to argue from what is directly observed to what best explains what is directly observed (or, better, to argue from the *more* directly observed to hypotheses about the *less* directly observed that best explain the more directly observed – how direct an observation is, is context-relative and a matter of degree; it is not an absolute notion). These examples also refuted verificationism. Talk about electrons is not analysable as talk about tracks in Wilson cloud chambers and the like, for it is talk about what *explains* those tracks.

Diagnosis of the behaviourists' error

Causal connection and conceptual connection

The other factor which led them to deny the causal truism was the belief that allowing that mental states are internal states that cause behaviour and dispositions to behaviour leads straight to identifying mental states with brain states – for among the internal states it is they that play the appropriately distinctive roles in causing behaviour. But then, it was thought, the conceptual connection between mental states and behaviour and behavioural dispositions would be lost. For it is contingent that a given brain state causes such-and-such a disposition to behaviour. Indeed, sometimes the point was put more directly. Because there is a conceptual connection between mental states and behaviour, it was argued, there *cannot* be a causal connection. Causal connections are by their very nature empirical, contingent connections.

So there are three principles, each of which seems plausible, yet which it seems difficult to reconcile.

1 Causal connections are essentially contingent.
2 Mental states cause behaviour.
3 There is a conceptual connection between being in a mental state and behaviour.

The poison example

There is, however, a way of reconciling these three principles. The key idea is to allow that what something causes or is disposed to cause is part of what makes it correct to describe it in a certain way. Here is a simple example of the idea. Ingesting a poison causes illness, and yet there is a conceptual connection between ingesting a poison and getting sick. Someone who thinks that it is merely an interesting empirical fact that ingesting a poison is often followed by getting sick does not fully understand what 'poison' means, or, equivalently, they have a defective concept of poisonhood. The explanation for the conceptual connection is that various events, which include ingesting arsenic, ingesting cyanide, and so on, get to be correctly called cases of ingesting a poison because they typically cause illness. The connection between each of ingesting arsenic, ingesting cyanide, and so on with getting ill is contingent, exactly as is required by the causal nature of the connection. But the various events count as cases of ingesting a poison because they typically cause illness. Applied to the mind, the idea would be that we allow, as is so natural, that mental states cause behaviour and dispositions to behaviour. But we insist that *what* they cause is part of what makes it right to describe them as the mental states they are, thus preserving a conceptual connection with behaviour.

The upshot is that there is no need to deny that mental states cause behaviour and dispositions to behaviour in order to respect the prime intuition that the mind is conceptually linked to behaviour, or in order to be scientifically respectable. The realization that the behaviourist's two reasons for denying that mental states are internal causes are weak ones was the first big step towards functionalism. The second big step arose from another problem for behaviourism, to which we now turn.

This final objection to behaviourism that we will discuss arises from the fact that it is impossible to pair individual mental states with behavioural dispositions. There is no one–one mapping from mental states to behavioural dispositions. Consider, for instance, the belief that there is a tiger nearby. What behaviour does that belief point to? There is no answer to this question. What there *is* an answer to is the question of what behaviour is pointed to by the belief that there is a tiger nearby *together with* the belief that tigers nearby are dangerous, the desire to go on living, the belief that a good way to get away from nearby tigers is to run in such-and-such a direction, the belief that there are no lions or animal traps, or anything you desire even less to be near than a tiger, in such-and-such a direction, and so on. It is a whole complex of mental states that points to running in a certain direction, not any one or another individual mental state. But that is to concede the failure of the behaviourist's programme. There can be no behavioural disposition which is one and the same as the belief that there is a tiger nearby, because we cannot match one–one dispositions with mental states. That is why it is impossible to complete the analytical programme of analysing mental states in terms of behavioural dispositions. The conceptual connection is not between mental states and behavioural dispositions but between complexes of mental states and behavioural dispositions.

The match-up problem

The problem is not merely that the behaviour which subjects are disposed to manifest depends on the totality of the mental states they are in. The way a particle moves under the influence of massive bodies depends on the totality of the component gravitational forces acting on it. Nevertheless, for each force there is a distinctive contribution specifiable in terms of the motion the particle would undergo if that were the one and only force acting on it – a contribution that is explicitly represented in the familiar diagrams for calculating resultant forces. Again, the action of a poison can be blocked by an antidote. Nevertheless, there is a result that taking a poison typically points towards; the existence of antidotes simply means that 'typically pointing towards' is not the same as ensuring. The problem for behaviourism about the mind is that there is no such thing as the distinctive behaviour associated with any mental state in itself, there just is no consistent behaviour that will typically follow any given mental state unless there is some sort of outside interference.

The path to functionalism via a causal theory

Mental states as causes of behaviour

The discussion of the causal objection to behaviourism tells us that we should think of mental states as inner causes of behaviour, and that, by making the typical causal role part of what makes a mental state the state it is, we can secure the conceptual link between the mind and behaviour. But we cannot secure it simply by saying that, say, pain is the internal state apt for pain behaviour. For the discussion of the match-up problem tells us that we should think of the conceptual tie to behaviour as being between complexes of mental states and behaviour. We must then think of pain as roughly (what follows is too simple but serves to give the general idea) the internal state apt for behaviour that will, by the lights of what we believe, minimize the bodily damage causing the pain, provided we desire to minimize that damage. It is not pain, but pain along with other mental states that causes behaviour.

History makes behaviour appropriate

Further, the behaviour that matters is environmentally embedded behaviour with the right causal history. What is behaviourally important about desire for beer is that it causes movement *towards beer* when combined aright with other mental states. But it had better be the case that beer typically plays a role in *causing* some of those mental states. Otherwise it would be a *fluke* that the movement was towards beer, and fluke movements towards beer are not signs of desire for beer. Every time you walk towards a car that has beer in its boot, you move in such a way that you get nearer to beer. But if your behaviour has no causal link to the beer (as would normally be the case unless you put the beer there yourself, or you have X-ray vision), it will be no sign of desire for beer. Again, belief that there is a bend in the road gets you round the bend other than by luck only if it is typically caused by bends in roads, and the like. The fact that the conceptual link between mind and behaviour is one between mind and behaviour inasmuch as behaviour orientates us with respect to our environment, means that there is also a conceptual link between the mind and antecedent conditions. There is a conceptual link upstream as well as downstream. For the downstream link only gets to be non-fluky inasmuch as there is a non-fluky upstream link.

The causal theory of mind

These points can be put together in a version of a **causal theory of mind**. Mental states are inner states with typical causes and effects. The causes may be environmental circumstances (a tiger in front of one in daylight typically causes the belief that there is a tiger in front of one), or they may be other mental states (perceptions typically cause beliefs); and the effects may be other mental states or behavioural responses. This picture of the mind makes very good evolutionary sense: the survival value of being such that bodily damage tends to cause a behavioural response that minimizes the damage is obvious; and that is what pain is (very roughly) on the causal theory. It also suggests a way of handling the difficult question (for behaviourists in particular) of what to say about the mental states of partially paralysed people. Paraplegics and quadriplegics may have a rich array of mental states despite the fact that they do not have behavioural dispositions in the sense in which we have them. Indeed, often there are many actions that we take for granted that they cannot even try to do. Just as most of us cannot even try to waggle our ears, they cannot even try to move their feet, for instance. True, they have behavioural dispositions in an attenuated sense – were they able to move their bodies in such-and-such a way, and knew it, *then* they would be disposed to move in certain ways – but this hardly accommodates our sense that there is something about how they *actually* are that makes it true that they are in such-and-such a mental state. A causal theory of mind can accommodate this sense by pointing out that paralysed people have that which *actually* causes the relevant dispositions in normally embodied people; that is, what goes on in their brains is essentially the same as what goes on in the brains of people who are not paralysed. The difference between them and those with full control over their movements lies in the pathways from the brain to the limbs, not in the central processor, and it is that, rather than any disposition *per se,* that matters on a causal theory of mind.

Mental states and paralysis

Functionalism as a certain kind of causal theory

A causal theory of this tripartite kind is called functionalism. That is, a functionalist theory of mind specifies mental states in terms of three kinds of clauses: input clauses which say which conditions typically give rise to which mental states; output clauses, which say which mental states typically give rise to which behavioural responses; and interaction clauses, which say how mental states typically interact. In the next chapter we address functionalism in some detail.

Annotated Reading

A very accessible, textbook-style, but not elementary, account of behaviourism's strengths and weakness is to be found in Keith Campbell, *Body and Mind*. There are a number of books that detail the path from behaviourism to some kind of causal theory of mind. The classic source is D. M. Armstrong, *A Materialist Theory of the Mind*, chapters 4 and 5. A good account is also given in Paul Churchland's *Matter and Consciousness*. For a recent presentation of the case against causal theories of mind, see Norman Malcolm's contribution to D. M. Armstrong and Norman Malcolm, *Consciousness and Causality*. Analytical behaviourism, though not under that name, is defended in Gilbert Ryle, *The Concept of Mind*. This work, along with Ludwig Wittgenstein's *Philosophical Investigations*, played an important role in forcing philosophers to take analytical behaviourism seriously, though you should be aware that it is a matter of some controversy whether Wittgenstein is rightly classified as a behaviourist. A methodological behaviourism of a distinctly revisionary stamp is defended in B. F. Skinner, *About Behaviourism*. Skinner's work had great impact among psychologists, though more recently some form of functionalism has become orthodoxy. An important figure in philosophical discussions of behaviourism, but one who is hard to classify definitively, is Daniel Dennett. His essays in, for instance, *The Intentional Stance* are clearly sympathetic to behaviourism, and in any case are well worth reading.

3

Common-sense Functionalism

Functionalists take mental states to be the internal causes of behaviour. They embrace the insight that there is some kind of conceptual connection between behaviour and the mind, but reject the simple account of this connection that the behaviourists gave. The basic idea is very simple. Mental states are, according to functionalists, internal states within us, but we identify and name them by the effect the world has on them, the effect they have on one another, and the effect they have on the world by causing our behaviour. Just as we saw that we could, without knowing the details of what is going on when people die after ingesting food, have a name – 'the poison' – for whatever it is which causes their death, we might, say functionalists, identify and name mental states by their characteristic causes and effects.

There are many kinds of functionalism, but there are some things about which most functionalists agree.

1   They agree about the general shape of the right theory of mind. *Some common* It has the three parts that we mentioned at the end of the last *ground for* chapter: input clauses – clauses that say what sorts of events *functionalists* cause mental states in people, output clauses – clauses that say what sorts of behaviours are caused by mental states, and internal role clauses – clauses that describe the internal interactions of mental states.
2   They agree that mental states are inner states that occupy or fill the roles specified by those clauses.[1]

---

[1]   There is a complication here which we set aside for the moment, but will consider in our discussion of the identity theory in chapter 6. Some who call themselves functionalists say that, strictly speaking, a mental state is the state of having the role filled, not the state that fills the role.

3   They agree that one of the great strengths of functionalism is that it allows for what is known as **multiple realizability**. This is the idea that these roles could be filled or occupied by quite different kinds of things in different cases.

There is a range of disagreements as well. Functionalists disagree about the nature of mental *properties*, and about how to specify the clauses in order to capture what is essential to having a mind or being in one or another mental state, or indeed whether functionalism is in the business of specifying what is *essential* in the first place.

We will start by saying something about multiple realizability, and will then address the question of what the functionalist should say about what is essential to being in one or another mental state. We will expound the answer to this question usually known as **common-sense functionalism**. The view is also known as **analytical functionalism**. We will discuss its relationship to other kinds of functionalism later in this chapter and in the next. The question of mental properties will be postponed until our discussion of the type–type identity theory of mind in chapter 6.

Multiple realizability

The world is full of states, devices, stations in life, objects, processes, properties and events that are defined wholly or partly by their functional roles. Thermostats are defined by how they control temperature by switching machines on and off; burglar alarms are defined by how they function to produce loud noises on being disturbed in various ways (only sometimes by burglars, unfortunately); the office of vice-chancellor is defined by its function in a university; filtration is defined as a process that takes as input solids in liquid suspension and delivers as separate outputs the solid and the liquid; a graduation ceremony is an event in part defined by its role of producing graduates; a dangerous corner is the kind that tends to take approaching cars and deliver accidents; and so on and so forth. In all these cases there is a distinction to be drawn between the functional role and what occupies or fills it. Some thermostats are bimetallic strips; some are more complex electronic devices. Either way, they count as thermostats provided they do the required regulating of temperature. Many different people might be vice-chancellor of the university. Burglar alarms come in many shapes and sizes. There are many ways a corner can be dangerous.

In the same way functionalists about the mind distinguish the functional roles specified by the input, output and internal role clauses from what occupies them, and insist that what matters for being in one or another mental state are the roles that are occupied, not what occupies them. Provided the right roles are occupied, it does not matter what occupies them. Sometimes it is claimed that as a matter of empirical fact what occupies the relevant roles most likely varies. It is claimed that what plays the belief-that-there-is-food-nearby role in dogs is most likely different from what plays that role in cats; or perhaps the occupant of the role varies from one kind of dog to another; or perhaps it is different in left-handed people as opposed to right-handed people. Sometimes the claim is simply that it is abstractly possible that what plays or realizes the role associated with a given mental state varies. What is agreed though is that what matters for being in a given mental state are the roles occupied, not what occupies them. This is the famous multiple realizability thesis distinctive of functionalist theories of mind. Multiple realizability is appealing for a number of reasons:

1 We ascribe mental states on the basis of behaviour in circumstances and without much regard to what realizes the various functional roles. Indeed, we do not know in any detail what realizes the roles, and until relatively recently we did not know even in broad outline.

We do not know what realizes mental states

2 We have all read science fiction stories about creatures – traditionally called 'Martians' in philosophical discussions – whose chemistry is, say, silicon-based, instead of carbon-based like ours, and who interact with the environment much as we do, plan our defeat, fall in love with some of us, admire characteristics that we abhor, shame us with their compassion and understanding, are vastly more intelligent than we are, or whatever. These stories strike us as perfectly coherent, despite the fact that it is part of the story that the states that realize the relevant functional roles in them are quite different from those that realize the roles in us. As the conclusion from these science fiction considerations is often put, we should not be **chauvinists** about the mind.

We can imagine beings unlike us, but with mental states

Human brains may be very diverse

3   There is considerable evidence that our brains start out in a relatively plastic state, and that as we grow and the environment impacts on us, states come to occupy new functional roles, those subserving language, for instance. The usual explanation as to why language cannot be learnt past a certain age appeals to this point. Past a certain age it is too late for the right changes in brain function to occur. This opens up the possibility that the way your brain changed to subserve the functional roles needed for language was different from the way my brain did. But, provided the job gets done, it does not seem to matter.

If a different part of the brain takes over a job, we do not mind

4   An important part of making a good recovery from a stroke is getting an undamaged part of the brain to do something previously done by the part damaged by the stroke. Stroke victims do not worry about whether the new part of the brain counts as a different realizer of the old role. What they worry about is whether the job will be well done, and that seems exactly the right attitude to take.

We might replace part of our brains with artificial aids

5   Prosthetic surgery for the brain seems no more problematic *in principle* than does prosthetic surgery in general. We can imagine that, as they degenerate, parts of someone's brain are progressively replaced by silicon implants. Provided the implants fill the same functional roles, surely the surgery would count as successful. But then it must be the case that mental life is preserved despite the radical change in what realizes the various functional roles.

Multiple realizability, then, in addition to being common ground among functionalists, is a point in favour of their theory. It is widely accepted that any theory of mind should accommodate multiple realizability, and it is very much a point in functionalism's favour that it does this so naturally. What is not common ground is the question of which functional roles are essential to which mental states and the more general question of where functionalism should stand on how we might answer this question.

Which functional roles matter

One response is to leave the question to someone else. Some functionalists hold that the question of which functional roles mental states occupy should be left to empirical psychology and neuroscience. We can distinguish very many functional roles played by mental states, and the study of the mind is the study of these many functional roles. But it is no part of functionalism, on this view, to argue for one or another answer to conceptual issues concerning how to analyse what it is to be in pain, believe that it will rain soon, or whatever. But if the key to the mind lies in functional roles, it seems fair to ask for some sort of guide as to which functional roles matter. A burglar alarm may play many functional roles. Perhaps it plays the role of being a drain on your bank balance, being a conversation piece at dinner parties, and making a loud noise when burglars are near. We know which role matters for its being a burglar alarm. The last role is the one that matters. That is why if it stops breaking down – and so stops being a drain on your bank balance – and if it stops being unusual in the neighbourhood – and so stops being a conversation piece – it will still be a burglar alarm. Among the various functional roles it has, we discriminate between those that matter for its counting as a burglar alarm and those that do not matter. The same is true for all the examples we gave earlier. Any particular vice-chancellor, thermostat or dangerous corner will play many roles, but only some will matter for being a vice-chancellor, a thermostat or a dangerous corner. Why, then, should it be impossible to make the same kind of discrimination in the case of mental states? We know that not all the roles which various mental states fill matter equally for its being the mental state that it is – for instance, pain's playing the role of being the example most often chosen for discussion by philosophers is irrelevant to its being pain; it wouldn't hurt any less if philosophers instead began to discuss itching – so surely it is fair to ask the functionalist for some guide as to which functional roles of a mental state matter for its being the mental state that it is.

The best answer, in our view, to the question of which functional roles matter is the answer given by common-sense functionalism. Common-sense functionalism aims to give an analysis of what it is to be in one or another mental state in broadly functional terms, in the same general way that we can give an analysis of being a burglar alarm in broadly functional terms.

Common-sense functionalism expounded

It is common knowledge which functional roles matter for being a burglar alarm or a thermostat. Common-sense functionalism says the same for the mind. We distinguish the roles that matter for having a mind, and matter for being in one or another mental

The roles that matter are common knowledge

state, by drawing on what is common knowledge about mental states. We extract the crucial functional roles from the huge collection of what is pretty much common knowledge about pains, itches, beliefs, desires, intentions, and so on and so forth, focusing on what is most central to our conception of what a pain is, what a belief is, what it is to desire beer and all the rest. And we can group the common knowledge into the three clauses distinctive of the functionalist approach. The input clauses will contain sentences like 'Bodily damage causes pain' and 'Chairs in front of people in daylight cause perceptions as of chairs'; the output clauses will contain sentences like 'Pain causes bodily movement that relieves the pain and minimizes damage' and 'Desire for beer causes behaviour that leads to beer consumption'; the internal clauses will contain sentences like 'Perception as of beer in front of one typically causes belief in beer in front of one' and 'Belief that if p then q typically causes belief that q on learning p'. There are also clauses that may not, strictly speaking, concern functional role. An example is 'Looking red is more like looking pink than looking green'. It is an open question, to which we will return in chapter 8 on phenomenal qualities and consciousness, as to whether the similarity here can be cashed out in causal-functional terms.

The meanings of mental state terms

The clauses of common-sense functionalism are thought of as giving the meaning of the various mental state terms. Just as the network of interconnections we associate with being a vice-chancellor, or the much simpler functional role that is crucial for being a burglar alarm, capture our conception of what it is to be a vice-chancellor or to be a burglar alarm, so common-sense functionalism maintains that the network of interconnections reflects our concepts of the various mental states. This is why common-sense functionalism is sometimes called analytical functionalism: it is an account of the meaning of the mental state terms – an elucidation of the mental state concepts – in functional terms. The fact that people tend to move in such a way that what they desire is satisfied if what they believe is true is more than an interesting truth. It is in part constitutive of our understanding of belief and desire. Again, the fact that pain is typically caused by bodily damage and tends to make people behave in a way that they believe will relieve the pain is part of our conception of pain. Yet again, the fact that perception typically leads to belief is taken to be part of our conception of perception and belief. Common-sense functionalism thus draws *inter alia* on the conceptual connections that behaviourism noted between mind and behaviour, but in a more moderate and thus more plausible form. The connections are governed by *ceteris paribus* clauses, hence the appearance of 'typically' or the like in many of our illustrations, and no part of the network is essential.

What then is a given mental state M, according to the common-sense functionalist story? It is the state that plays the M role in the network of interconnections delivered by common knowledge about the mind. The network in effect identifies a role for each mental state, and thus, according to it, a mental state is simply the state that occupies the role definitive of it. The situation is similar to that which applies when we elucidate our concept of being a bank teller. There is a network of interconnections between inputs involving customers entering the bank, outputs involving loans approved and cash handed over, and internal connections between tellers, accountants, managers, and the like. What then is a teller? Anyone who occupies the relevant role in the network. And, as is the case with the mind, there is no neat, cut and dried formula that describes the functional organization that is necessary and sufficient for being a bank, and so no neat, cut and dried account of the tellers' place in the organization. We allow a good deal of variation between banks, and how much variation is allowed consistent with something's being a bank rather than a credit union, say, is vague and elastic. But it is not so vague and elastic as to be without content. Language is a flexible, open-ended instrument, but it is not so flexible and open-ended as to allow *anything* to count as *anything*. It would not be much use for telling us about how things are if it were. When you are told that someone is a bank manager and not a bank teller, the interest of the remark derives from the fact that your understanding of the words tells you that the functional roles definitive of being a bank manager and being a bank teller are very different.

Multifaceted concepts – sometimes called **cluster concepts** – are typically like this. There is a list of features that we regard as paradigmatic of pens. Something that satisfies every single one is by definition a pen. If it uses ink, is small enough to fit in the hand, is used to write with, is called a 'pen', is barrel-shaped, and has a nib, then it is a pen. That follows from our concept of a pen. But nothing in that list is sacrosanct. Any single feature on the list can be absent and yet the object still be a pen. For instance, a pen set aside at the factory for putting in a display cabinet may never be used for writing, yet is still a pen. What matters is that enough of the list is satisfied or near enough satisfied, and what counts as

Cluster concepts

enough may itself be a vague matter, and may change with time. But enough of the list must be satisfied or near enough satisfied. A table is not a pen, and that is not an interesting discovery about tables and pens.

The crude understanding of conceptual analysis

One thing needs to be made clear here. What we are talking about is conceptual analysis *of a sort*. There is a crude story about conceptual analysis that we know won't do, thanks in part to philosophers like Quine and Wittgenstein. On this view, when we analyse a concept, we can give a firm, cut and dried list of features each of which must be possessed to count as falling under that concept, and the conjunction of which is sufficient for falling under it. To hark back to the pen example, the crude conception would require the analyst to produce a list of properties, each of which is required for something to be a pen, and the possession of all of which is enough for something to be a pen, regardless of what else is true of it. This cannot be done in general. But it doesn't mean that analysis fails to delimit a concept in *any* way. Language is often vague, so good conceptual analysis must capture that vagueness. But if you announce that what you mean by 'pen' is a device which can be used to destroy cities by nuclear fusion, then you have simply changed the subject. You're talking about H-bombs, not pens. Now you are free, if you don't mind muddying the waters, to use the word 'pen' to refer to H-bombs, but it is a conceptual matter that 'pen' as *we* ordinarily use it does not pick out H-bombs, and we can grasp this by interrogating our concept of pen. There may be some latitude in what counts as a pen, but not so much as to include thermonuclear devices that you can't write with! To repeat a point that we made earlier, if just about *anything* counted as a pen, we couldn't give much useful information by using the word 'pen' – and clearly we can and do.

There are three questions to be asked immediately of common-sense functionalism. One is whether there is an objectionable circularity in the way the clauses interconnect, and so interdefine, the various mental states; a second is how to characterize the behaviour mentioned in the output clauses; and a third question – the hardest – is about how, precisely, to specify the raft of common-sense opinions about mental states that are taken to define them. We will address these concerns in turn. In the next chapter we will consider a more general worry about common-sense functionalism, the worry that it is committed to a discredited theory of reference, the description theory of reference.

Interconnections without circularity

Any plausible spelling out of the clauses of a common-sense functionalism reveals them as spelling out interconnections between
various mental states. This is obviously true of the internal role
clauses – a clause that says that perception typically causes beliefs
about the environment is transparently telling us about interconnections – but the point also applies to the input and output clauses.
Pain causes behaviour that relieves *pain*. A desire causes behaviour that is *believed* will satisfy *it* provided that there is not some
stronger *desire* that is *believed* to call for distinct behaviour. The
beliefs that are caused by a given perception depend on what is
already believed. And so on and so forth. The point is sometimes
put by saying that mental terms come as a package deal, just as, to
take a very simple example, the terms 'husband' and 'wife' come
as a package deal. There is no understanding one without understanding the other.

Is all this interdefinition circularity by a polite name? There are   *Machine tables*
two ways to see that the answer to this question is no. One can be
introduced in terms of the notion of a machine table, a notion we
will need shortly anyway.

Suppose, to borrow a famous example, that you want to make a
machine which fulfils the following requirements:

1   It gives a coke in return for $1.
2   It accepts both $1 coins and 50 cent coins.
3   It is forgiving to people who put in a 50 cent coin followed by
    a $1 coin.

What you have to do is make a machine which keeps track of its
credit and debit status. It needs to have an internal state, S_1, which
records the fact that it is all square, and a state, S_2, which records
the fact that it is 50 cents ahead. We can summarize these requirements in a table (see table 1). This is an *extremely* simple example

Table 1   The coke machine example

	S_1	S_2
Insert 50c	Go to S_2.	Emit coke. Go to S_1.
Insert $1	Emit coke. Stay in S_1.	Emit coke and 50c. Go to S_1.

of a machine table. For each internal state (S_1 or S_2) and each possible input ($1 or 50 cents), the table tells us which internal state the machine moves to or stays in and which possible output (coke, coke and 50 cents, or nothing) we get. S_1 and S_2 are functionally identified internal states, and they are identified by the ways they are interconnected, as shown in the table. Any functionalist theory of mind can be thought of as an account of the mind that represents it in terms of a machine table. For a machine table is simply a way of giving the input, output and internal role clauses. Of course, in the case of the mind, the table will be very much more complicated than the one illustrated.

Does the fact that S_1 and S_2 are identified in terms of each other mean that there is some kind of vicious circularity in the account of what S_1 and S_2 are? What is S_1? We tell you in part in terms of S_2. But then if you ask us about S_2, we tell you a story involving S_1! Nevertheless, the circularity is not vicious. For we could easily enough dive into the machine and identify which state is S_1 and which state is S_2. The same is true when we explain the workings of a bank. In addition to mentioning the financial inputs and outputs, we will have to mention the interconnections between tellers, accountants, loan officers, managers, and so on. But despite the interconnections, there is no vicious circularity, and what shows this is that you could use the story to identify who the tellers, accountants, loan officers and manager are. Indeed, you implicitly use your knowledge of the story every time you go into a bank and succeed in identifying the tellers, the managers and so on.

How exactly do we pull off the trick of identifying S_1 and S_2? When we investigate the internal workings of the coke machine, we will discover enough to be able to write a second table (table 2). This table is exactly the same as the first except that it has 'M_1' for 'S_1' and 'M_2' for 'S_2', where 'M_1' and 'M_2' are machine state names. M_1 might be 'the levers are arranged thus-and-so', for example, or perhaps 'the potential distribution across that part of the circuit board is so-and-so'. We then simply identify S_1 with

Table 2 The coke machine after investigation

	M_1	M_2
Insert 50c	Go to M_2.	Emit coke. Go to M_1.
Insert $1	Emit coke. Stay in M_1.	Emit coke and 50c. Go to M_1.

M_1 and S_2 with M_2. This is how we discover what S_1 and S_2 are. In the same way, enough knowledge of a bank will enable us to match up the story we know from our grasp of how banks are organized, the story that contains sentences like 'The manager tells the accountant what to do when the loan requested is high', with the story we learn by investigating the bank, the story that contains, say, 'Robinson tells Jones what to do when the loan requested is high'. We can then identify the manager with Robinson and the accountant with Jones. In sum, the stories about how various states or people relate to inputs, outputs and interconnections are stories that say that *there are* states or people standing in such-and-such relations, and we make the identifications by finding which states or people stand in the relations. The fact that we can make the identifications shows that the networked nature of the story is not viciously circular.

*Explicit definitions and Ramsey sentences

There is a second, more technical way to see that there is no vicious circularity. It is possible to write down an *explicit* definition for each term that is defined by its place in a network. (Readers with no background in logic can go straight to the next section if they are prepared to take this on trust.)

An explicit definition in non-mental terms of the conditions under which Jones is in some mental state M_i is a sentence of the form 'Jones is in M_i if and only if . . .', where the dots are filled in by non-mental terms. We can use the network story told by common-sense functionalism to construct a definition, as follows. Let **M** be the long conjunction that includes all the clauses of common-sense functionalism as applied to Jones, and suppose, for convenience, that the mental state terms, M_i, are all in the form of names of mental states rather than predicates. Thus, instead of 'If Jones desires beer and believes that moving in such-and-such a way will lead to beer, Jones will tend to move in such-and-such a way', we have 'If Jones has the desire for beer and Jones has the belief that moving in such-and-such a way will lead to beer, Jones will tend to move in such-and-such a way'. Thus, what we will deliver will be an explicit definition of 'Jones has M_i' rather than 'Jones is in M_i'. Now replace each distinct mental property name, 'M_i', by a distinct variable to give:

$$\mathbf{M}(x_1, \ldots, x_n)$$

then

$$(\exists x_1)(\exists x_2) \ldots \mathbf{M}(x_1, x_2, \ldots)$$

Ramsey sentences introduced

gives the content of common-sense functionalism as it applies to Jones. It is known as the **Ramsey sentence** of **M**, after F. P. Ramsey. It says that there are states of Jones that stand in the specified relations; and of course if what it says about Jones is false, then, according to common-sense functionalism, Jones does not have mental states. But now we can give the conditions under which Jones has M_i:

Jones has M_i if and only if $(\exists x_1)(\exists x_2) \ldots$ [Jones has x_i & $\ldots$ $\mathbf{M}(x_1, x_2, \ldots)$)], where '$x_i$' replaces '$M_i$'.

As all the mental state terms 'M_i' have been replaced by variables 'x_i', the right-hand side of this definition contains no mental vocabulary. This shows that there is no vicious circularity in common-sense functionalism. Although the most natural way of stating common-sense functionalism *interdefines* the mental, we can recast the story so as to yield an account of when a subject, our Jones, say, is in any particular mental state that makes no explicit reference to any other mental state. The essential idea shorn of the technicalities is that common-sense functionalism defines mental states holistically by their place in a network. This amounts to treating it as asserting that for a subject to be in any particular mental state is (a) for there to be a set of states interconnected in a certain way, and (b) for the state the subject is in to be in the relevant place in that network. And the crucial point is that the network can be described in non-mental terms.

Behaviour characterized in terms of environmental impact

Characterizing inputs and outputs

We can characterize the inputs in the common-sense functionalist story without recourse to the mental states they typically cause. The inputs are characterized as chairs in daylight, bodily damage, tigers, trees in the quad and so on. The situation is not so straightforward in the case of the outputs. We often characterize the outputs in intentional terms, as *actions* rather than mere bodily movements: we reach for beer, we signal for a taxi, we scratch our leg, and so on and so forth. And reaching, signalling and scratching are all intentionally characterized actions; they are things we do. Many have urged that this is an ineliminable feature of any viable form of functionalism. It arises, it is argued, from the fact that there is no non-intentionally capturable pattern in our behavioural responses. Too many quite distinct bodily movements are produced by the desire to get a taxi for there to be any discernible pattern capturable in the language of bodily movements. The only pattern is that captured by saying that desire for a taxi typically causes signalling a taxi, but that may be done by whistling, waving, raising an arm, stepping off the kerb, and so on and so forth – all of which involve very different bodily movements.

This is a problem for common-sense functionalism's claim to be able to give an explicit definition of '*x* is in *M*', for any *M*, in non-mental terms. Crucial to that enterprise is the supposition that the behavioural outputs can be specified in non-mental terms. Only then will '$(\exists x_1)(\exists x_2) \ldots \mathbf{M}(x_1, x_2, \ldots)$' be devoid of mental terms. But if the outputs have to be specified as actions, then their specification is in part mental. To specify bodily movements as constituting actions of one or another kind is to specify them as having mental causes, or at the least is specifying them in psychological terms. Entities that lack a psychology do not *signal* taxis: they move but do not literally act.

There is, moreover, a problem for anyone who takes the natural and common view that the justification for our beliefs about the mental states of others ultimately depends on being able to construe them as reasonable inferences from their behaviour in circumstances: the view we might tag 'the denial of telepathy'. The problem is that the behaviour can hardly be good evidence for the mental states if we can only make sense of it by presupposing mental states. A 'best explanation' argument from behaviour to mental states requires that the behaviour exhibit some characteristic that would be left without a good explanation in the absence of the relevant mental state. But this is not the case if the feature in question *would not exist* in the absence of the mental state.

Luckily there is a way of identifying patterns in behaviour described in 'raw' terms. The behaviour associated with psychological states, the behaviour explained by ascribing one or another mental state to a subject, is relational behaviour; it is behaviour

Behaviour non-intentionally characterized

that has a characteristic impact on the situation of the subject. The many movements associated with signalling a taxi all have the following property: the body of the subject tends to end up inside a taxi. The various movements that lead us to posit desire for beer may be very different, but they display the not insignificant commonality that they are such that the subject ends up with beer inside him or her. We will see later (in the discussion of content in chapter 11) that in fact we can do better than this by way of capturing patterns in bodily movements 'from the outside' if we draw on hypotheses of a more complicated kind. Instead of asking what effect a movement has on Jones's situation, we ask what effect it *would* have if things were thus-and-so.

There is a second reason for describing the behaviour in relational terms. We saw earlier (in the discussion of multiple realizability) that we should not be chauvinists about what realizes the various functional roles. Equally, we should not be chauvinists about the kind of body and, accordingly, the kind of bodily behaviour that are distinctive of creatures with a mental life. Martians might have mental lives like ours despite having very different bodies from ours. We have thus to think of what is crucial about the behaviour in terms that abstract away from the kind of body that displays it. The way to do this is to think of bodily behaviour in terms of environmental impact.

What does common sense say about the mind?

As we noted, common-sense functionalism selects its input, output and internal role clauses from what is regarded as most central among the common opinions about the various mental states. But how do we decide what counts as most central? This is the most pressing question that faces common-sense functionalism. David Lewis, a principal architect of common-sense functionalism, gives the following recipe for writing down the clauses:

Collect all the platitudes you can think of regarding the causal relations of mental states, sensory stimuli, and motor responses. . . . Add . . . all the platitudes to the effect that one mental state falls under another – 'toothache is a kind of pain', and the like. Perhaps there are platitudes of other forms as well. Include only platitudes which are common knowledge among us – everyone knows them, everyone knows that everyone else knows them, and so on. (Lewis, 'Psychophysical and Theoretical Identifications', p. 256)

The reason for setting the standard for inclusion so high – at the level of a platitude that is known and is known to be known – is to make it plausible that common-sense functionalism captures the meaning of the mental terms, that it elucidates the mental concepts.

It is important to make it neither too hard nor too easy for something to fall under a concept. If we include too much, then we make it too hard for things to fall under that concept. It was, for example, once widely believed that the heart played a special role with respect to the emotions, but it was not plausibly part of our concept of jealousy that it stemmed from the heart – otherwise the discovery that it is the brain that is the seat of mental activity would have shown that people are never jealous! On the other hand, if we include too little, then it will be too easy for someone to count as jealous. It is important that the common-sense functionalist preserve the distinction between what is a common opinion about one or another mental state and what is definitive of that state. For example, common-sense functionalism is a theory of the mind explicitly designed to be compatible with physicalism – indeed, to lead inevitably to physicalism, given the empirical facts; yet common opinion held for many years that the mind was different in kind from anything physical or material. At the same time we should recognize that there will be borderline cases where it is indeterminate whether something is mere common opinion about some mental state, or is constitutive of our concept of that state. A distinction can be important and still have borderline cases, as anyone worrying about becoming bald well knows.

There is, however, a problem with setting the standard as high as Lewis does in the passage quoted. There may not be enough clauses that meet the standard. Consider the difference between pride and vanity. This is a subtle matter. Is it really plausible that the difference is captured by what we can write down that meets the standard of being a platitude that is common knowledge and is known to be common knowledge? Or consider the difference between knowing something and having a true, justified belief about something. This is a subtle matter, proof of which is the fact that the difference eluded philosophers for many years, and that there is still no general agreement about how to spell out the distinction between true, justified belief and knowledge.[2]

What common-sense functionalists should do, it seems to us, is appeal to implicit or **tacit** knowledge. The classic illustration is

---

[2] It took Edmund Gettier's examples to convince philosophers that knowledge is importantly different from true, justified belief.

our knowledge of grammar. Most of us can write down a few rough-and-ready grammatical rules – 'Verbs should agree with their subjects', 'Most sentences should have a verb', and the like – but anything remotely approaching the full story is beyond us. But most of us can distinguish the grammatical from the ungrammatical, and our ability is no fluke. We have an implicit mastery of the rules of grammar. The job of the grammarian is the not inconsiderable one of making explicit what we know implicitly. In the same way, the common-sense functionalist should maintain that we have a rich and complex implicit knowledge (along with our explicit knowledge) of the interconnections between our mental states and their inputs and outputs. What reveals our implicit knowledge in the case of grammar is our ability to classify sentences as grammatical or ungrammatical. What reveals our implicit knowledge in the case of the mind is our ability to predict and explain behaviour in circumstances in terms of mental states.

Implicit knowledge as predictively powerful

This ability is a very remarkable one, although the way familiarity breeds contempt can mask this fact. Trees and planets behave in relatively regular ways. When the wind blows a tree moves in much the same way each time. Mars moves through the sky in a highly predictable way. By contrast, human beings move in a quite bewildering variety of ways, as we have already noted. Nevertheless, we often succeed in predicting what they will do. How do we do this? By treating them as subjects with mental states. By observing what they do and say, we arrive at views about what they are thinking, what they desire, and closely associated views about their characters, mental capacities, and in general their psychological profiles. We then, in terms of these views, predict what they will do. We have, then, great facility in moving backwards and forwards from behaviour in situations to mental states. Think of what is involved in playing a game of tennis, crossing a road at traffic lights, or organizing a conference. The antecedent probability that Jones will move her body in such a way that the ball will land where you have most trouble retrieving it, or that drivers will move their bodies in such a way that their cars will stop when the light turns red, or that a number of human bodies will move from various corners of the globe to end up at the same time in one conference centre, is fantastically small. Yet we make such predictions successfully all the time. True, we cannot write down the rules we follow (although we can give some rough examples), and from an evolutionary point of view, that is to be expected. Making predictions, rather than theorizing about how we make them, is what matters for survival. But the fact that we can make the predictions shows that we have cottoned on to the crucial regularities – otherwise, our predictive capacities would be a miracle. They show that we have an implicit mastery of a detailed, complex scheme that interconnects inputs, outputs and mental states. Or take the earlier example of vanity and pride. Many of us cannot *say* in detail what the difference is. But we can tell the difference between vain people and proud people; we can tailor our predictions of behaviour to fit the difference; and although we cannot say in detail what the difference is, we can recognize when someone else has done a good or a bad job of saying what it is. What is most fundamental in guiding us when we distinguish proud people from vain people is there waiting to be elucidated. This does not, of course, mean that that we must have a theory of pride and vanity *explicitly* worked out in our minds but somehow hidden from view and guiding our actions from its hiding-place. Rather, it means that our responses to situations and our judgements about pride and vanity are governed in most cases by our existing networks of interrelated powers of discrimination. Our judgements are not usually random; nor are they controlled by new dispositions which are not themselves the product of existing dispositions. So there is a theory to be had in principle about what the regularities underlying those judgements are.

The common-sense functionalist has to appeal to the idea that we have a partially implicit and partially explicit shared knowledge of the essentials of a certain complex, detailed story about situations, behavioural responses and mental states. Perhaps one day the story will be made fully explicit – what is there waiting to be elucidated will be elucidated – though the trouble grammarians have had making the rules of grammar explicit and the fact that that task is obviously a *much* smaller and easier task hardly make one optimistic. This is the partially implicit and partially explicit story we use when we predict behaviour in circumstances, and our remarkable success in making these predictions shows that there is such a story, that it is coherent, and that it gets an awful lot right. (We will return to the question of what entitles us to hold that it gets an awful lot right when we discuss eliminativism in chapter 13.) This is the story the common-sense functionalist should appeal to. It means that the common-sense functionalist's claim to have a definition of what it is to be in M_i for each M_i via the Ramsey sentence approach needs to be carefully circumscribed. There is no definition that anyone can write down. But there is a

definition available in principle. Theory **M** is not something anyone can yet write down, but it exists to be written down in theory.
Or so the common-sense functionalist must hold.

Annotated Reading

Good places to begin some further reading on functionalism include chapter
6 of Keith Campbell, *Body and Mind,* and chapter 3 of Paul Churchland,
Matter and Consciousness. Two of the most influential expositions of
common-sense or analytical functionalism are David Lewis, 'Psychophysical
and Theoretical Identifications', in which the Ramsey sentence approach
is spelt out very clearly, and various papers in Sydney Shoemaker, *Identity, Cause and Mind.* Further (and second!) thoughts on common-sense
functionalism are to be found in the early parts of Lewis's 'Reduction of
Mind'. For a version of common-sense functionalism that differs from
ours on the possibility of defining mental states in non-mental terms, see
O. Jones and P. Smith, *Philosophy of Mind.* Two collections that contain
a number of the important papers on functionalism and also helpful intro-
ductions to the material by their editors are Ned Block, ed., *Readings in
the Philosophy of Psychology*, vol. 1, and W. G. Lycan, ed., *Mind and
Cognition.* The paper that taught us that knowledge is not true, justified
belief is Edmund Gettier, 'Is Justified True Belief Knowledge?'

Part II
Rivals and Objections

4

Theory of Reference

We now make something of a detour through terrain in the philosophy of language. This is required partly because many hold that common-sense functionalism depends crucially on a discredited **theory of reference**. A theory of reference is a theory of relations between words and the world, a theory of how the word 'cat', say, gets to pick out or refer to those furry things that cause such damage to native wildlife in Australia. Common-sense functionalism, as we noted in the previous chapter, says that pain is whatever satisfies the central tautologies that we associate with pain. This is in effect a theory of reference for the word 'pain': namely, that the word picks out whatever satisfies the central tautologies. Many hold that any theory of reference of this kind is mistaken. We aim to show that to the extent that the theory is mistaken, common-sense functionalism does not inherit its faults, and to the extent that it is right, common-sense functionalism shares in its virtues. But the theory of reference has a wider importance for our project. In the next chapter we distinguish versions of functionalism importantly different from common-sense functionalism. These versions are best understood with the aid of some conceptual tools that we will introduce in our discussion of reference. Moreover, in our view, some common mistakes in contemporary philosophy of mind depend on taking home the wrong message from the recent debate over the theory of reference.

It would be nice in a text in the philosophy of mind to steer clear of the philosophy of language, but much of the current debate in the philosophy of mind hardly makes sense in the absence of some understanding of recent work on reference.

The description theory of reference

Why do we have the word 'conference' in our language? The answer is that it would be a nuisance to say 'I am going to a place where a number of other people with similar interests will be located and where some of us will read papers and exchange views'. It is simpler to say 'I am going to a conference'. We use the single word to stand in for a string of words. The same goes for words like 'car', 'weekend', 'university', and 'political party'. They save us a lot of talking and writing. Many words in our language can, that is, be thought of as essentially devices of abbreviation. It is tempting to think of words like 'heat', 'aluminium', 'gold', 'water', 'electron' and so on in terms of this model. We associate gold, water and so on with characteristic lists of properties – the properties we would cite if someone asked us what gold, water and so on are. Hence it is tempting to regard the terms as short for 'the stuff that has . . .', where the ellipsis is filled in with a list of descriptive terms for the characteristic properties. For instance, we associate water with the following properties: being colourless and odourless, falling from the sky, being liquid, being called 'water' by (English-speaking) experts, being essential for life, filling the oceans, and so on. The definite description theory of the meaning of theoretical terms takes precisely this view: 'water', according to this theory, means 'the colourless, odourless liquid that falls from the sky . . .'; and this, or something like it, is in fact what you find in most dictionaries. From this we derive a theory of reference for these theoretical terms: the reference of a theoretical term is to whatever has the characteristic properties. Thus, 'water' refers to the colourless liquid that falls from the sky, and so forth.

Part of the appeal of this combined theory of meaning and reference for theoretical terms rests on the fact that we used and understood words like 'water', 'gold' and 'heat' long before we knew what water, heat, or gold are. But if we used the word 'water' before we knew that it was H_2O, clearly the word cannot mean 'H_2O'. What else then can it mean but something like 'the stuff that is . . .', where the ellipsis is filled with terms for properties we *did* know about and associated with water, and which we subsequently discovered to be the properties of H_2O? When scientists discovered that the odourless, colourless stuff that falls from the sky, is essential to life, fills the rivers, and so on, is H_2O they did not consider that they had more work to do to show that water is

H_2O. The job was done, and, note description theorists, our theory explains precisely why this was so.

Definite description theorists emphasize that terms like 'water', 'gold' and, for that matter, 'conference' and 'university' should be regarded as **cluster terms**. What is needed for something to be water, say, is not that every single property on the list of characteristic properties be possessed by that thing; not every single description needs to be apt. All that is needed is that most of the properties be possessed. A tele-conference is still a conference, despite the fact that the participants are not located at the same place, because enough of the other distinctive features we associate with conferences are satisfied. The point here is similar to the one we noted in discussing conceptual analysis in the preceding chapter. Language is flexible and vague. It is a mistake to seek out neat lists of necessary and sufficient conditions. Although the description theory was in part inspired by the idea that certain terms are abbreviations for a cluster of *descriptions*, it is important to note that it must allow that the reference of many terms is determined by what has enough of the *properties* associated with the term independently of whether there are separate terms for the properties themselves. Otherwise, it would be involved in a vicious infinite regress. The reference of a given word would be determined by the reference of certain other words, which would in turn be determined by the reference of still other words, and so on. Moreover, it is obvious that we do not always have words for every property we associate with some word. For instance, although we can recognize a cat easily enough, often all we can say in words about the properties that enable us to recognize it is something relatively uninformative such as 'has a cat-like walk'. The description theory holds that referential terms are associated with bundles of properties whether or not we have words for the individual properties; but when we do have words for the individual properties, the terms can be thought of as abbreviations.

Description theorists also emphasize that near enough is good enough in many cases. The term 'atom' was introduced in terms of indivisibility. But it turns out that atoms can be split. Nevertheless, it is very hard to split them, and that is near enough. They also emphasize that terms change their meaning. It is plausible that 'acid' has changed its meaning as science has refined its notion of an acid. It once meant a substance that burns on contact. It now means proton donor. They emphasize that questions of change of meaning are sometimes indeterminate. We said a moment ago that

Descriptions and properties

there are atoms because being very hard to split is near enough. But maybe we should have said that, strictly speaking, the meaning of 'atom' has changed slightly. Or maybe this question has no determinate answer, just as questions about whether someone is bald, or exactly when a war ends, may have no determinate answer.

Objections to the description theory

The associated descriptions differ from person to person

An immediate problem for description theories of meaning is that the person in the street, and philosophers of language if it comes to that, often do not know much about, for instance, aluminium, and that what one person knows may differ markedly from what another person knows. Indeed, perhaps the only bit of common knowledge about aluminium among English speakers is that it is a metal called 'aluminium' by experts. Hence, the cluster of descriptions (or properties) associated with the term 'aluminium' will vary markedly from speaker to speaker, and so the meaning, on the description theory, will vary markedly from speaker to speaker, the only near to common thread being the description 'is called "aluminium" by experts'. We can live with this result. We should distinguish the meaning of a theoretical term for some particular speaker from what might be called the 'official meaning'. The meaning for a speaker will vary from individual to individual, whereas the official meaning in a given language will be given by the kind of cluster of descriptions to be found in a dictionary for that language. The idea here is nothing more radical than that a commonplace remark like 'What I mean by "acid" is something that burns on contact, but I know that chemists have a more precise meaning' may be the literal truth of the matter.

Ignorance of unique specifiers

A common objection to the description theory is that you can refer to something despite not knowing enough about it to distinguish it from a host of other things. How so, if, as the description theory holds, what you refer to is *the* thing that has enough of the properties you associate with it? Polyethylene is a case in point. You can refer to it – as in the sentence 'I know almost nothing about polyethylene' – despite having no way of uniquely specifying it. But of course you *do* know something that only it satisfies – only it is called 'polyethylene' by experts. Hence, the description theorist can hold that in my mouth 'polyethylene' means 'the chemical compound called "polyethylene" by experts', whereas the official meaning is 'a thermoplastic polymer of ethene with a repeating group of–CH_2-CH_2–'. A similar point applies to the example Hilary Putnam made famous. He admitted to not knowing how to distinguish an elm from a beech, but pointed out that surely he could still refer to elms. But of course he did know a feature of elms that distinguishes them from beeches – only they are called 'elms' by those in the know. A description theorist who makes this point must allow that in some reasonable sense of 'concept' an English speaker who knows only that elms are called 'elms', and a French speaker who knows only that elms are called 'orme' have different elm concepts. Some see this as a serious problem, but to our ears it sounds a very natural claim. It shows only that different concepts can be used to track the same actual things. Of course, the description theorist cannot hold that a person sometimes secures reference to an A via its satisfying 'is called "A"' by *that very* person. That would be circular. But this does not mean that a person cannot secure reference to an A via its being called 'A' by others that the person defers to as being experts, or at least as being more expert than they are, on the subject of As.

The really serious problem for the description theory arises from *Twin Earth* the famous Twin Earth case. It refutes the description theory for 'water', 'gold' and, indeed, for natural kind terms in general. It shows that the words we use for kinds in nature – water, gold, energy, hydrogen and so on – are not abbreviations of definite descriptions made from the words for the properties we associate with the respective kinds.

Take our stock example, the description theorist's story about the meaning of 'water'. It follows from it that something that does not go close to having *a single one* of the characteristic properties associated with water cannot possibly be water. It also follows from the story that something that has *every one* of the characteristic properties is water. The fact that the description theory allows that meanings may vary from speaker to speaker, and that not every member of any given cluster of properties needs to be possessed for some substance to be water, say, does not alter the fact that if not a single property that might plausibly be associated with the term 'water' is possessed by x, then x is not water, according to the theory; and, conversely, if every property that might plausibly be associated with the term 'water' is possessed by x, then x is water, according to the theory. The case of Twin Earth refutes these two consequences of the theory.

Twin Earth is superficially like Earth. Sometimes it is imagined that Twin Earth is in our possible world and is, say, on the opposite side of the Sun from Earth so that we never get to see it in the night sky; sometimes it is supposed to be in another possible world altogether. We will suppose that it is somewhere else in our world. Just as Earth is populated by Earthians, Twin Earth is populated by Twin Earthians. They look pretty much like us. Their language is superficially like English. Their world is superficially very like ours: their sky looks blue, they have things they call 'rivers' that flow, their sea tastes salty, and so on and so forth. The important difference between Earth and Twin Earth lies in the stuff they call 'water'. Their water – 'retaw', as we will call it in *our* language – is superficially like our water. Retaw is liquid, odourless, colourless, falls from the sky, is called 'water' by (their) experts, is essential to life (on Twin Earth), and so on. However, its chemical composition is not H_2O. It is, let us say, XYZ. There is, however, some H_2O on Twin Earth, but there it is a black, tarry substance. There are, no doubt, subtle reasons that explain why it is XYZ, not H_2O, that is essential to life on Twin Earth and why H_2O is black and tarry there. We need not enquire into them here. What matters for us is the answer to the question, as asked in our language, in Earth English as opposed to Twin Earth English: What stuff is water on Twin Earth?

The answer is clear. Water on Twin Earth is *not* the stuff that satisfies the list of characteristic properties. It is rather the black tarry stuff, for it is that which is H_2O. The right thing to say in our language is that water on Twin Earth is, for reasons we may or may not understand, black and tarry, and that the stuff, retaw, which is superficially like our water and which the Twin Earthians call 'water', is something else altogether: namely, XYZ. But then it cannot be the case that 'water' in our language is an abbreviation for the definite description 'the liquid that satisfies the characteristic properties' or, for short, 'the watery stuff', and refers to whatever has the characteristic properties. For it is retaw, not the black tarry stuff, that satisfies the definite description, and has the characteristic properties – that is to say, is the watery stuff – on Twin Earth.

The causal theory

What can we put in place of the description theory? What follows is a brief account of one popular, and to our mind highly attractive, alternative to the description theory. It is a version of the causal theory of reference. We will present it as applied to natural kind terms like 'water' and 'gold'. This is sufficient for our pedagogical purposes here.

There are certain paradigm examples of bits of water – exemplars of water, or water stereotypes, as they are sometimes called. The sea, puddles after rain, and rivers would be examples. We come across them regularly, and when we do they often interact causally with us. We have long supposed that they are all made up of the same fundamental kind of stuff, that they are examples of a single natural kind. This supposition predates our knowing that they are all bodies of H_2O. We use the word 'water' for the natural kind that causally confronts us when we view, drink, swim in (or whatever) these exemplars of water.

Water stereotypes

This theory explains why the black tarry substance on Twin Earth is water. It is of the same natural kind as the exemplars of water on Earth – as, that is, the exemplars that confronted us when we introduced the term 'water' (and the French introduced the term 'eau', and so on for the other natural languages). For the chemical composition – what matters for natural kind-hood – of the black tarry stuff is H_2O, and it is H_2O that acted on our sense organs when we named the kind in common to the exemplars of water. The causal theory also explains why the watery substance on Twin Earth is not water. It is not of the same natural kind as the exemplars of water on Earth, despite its superficial similarities to water. We have never drunk or swum in XYZ, and it was not what we are responding to, though it is what the Twin Earthians are responding to, when we use the term 'water'.

The theory is plausible for a whole range of natural kind terms: 'gold', 'aluminium', 'lemon', 'heat' and so on. Take gold. We associate gold with a whole range of characteristic properties: yellow, malleable, valuable, resistant to corrosion, found in the ground, and so on. The description theory accordingly says that 'gold' is a cluster term with constituent descriptions like 'is a yellow metal', 'is malleable', 'is valuable', and that its reference is determined by what near enough satisfies enough of these descriptions or near enough has the corresponding properties. But suppose that on Twin Earth, owing to the different conditions there, the element we call 'gold', the element with atomic number 79, is easily corroded, is of little value, and is usually grey in colour. Is it gold? The answer is, Yes. True, it would be sensible not to take gold with you on a trip to Twin Earth, but the reason would *not* be that the gold would turn into another element. It would be the rather bad effect the trip would have on the properties we value gold for. How can we explain the fact that the meaning of the word 'gold' is such that it names the element with atomic number 79 on both Earth and Twin Earth? The description theory has no hope of explaining this fact, whereas on the causal theory the explanation is straightforward. 'Gold' names the natural (chemical) kind exemplified in certain samples that we on Earth have come across. That kind is, as it happens, the element with atomic number 79, and thus it is the element with atomic number 79 that counts as gold on Twin Earth.

There are many questions to be asked about the causal theory. What should be said about cases where the presumption of a natural kind in common fails? What do we say about someone who travels to Twin Earth and uses the word 'water' for XYZ? – Does the word 'water' come after a time to pick out retaw, or does the initial causal link to H_2O trump all subsequent causal interactions with XYZ in settling what 'water' refers to in his or her mouth? For our purposes, though, there are just two points that call for elaboration.

Extreme versus moderate causal theories

First, the causal theory just described is not an extreme causal theory. The superficial properties associated with water, and not just the causal facts, play an important role in settling what the word 'water' refers to. When we called the exemplars of water 'water', we were responding to a huge range of factors that came together to cause us to use the word 'water', including: a certain pattern of retinal stimulation, a kind of wave packet reflecting from the exemplars, the weather conditions that caused the water to be in front of us to begin with, the position of our heads, the factors that led us to use 'water' and not some other word, and the ambient lighting. How then did the word come to pick out water, and not, say, the retinal stimulus pattern? And how did it come to pick out water and not liquid or being essential to life?

There are two problems here: a **depth problem** and a spread problem. The depth problem is to explain why 'water' picks out a property of something at a certain point, at a certain 'depth', in the causal chain that ends up with our using the word 'water'. The spread problem is to explain why 'water' picks out from the very many properties of water the property that it does. Samples of water are also samples of liquids, of stuff essential to life, of what is colourless, and so on. How come 'water' names the natural kind distinctive of samples of water rather than being liquid or being

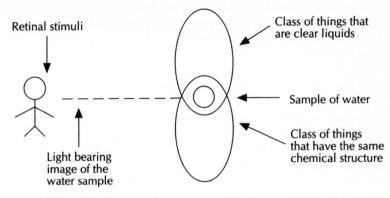

Figure 3   The depth problem: why does 'water' pick out a property of something at a certain point, at a certain 'depth', in the causal chain that ends up with our using the word 'water'? The spread problem: why does 'water' pick out from the very many properties of water the property that it does?

essential to life or being colourless? The spread problem is also known as the *qua* problem, for it is the problem of explaining why 'water' picks out water *qua* water rather than *qua* something essential to life, colourless or liquid. The two problems can be thought of in the terms shown in figure 3.

It is hard to see how causal considerations alone could solve either the depth problem or the spread problem. The obvious answer to the two problems is to insist that our grasp of the meaning of the word 'water' involves knowing that 'water' picks out a cause of a *certain kind*, the natural kind whose exemplars have the associated properties, the very properties that the description theory is framed in terms of. We use 'water' for the liquid, odourless etc. natural kind – the *watery* natural kind, as it is sometimes called – that was before us and with which we were interacting in various ways, and not, for example, the retinal stimulus natural kind or the kind of weather conditions that lead to water being around. The same goes for the other examples of natural kind terms. 'Gold' refers to the malleable, yellow, etc. kind that is common to the exemplars of gold with which we have interacted on various occasions and that we use the word 'gold' for. The idea is, that is, that the reference of natural kind terms depends on a *mixture* of causal and non-causal factors: natural kind terms pick out a certain sort of cause, and the certain sort is specified by the features that the description theory appealed to.

The second feature of natural kind terms that is important for what follows is that they are **rigid designators**, and this is a point that needs a little elaboration.

Rigid designation

There are *two* things wrong with the classical description theory as applied to natural kind terms, though the description theory is clearly right for *some* terms; we *do* sometimes abbreviate longish, complex descriptions. One thing which is wrong is the neglect of the role of causal interaction with the natural kind common to the exemplars in settling what it is right to call 'water', say. This is the point we have been emphasizing so far. This is what stopped XYZ from being water. XYZ was not what we were causally acquainted with on the relevant occasions. The other thing wrong with the classical description theory is that it makes 'water' out to be a non-rigid designator.

Definite descriptions are non-rigid

An expression like 'the tallest man alive' is a non-rigid designator. It designates different persons in different possible worlds. Suppose that Tom is taller than anyone alive except Dick. Then 'the tallest man alive' designates Dick. But (let's suppose) had Dick not eaten up his Weeties, then Dick would have been shorter than Tom. In that case Tom would have been the tallest man alive. Hence, 'the tallest man alive' might have failed to designate Dick; it might have designated Tom instead. Which is to say that the reference of 'the tallest man alive' varies from possible world to possible world according to who is the tallest man in any given world. Definite descriptions are typically non-rigid designators simply because 'the F' refers in w to the one and only F in w (or the one and only F salient in the context of utterance, but we will neglect this sort of complication), and in general the one and only F in w need not be the same thing as the one and only F in w'. There are exceptions. For instance, 'the smallest prime' designates 2 in every world, but these are special cases. In particular, the definite description 'the watery natural kind' is non-rigid. It designates H_2O in the actual world, but in a possible world where some other natural kind, XYZ, say, is the natural kind that falls from the sky, etc., then it designates XYZ, not H_2O.

'Water' is rigid

Now we saw that in Twin Earth it is H_2O, not XYZ, that 'water' refers to. But the point could be thought to turn *solely* on the fact that the reference of 'water' in our mouths and from our pens is in part determined by what interacts with us, and it is H_2O, not XYZ, that interacts with us. XYZ interacts only with the Twin Earthians. What then should we say about a possible world – not our world obviously – where it is *we* who interact with XYZ, and where it is XYZ that is the stuff that is watery? The answer is that it makes no difference. XYZ is not water in that world either. The reference of 'water' is fixed on the watery natural kind we named 'water' in the actual world. 'Water' is, we say, a rigid designator. It names the *same stuff in every world*: namely, H_2O. One way of putting the point is to say that there is an indexical element in our use of the term 'water' – 'Water is *that* kind of stuff there' – where the role of the demonstrative is to make the reference of the term the same in all possible worlds.

When we first introduced the Twin Earth case, we noted that it comes in two varieties. In one, Twin Earth is somewhere remote from Earth but in our possible world. In the other, it is in another possible world altogether. We used the first version to show the importance of causal acquaintance with exemplars in settling the reference of 'water'. We are in effect using the second version to show that 'water' is a rigid designator.

It follows that there is an important addition to make to the causal story about how the word 'water' comes to refer to H_2O. 'Water' does not just refer to whatever has the associated properties and stands in the right causal relation to us in the actual world. It refers to that very kind in every possible world. We saw that a pure causal theory cannot account for why 'water' refers to H_2O rather than to a certain retinal stimulus pattern or to being essential for life. We need to require in addition that water satisfy the cluster of associated properties that figure in the classical description theory. But we must not interpret this as requiring that water possess the associated properties in every possible world. If in some possible world H_2O is black and tarry, it is nevertheless water. We must interpret the requirement as that 'water' denotes whatever kind in the actual world has the associated properties and has the right causal connection. The answer to what 'water' denotes in some other possible world is then simply that it denotes the very same kind that it denotes in the actual world, *whether or not* it possesses in that world the associated properties or the causal connections to us.

The key idea is that definite descriptions can be turned into rigid designators by a device known as **rigidification**. Consider a remark like 'If the tallest man had not eaten up his Weeties, then

'Actually' as rigidification device

he would not have been the tallest man'. Read one way this is nonsense. Regardless of Weetie consumption, in every possible world the tallest man is the tallest man. But there is, of course, another way of reading the remark. You might read it as saying that the man who is *actually* or *in fact* the tallest would not have been the tallest had he not eaten up his Weeties. The role of the words 'actually' and 'in fact' is to tell us that what is being said is that the tallest man in the actual world is not the tallest man in the world where he does not eat up his Weeties. Or think of the remark 'I would be earning more than I am had I only . . .'. Someone who says this is not saying that there is a possible world w in which she earns more in w than she does in w. What is being said is that what she earns in the actual world – that is, what she actually or in fact earns – is less than what she earns in some other possible worlds – the worlds that would have been actual had she taken up tax law, say, or won the lottery. The role of the terms 'actually' and 'in fact' is to fix the reference on what satisfies the relevant description in the actual world. A final example: the word 'now' serves to pick out the time of speaking. If Mary says 'I am now pouring the champagne', she tells you that the time of champagne pouring is the time of speaking (near enough). But 'now' does not *mean* 'the time of speaking', for if it did, the sentence 'I might not be speaking now' would be nonsense. What it means is 'the *actual* time of speaking', and Mary's sentence 'I might not be speaking now' says that there is a possible world where the time that she is speaking in the actual world is not a time at which she is speaking in that world. The crucial distinction can be captured as follows: whereas 'the F' denotes in every possible world w the one and only F in w, 'the actual F' denotes in every possible world w the one and only F in the actual world. Inserting the word 'actual' serves, as we say, to rigidify the definite description. It turns a definite description into something that works more like a name.

Giving the meaning versus fixing the reference

In sum, the situation is as follows. Associated with water – and similar remarks apply to a whole range of natural kind terms – are a number of exemplars with which we are acquainted, which are all samples of a natural kind that is liquid, odourless, falls from the sky and so on, and which we baptised 'water'. We will use 'watery' from now on for this cluster of features (so, from now on, we include the causal link involved in the baptismal acquaintance as part of the cluster). The word 'water' does not mean 'the watery kind'; it means 'the actual watery kind'. It is a rigidified definite description that incorporates a causal element. In an alternative terminology, we distinguish giving the meaning of 'water' in terms of a definite description like 'the watery kind' from fixing the reference of 'water' in terms of 'the watery kind'. To fix the reference of 'water' in terms of its being the watery kind is to set the reference of 'water' in any world w as the kind that is watery in the actual world. We have here two ways of saying the same thing. To say that a term functions as a rigidified definite description is the same as saying that the term's reference is fixed via the definite description.

A fair question at this stage is whether the causal theory of reference for natural kind terms as we have developed it can be seen as a sophisticated development of the old description theory. The inspiration behind the old description theory is the idea that a word W refers to x just if associated with W is a set of properties and x has enough of those properties or something close to those properties. The description theorist can well insist that what the first version of the Twin Earth argument teaches us is that important among the associated properties is the relation of causal acquaintance with exemplars; and the second version teaches us is that reference in a non-actual possible world w is sometimes a matter of the properties possessed in the actual world, not in w itself. We are happy to leave this bit of turf marking to the philosophers of language.

The importance of the causal theory of reference for the philosophy of mind derives from, first, its impact on the discussion of what is and what is not necessary, and, second, the fact that it opens up the possibility that a term associated with some set of distinctive features may not be a term for whatever has those features, or enough of them, or near enough of them, but may rather be a term whose reference is fixed by those features. It may be, that is, a term like 'water' or 'gold' or like 'the person who is *actually* the tallest'. In particular, it serves up the possibility that we should think of the common-sense roles of common-sense functionalism as fixing the reference rather than giving the meaning of the mental state terms. The next chapter starts with a consideration of this idea. We will close this chapter with some more general comments on the impact of the causal theory on discussions of what is and what is not necessary. The general thrust of our remarks here, and throughout the rest of this book, will be rather deflationary in tone. The causal theory of reference is without question important, but we think, contrary to much current opinion, that it leaves the main issues in the philosophy of mind and of necessity much as they were.

The necessary *a posteriori*

In our discussion in chapter 1 of the possible worlds way of eluci-dating various central notions, we said that a sentence *p* is neces-sarily true iff *p* is true in every possible world. Thus 'Nothing is bigger than itself' and 'Everything is identical with itself' are nec-essarily true because they are true in every possible world. It is also a feature of these two sentences that they are *a priori* know-able. We do not need to undertake empirical investigation of what the world is like in order to ascertain that they are true: our under-standing of the relevant words plus logical acumen are enough to tell us that they are true. Indeed, we would think it very strange if someone were undertake a series of experiments to try to show that they are true. The phenomenon of rigidified definite descrip-tions means, however, that there are clear cases of sentences that are both necessarily true and *a posteriori*.

Rigid designation and necessity   Consider, for instance, the sentence 'Water = H_2O'. If we ne-glect the issue of what to say about worlds where there is no water as raising here irrelevant issues,[3] this sentence is true in all poss-ible worlds. For the terms 'water' and 'H_2O' designate the very same stuff in the actual world. This follows from the fact that 'Water = H_2O' is true. But then they designate the very same stuff in all possible worlds, because, by rigidity, what they designate does not vary from world to world. But then the sentence 'Water = H_2O' is true in all possible worlds. Indeed, it is easy to see that any identity sentence formed with rigid designators flanking the identity sign is if true, necessarily true, and if false, necessarily false (again ignoring the issue of what to say about worlds where the terms do not refer). But, of course, the sentence 'Water = H_2O' is not *a priori* true. It took empirical investigation to show that it was true. It is, that is, *a posteriori*. Equally, although the sentence 'Water = XYZ' is necessarily false, it is not *a priori* that it is false. Both 'Water = H_2O' and 'Water = XYZ' are *a posteriori*, though the first is necessarily true and the second is necessarily false.

---

[3]   If you want a sentence that does not raise this issue to start with, replace 'Water = H_2O' with 'If there is water, water = H_2O' or 'Any water = H_2O'.

What is the relevance of this point to the philosophy of mind? Often claims about what is possible play a central role in establishing important conclusions in the philosophy of mind. A simple example is the famous, plausible thesis of multiple realizability that we discussed in the previous chapter. This thesis is the thesis that it is *possible* for two creatures with very different internal natures – perhaps one is carbon-based like us, and the other is silicon-based like the imaginary Martians – to be alike psychologically. In other words, although it may be true that all creatures with a psychology are carbon-based, it is not necessarily true. Creatures with a psychology might have been silicon-based (and perhaps will be one day if computers that think are developed). What we learn from the fact that being necessary is different from being *a priori* is that it would be a mistake to argue for this possibility as follows. It is *a posteriori* that creatures with a psychology are carbon-based (it took experiments to find this out). Therefore it is not necessarily true that creatures with a psychology are carbon-based; that is, creatures with a psychology might not be carbon-based.

However, it does *not* follow that we should not be guided by our intuitions in deciding what is or is not possible. And this indeed is what we did when we discussed the thesis of multiple realizability. We noted for instance that the intuitively right thing to say about the Martian is that it has a psychology that may well be very like ours. It is sometimes supposed, or seems to be supposed, that divorcing the question of what is possible from what is *a posteriori* means that we can no longer rely on intuitions for guidance concerning what is possible. However, this would be an internally inconsistent position. The reason for believing in the phenomenon of reference fixing, the phenomenon that generates the necessary *a posteriori*, is our *intuitions* about what to say about Twin Earth and like cases, and these are intuitions about possible cases (Twin Earth does not actually exist). What is true is that we need to be careful that we do not move from the fact that something is *a posteriori* to the conclusion that it might be true and it might be false. Thus, although it is *a posteriori* that everything with a psychology is carbon-based, the reason for thinking that psychology is not necessarily linked to being carbon-based is not that fact, but our intuitions about what should be said about Martians and the like.

Some worry about the role of intuitions here (paradoxically, some of these worriers are the very same people who appeal to

Intuitions about possibility

intuitions about Twin Earth elsewhere in their work), but what can we do but be guided by our intuitions? For to be guided by intuitions is nothing more than to follow the principle that it is better to say what seems plausible than to say what seems implausible. This does not mean that our intuitions about possibility are sacrosanct – far from it – but it does mean that they are where we must start, and that the onus of proof is on one who denies the possibility of something – like a silicon-based thinker – that seems clearly possible.

A new kind of possibility and necessity? We promised earlier that we would return to the distinction between metaphysical and logical possibility, and the correlative distinction between metaphysical and logical necessity. Taking this distinction seriously may be part of the explanation of the views of those who think that we do not need to start with our intuitions about possibility. They imagine that metaphysical possibility is a special kind of possibility, distinct from logical possibility. Metaphysical possibilities, and likewise necessities, they think, are discovered *a posteriori*. You look into the world, and the world itself reveals that, for example, water is necessarily H_2O.

On our picture, though, water is necessarily H_2O because it is part of our concept of water that it has necessarily whatever properties science tells are the most intrinsically important ones possessed by the stuff around us that is watery. Those properties turn out to be ones of chemical structure, in particular being H_2O. But this is straightforward logical necessity. In every (logically) possible world that contains water, it is H_2O: not because of a new kind of necessity, but because, given what we mean by 'water', something has to have the same chemical structure as the watery stuff to earn the right to be called (by us) water. As it happens, that chemical structure is H_2O.

Of course, we *learn* which properties water necessarily possesses *a posteriori*. But that does not mean that there is a special kind of necessity that only reveals itself *a posteriori:* it's the same kind of necessity, but because something in our concept appeals to contingent facts about the actual world to determine the properties that water has necessarily, we only learn what these properties are through experience.

The necessary a posteriori On our view, then, the fact that 'Water = H_2O' is necessary *a posteriori* does not mean that it has a different kind of necessity from that possessed by, say, 'Water = water'. We take the view that they have the same kind of necessity, the strongest kind, which can equally be called metaphysical or logical, and that they differ merely in whether their possession of this property is or is not knowable *a priori:* in the first case it is not, in the second it is. The necessity they have is the same; the access we have to it is not.

Our reason is in part a desire to avoid multiplying kinds of necessity, but mainly that the explanation of how 'Water = H_2O' gets to be necessary does not involve recognizing a new sort of necessity. Instead, it turns on a *semantic* point: namely, that the term 'water' is a rigid designator. Had the term been, as many used to believe, a standard (and so non-rigid) definite description, then 'Water = H_2O' would have been contingent. But a fact about the way we use words is not a reason for believing in a new kind of necessity.

There is a separate issue which it is important to disentangle from these considerations. Even if 'Water = H_2O' were not necessary, it might still be true that the water in our world is a substance that is *essentially* H_2O. Though you can lose a few hairs from your head and remain the same person, this substance cannot lose its chemical nature and remain the very same substance – its chemical nature is bound up in its very identity. *The issue of essential properties*

This is quite separate from whether 'Water = H_2O' is necessary. If the semantic facts were different, and 'water' were a definite description, then indeed 'Water = H_2O' would not be necessary. This is because 'water' would not then be a rigid designator, it would not designate H_2O in all worlds, and so 'Water = H_2O' would be false in some worlds. Nevertheless, it would still be true that the chemical substance we call 'water' is essentially H_2O, that it could not be the chemical substance that it is without being H_2O. The difference would be that that substance is not correctly called 'water' in all worlds. The issue of the essential nature of the substance we call 'water' thus comes apart from the issue of the **semantics** of 'water', and in particular from the question of whether 'water' is a rigid designator. There is the further question as to whether the issue of essences comes apart from *all* semantic facts (e.g. the semantics of the phrase 'same substance'), but nothing we say here depends on the answer to that question.

The attribution of essential properties in this way does not require a separate kind of necessity. Our judgements about essential properties are based in the usual way on our *a priori* intuitions. Science *per se* does not show us that the water around us is a substance which is essentially H_2O. It shows us only that it *is* H_2O. The step to its being an essential property is made by reflecting that anything in any possible world which was not H_2O would not count as the same substance; and the notion of possible world that we use in these reflections is the standard, univocal one.

Annotated Reading

The two classic challenges to the description theory of reference are Saul Kripke, *Naming and Necessity,* and Hilary Putnam, 'The Meaning of "Meaning"'. Kripke's book is the classic source for rigid designation, fixing the reference, and the necessary *a posteriori*; Putnam's for Twin Earth, the elm–beech example, and stereotypes. They have spawned an enormous literature. One place to start is Michael Devitt and Kim Sterelny, *Language and Reality*. Devitt and Sterelny are very sympathetic to a style of causal theory that concedes little to the claims of the description theory. For a defence of the importance of associated properties for settling reference see John Searle, *Intentionality*, chapter 8. An important but difficult discussion is Gareth Evans, *The Varieties of Reference*. A good collection of readings is A. W. Moore, ed., *Meaning and Reference*. For 'actually' as a rigidifier, see Martin Davies and I. L. Humberstone, 'Two Notions of Necessity'.

The most elegant account of the necessary *a posteriori* does not require distinguishing two kinds of necessity and possibility, and is given in terms of what is known as two-dimensional modal logic. If you are interested in pursuing this further, the paper by Davies and Humberstone is a good beginning, as also is Robert Stalnaker's 'Assertion'.

5

Empirical Functionalisms

There are many varieties of functionalism and doctrines that are called functionalism on the market. In chapter 3 we expounded the well-known and, to our minds, appealing variety known as common-sense or analytical functionalism. But many popular positions in the philosophy of mind and cognitive science take as their starting point other versions of functionalism. The purpose of this chapter is tell you about some of the other varieties and to map out the intellectual terrain surrounding these versions and common-sense functionalism. We will draw on the discussion of reference in chapter 4 at a number of points.

Common-sense functional roles as a reference-fixing device

Most people understand the word 'thermostat'. It is not like the terms 'second-order differential coefficient' or 'ganglion'. This places a constraint on any account of the word's meaning: it had better make sense of the fact that most people understand it. The same goes for mental state terms. Most of us understand them – we know what we are saying when we say that someone is in pain, believes in God, or desires a pay rise – and so any account of their meaning should respect this fact. One strength of common-sense functionalism is that it does respect this fact. Most of us know that bodily damage typically causes pain, and that pain typically causes behaviour that the subject believes will minimize the damage and the pain, and most of us know what behaviour belief in God or the desire for a pay rise typically causes. More generally, the functional roles in terms of which mental states are specified in common-

The knowledge constraint on understanding

sense functionalism are ones which are common knowledge –
though, as we saw, this common knowledge must be construed so
as to include implicit knowledge as well as explicit knowledge.
The roles are, that is, common-sense or folk functional roles. Thus,
when common-sense functionalists tell their story about the meanings of the mental state terms, they meet what we might call the
knowledge constraint by virtue of the fact that their story is one
told in terms of what is common knowledge.

The distinction between *giving the meaning* and *fixing the reference* means, though, that there are *two* ways you might meet the
knowledge constraint: you might think of the folk roles as giving
the meaning of the mental state terms, or alternatively as playing
a reference-fixing role. Common-sense functionalism, of course,
thinks of the folk roles as giving the meaning: to be in mental state
M is to be in the state that fills the folk role associated with M. But
you might think of the folk roles as fixing the reference instead.
After all, we understood the term 'water' when all we knew about
water was that it is watery, and yet, as we have seen, to be water is
not to be the watery stuff – XYZ is the watery stuff on Twin
Earth, but it is not water. So you might say that we understood the
term 'water' before we knew it was H_2O because (a) its reference
is fixed by being watery, (b) we knew about being watery, and (c)
a term's having its reference fixed in terms of something we know
about is good enough for understanding it.

Empirical functionalism

Empirical functionalism typically meets the knowledge constraint by having the folk roles fix the reference. It comes in two
forms. In one the folk roles fix reference on the relatively categorical nature of the states that play the roles – on, for example, the
relevant neurophysiological states. This form is thus committed to
denying the multiple realizability insight: it makes it necessary *a
posteriori* that silicon-based creatures do not have mental states. As
far as we know, very few now subscribe to this version explicitly.

In the most plausible versions of empirical functionalism, the
versions we will be focusing on, the folk roles reference fix on
further functional roles that it is then the task of empirical science
to discover. The idea is that there is something relatively abstract
about the internal nature of the actual exemplars of thinking beings – we humans – that is essential to having mental states. The
questions of how abstract these states are and which science (or
which faction in cognitive science) gets to describe their natures
determine some of the axes of variation among these views. But
the general idea common to the various versions is that although

we identify who is in mental state M by identifying who has inside them various states playing the folk functional roles we associate with M, it is *not* the nature of the state that occupies the folk role, and it is not the folk role itself that determines that a subject is in M. What settles that a subject is in M is the internal functional role that underpins the folk functional role associated with M. The nature of these underpinning roles is an *a posteriori* matter. It is something discovered by investigating how we exemplars of beings in M work. So when we discover that it is, say, F that underpins the folk roles associated with M, we will have discovered the necessary *a posteriori* truth that a subject is in M if and only if the subject's internal states occupy F.

Sometimes empirical functionalism is put forward without the digression via reference fixing by folk roles. The claim is simply that (a) mental states are occupants of functional roles, and that (b) which functional roles determine which mental states a subject is in is a matter for neuroscience alone. There is no mention of the folk roles in the story. But then how do we come by our opinions about what, say, President Clinton thinks? We do not have a clue as to the neuroscientific functional roles his states are occupying! The folk roles have to come into the picture. But what we learn from the causal theory of reference is that they can come into the picture without thereby forcing the functionalist into holding that the folk roles give the meaning of the mental terms; maybe they merely fix the reference instead. In the case of gold, the descriptions (which include 'the stuff we baptised "gold"') we associate with gold settle the exemplars or paradigms; then we look for some internal feature of these paradigm samples that we require to be present for something to count as an instance of gold (having atomic number 79, as it turns out). When we know the relevant natural kind, it may, of course, turn out that some of our exemplars were fool's gold. In the case of pain, the corresponding story would be that the folk roles we associate with pain settle the paradigm cases of pain; then we look for some internal *functional* feature that we require to be present for something to count as pain. Fool's pain will then occur when the folk roles are occupied, but not in the right kind of internal functional way.

We can put the same idea in terms of *essences*. The essence of *The essences of* gold is the property gold has in any possible world: namely, having *mental states* atomic number 79. The essence of water is the property water has in any possible world: namely, being H_2O. The essences of gold and water are *a posteriori* matters. The role of the descriptions we associate with water and gold, the descriptions that appear in dictionary definitions of the words 'water' and 'gold', is to tell us which samples need to be investigated when we find out what the essences of water and gold are. Likewise, empirical functionalism holds that the functional essences of the various mental states are an *a posteriori* matter, not something given by the descriptions, the folk functional roles, that we associate with the various mental states. And it is their functional essences that determine, settle without remainder, questions about which mental states subjects are in, according to empirical functionalism in its most plausible versions.

Chauvinism and empirical functionalism

We noted when we first broached the subject of functionalism in chapter 3 how strong the case for multiple realizability is, and how the multiple realizability of functional roles means that functionalist theories of mind can avoid the charge of chauvinism. The two problems we now raise for empirical functionalism both turn on the fact that the cost of making empirical functionalism significantly different from common-sense functionalism is chauvinism of one kind or another. We call the two problems the chauvinism–liberalism dilemma and internal architecture chauvinism.

The chauvinism– liberalism dilemma

Functionalism of any variety is characterized by there being three kinds of clause: input, output and internal role. The chauvinism–liberalism dilemma arises from the way that certain versions of empirical functionalism differ from common-sense functionalism in the characterization of the inputs and outputs of the functional roles it sees as crucial. Common-sense functionalism, as we saw, characterizes these clauses in the terms familiar to common-sense: the inputs are described as tigers and cups of coffee, the outputs in terms of the way movements affect how we relate to tigers and cups of coffee. Empirical functionalists, by contrast, typically fix on the inputs to and the outputs from the central nervous system. We know that what happens there is particularly important; specifically, it is how the central nervous system transforms what goes into it into what comes out of it that underpins the behavioural capacities that mark us off as creatures with minds. The central nervous system is thus the obvious place for empirical functionalists to find the underpinning functional roles that they see as crucial. But how should we describe these inputs and outputs? We could, of course, describe them in terms of their relatively remote origins and outcomes: as the sort of input to the central nervous system typically produced by a tiger, and as the sort of output from the central nervous system typically causing the body to move further away from a tiger. But that would turn empirical functionalism into a style of common-sense functionalism. Hence empirical functionalists, who want to emphasize the distance between empirical functionalism and common-sense functionalism, seek an alternative, more 'local' characterization of the inputs and outputs.

The trouble is that any characterization of the inputs and outputs interestingly different in being suitably local leads either to chauvinism or to excessive liberalism. If we describe them *qua* inputs and outputs to the central nervous system, that is, in neurophysiological terms, we force empirical functionalists to embrace a form of neurophysiological chauvinism. Only creatures with neurophysiologies like ours, or anyway like ours in inputs and outputs, can have minds. Machines and Martians, simply by virtue of the fact that the inputs and outputs to their central processors are so different from ours, cannot have minds.

An unacceptable chauvinism also results if we characterize the inputs in terms of peripheral stimulations at the sense-organs and the outputs in terms of in terms of bodily contortions. How much of a mental life bats enjoy is open to debate, but the debate is not closed merely by noting that the inputs that matter for them are importantly different from those that matter for us (sound is important for them in the way that light is important for us) – it is what they do with the peripheral inputs, or rather what they fail to do, that makes us suspect that they lack a rich mental life. Again, although the mental life of dolphins is a matter of debate, it would clearly be wrong to dismiss the suggestion that they are intelligent simply on the ground that their bodily contortions are very different from ours or on the ground that they are responding to vibrations transmitted through water, vibrations that have no interesting effects on we exemplars of the intelligent.

There is, however, a way of characterizing the inputs and outputs that allows empirical functionalists to stand up to the chauvinism challenge without falling back on the way common-sense functionalism characterizes the inputs and outputs. They can view the common-sense functional roles as reference-fixing on a highly abstract feature of us exemplars of the minded, and accordingly give a highly abstract characterization of the inputs and outputs. We will refer to this style of empirical functionalism as **machine**

Machine functionalism

functionalism, and will argue that it avoids the charge of chauvinism at the cost of being excessively liberal about what counts as having a mind. This objection calls for a little stage setting.

Two notions of multiple realization

We described the machine table for the coke machine in chapter 3 in relatively concrete terms. The inputs were described as money and the outputs as money and cokes. Only the internal states were assigned schematic letters. But, of course, we could have described it in completely abstract terms, using, say, '1' for '50c', '2' for '$1', '3' for 'coke', and so on. And it might well be that this abstract description fitted some other machine with different functional roles in the sense that its outputs were hot chocolate or parking vouchers instead of coke, and the inputs were 50p and £1. There are thus *two* notions of multiple realizability that can be distinguished in discussions of functionalism. One is the possibility of different *states or things* occupying the same, relatively concretely specified functional role: for example, a valve amplifier and a transistor amplifier may generate roughly the same outputs from the same kinds of inputs. But it is also possible to have different, relatively concretely specified functional *roles* realizing the same abstractly described functional role: the inputs and outputs may be totally different, and, in consequence, the functional roles typed by kinds of inputs and outputs may be quite different; nevertheless what is happening is the same at some highly abstract level of representation. Our earlier support for the thesis of multiple realizability was support for the view that creatures like us in the relatively concretely specified functional roles occupied, but differing in what occupies them, are psychologically like us. But what about an entity like us merely in having the same *abstractly specified* machine table?

Suppose, for instance, we take the common-sense functionalist story about us – though the points that follow could be made on any reasonable account of the functional roles that matter for having a mind – and code each distinct input, each distinct internal state, and each distinct output with different numbers. We then build a machine that shuffles numbers exactly in accord with the story we have just constructed. This machine will be like us in having the very same machine table, abstractly specified, as we do, and in having states occupying the same roles, *abstractly specified*, as we do. According to machine functionalism, it will then have the same mental states as we do.

Excessive liberalism

This seems to us to be jumping from the frying pan of chauvinism into the fire of an excessive liberalism. A machine that crunches numbers according to a table that matches the way we 'crunch' environmental inputs and outputs described in environmental terms just crunches numbers. Part of what is involved in having beliefs about tigers is responding to tigers in the right way, or at least being of a kind that would respond to tigers in the appropriate circumstances. The machine does not respond at all to tigers. It only responds to numbers. Again, part of what it is to be in pain is to be in a state that typically follows bodily damage and causes limb withdrawal, whereas the machine's states play causally intermediate roles only between numbers. The objection is sometimes put by imagining that some highly artificial, abstract description of the economy of Bolivia or a pail of water represents them as realizing the same machine table, abstractly specified, as President Clinton. It would clearly be ridiculous to suppose that the Bolivian economy or the pail of water has thereby the same detailed beliefs about Congress that President Clinton has. We should, that is, take the same view about having a mind as we take about being a thermostat. We might describe the way a thermostat mediates between temperature changes in a refrigerator and the turning off and on of its motor in a highly abstract table with numbers for the various inputs and outputs, but this does not make a device that operates on numbers according to the table a thermostat – as anyone who has replaced the thermostat in their refrigerator with such a device can tell you.

Empirical functionalists have, it seems to us, no alternative but to reduce the distance between their view and common-sense functionalism by accepting the common-sense functionalists' essentially distal way of characterizing the relevant inputs and outputs. They must think of the mental state terms as reference fixing on the nature of the internal information processing, the internal architecture, that underlies the path from environmentally characterized inputs to environmentally characterized outputs in certain exemplars – us – of the various mental states. A computing analogy may help to give the essential idea. Two computer programmers set the task of writing a word processing package that will perform a given set of tasks may deliver very different packages. The two packages may do exactly the same things as described in distal terms – the same key strokes may lead to the same footnotes, font changes, spelling corrections, and so on in some final print-out – but in very different ways. They differ in the general way in which they process information, in their internal architecture, to produce the required results. The difference need not merely be at the level

Internal architecture chauvinism

of implementation – in what happens when the two programs are run on computers – for the difference may be obvious from their abstract representations, from the written versions of the programs. Or consider the difference between Apple™ Macintosh™ computers and those running Microsoft™ Windows™. What they do can be much the same in terms of distally described inputs and outputs, but they do it in very different ways. The empirical functionalists' suggestion, then, in the version under discussion, is that to have one or another mental state is to process the environmentally characterized inputs that give rise to the environmentally described outputs in much the way that we exemplars of creatures in the mental state in question do.

But suppose that we differ from Martians in this kind of way – not, as in the earlier case, in that they are silicon-based whereas we are carbon-based – but in the way we process information from our surroundings in order to find our way around. Nevertheless, we and the Martians respond to and interact with our environments in very much the same way; it takes dissection and theorizing about the results of dissection to reveal the significant differences in the way we process the information. It seems unacceptably chauvinistic to refuse these Martians minds on this account. Indeed, perhaps the main difference between us and the Martians is that they process the information much more efficiently than we do. They are to us as RISC processors are to early CISC processors. It makes good sense from an evolutionary perspective that the way we process information should be highly inefficient from an engineering point of view; we are rather like a very old institution that grew very slowly in response to immediate pressures and whose operations have never been properly reviewed. Should we penalize the Martians for being efficient processors by denying them the compliment of describing them as thinkers? Is the reward for efficiency to be declared as lacking in intelligence? Or take the case of dolphins. Because their inputs and outputs are *locally* so very different from ours, it is likely that they run very different programs from those we run, but that should not *in itself* rule them out as subjects of mental states.

So far we have given imaginary examples of possible differences in the architecture of cognition. But there is a lively empirical debate going on about how exactly our brains process information. Classical computational models, models that assume something like the internal sentence theory which we discuss later in chapters 10 and 11, compete with models such as connectionist parallel distributed processing models. The differences between these models need not detain us here. The important point is that it is far from settled which of these models gives the right picture of how humans in fact do their thinking. An empirical functionalism that reference fixes on our internal architecture says that whichever of these models is true of us describes a necessary condition for thought in general. Suppose that connectionism turns out to be the right picture of human cognition. Then, if we ever came across beings for whom the internal sentence theory is true, we would be committed to denying that they had thoughts, however much like us they were in culture, science and communicative ability. Conversely, if the internal sentence theory turns out to be true of us, then any connectionist species would have to be regarded as mere simulations of thinkers.

The issue here is not whether the nature of what goes on inside our heads matters. It is common ground that it matters. It is part of folk opinion about the mind that there are memory traces, that perceptions cause beliefs, that beliefs combine with desires to cause actions, that one thought leads to another, and so on and so forth. It is a feature of common-sense functionalism as well as of empirical functionalism that there are internal constraints governing mental states. Moreover, in chapter 7 we will discuss what is known as the Blockhead example, which shows, quite decisively in our view, that a being might be behaviourally exactly like a normal human subject in all actual and possible situations, yet, owing to internal differences, not have a thought in its head. The issue is whether it is right to let the *particular* way that we handle the informational problems set by the world dictate what is to count as having a mind. It is to this question that we give a negative answer.

One response to this objection might be to move to a relaxed standard of identity of internal architecture. Very rough similarity in internal architecture to us, the paradigm mental beings, is enough. But how rough is rough? And how are we supposed to decide? It is hard to see how to address this question without relying on our intuitions about what is involved in being in one or another mental state but to do this is to reduce the difference between empirical functionalism and common-sense functionalism to no difference at all. Empirical functionalism then becomes common-sense functionalism, for common-sense functionalism just is the version of functionalism that is driven by our intuitions – our folk theory – about mental states.

We have covered a lot of ground in this chapter. Table 3 is offered as a summary of the various positions we have considered.

Table 3 Varieties of functionalism

	The place of folk roles	Inputs and outputs	Necessary constraints on internal nature	Problems
Common-sense functionalism	Give the meaning of the mental state terms.	Environmentally characterized.	Whatever it takes to realize the folk roles so long as the states are non-fluky, not externally controlled, non-Blockhead (see ch. 7).	Specifying the relevant folk roles. Qualia (see ch. 8).
Empirical functionalism I	Fix the reference of the mental state terms on the states that fill the roles.	Environmentally characterized or as inputs and outputs at the periphery of the brain.	The categorical states that realize the roles.	Contradicts multiple realizability in its most plausible manifestation. Qualia.
Empirical functionalism II	Fix reference to internal functional roles (on some views these role states are mental states, on others the roles are occupied by mental states).	Peripheral states of the brain.	At least enough to ensure the right peripheral relations.	Input–output chauvinism. Qualia.

Empirical functionalism III	No role.	Peripheral states of the brain.	At least enough to ensure the right peripheral relations.	Input–output chauvinism. Silence on how to identify mental nature. Qualia.
Empirical functionalism IV (machine functionalism)	Fix reference on machine table.	Anything provided the machine table comes out right via highly abstract mappings.	At least enough to realize the machine table (perhaps alarmingly few).	Bucket of water objection; i.e. excessive liberalism. Qualia.
Empirical functionalism V (cognitive science functionalism)	Fix reference on something like the internal architectures of us exemplars.	Via connection to the environment.	Internal natures must be the same as that described by the most explanatory story given by an empirical science of how paradigm thinkers actually work.	Internal architecture chauvinism. Qualia.
Empirical functionalism VI	Fix reference on internal functional nature.	Via connection to the environment.	Similar in architecture to us on a *loose* account of the appropriate level which ensures no architectural chauvinism.	Collapses into common-sense functionalism. Qualia.

Annotated Reading

Now that you have the contrast between empirical and common-sense functionalism before you, it would be worth reviewing briefly the text-book presentations of functionalism we listed at the end of chapter 3 and asking yourself of each whether it is a presentation of common-sense functionalism or empirical functionalism, or whether this is a question without an answer. Probably the best first port of call for the chauvinism—liberalism debate and for the difference between common-sense and empirical functionalism is Ned Block, 'What is Functionalism?' and 'Troubles with Functionalism'. You should note that Block uses the term 'psychofunctionalism' for a certain kind of empirical functionalism. The volume containing these papers also includes a good selection of papers on functionalism, as do the other anthologies we mentioned in the first annotated reading list: W. G. Lycan, ed., *Mind and Cognition*, and David Rosenthal, ed., *The Nature of Mind*. The Lycan volume also has a helpful, though tantalizingly short, introduction to the section on functionalism. Some of the papers in these volumes are fairly demanding. The classic early presentation of machine functionalism is Hilary Putnam, 'The Nature of Mental States', which is reprinted in both Lycan and Block. Interestingly, some of the most trenchant recent criticism of functionalism is to be found in later work of Putnam's, especially chapters 5 and 6 of his *Representation and Reality*.

6

The Identity Theory

We now come to a theory which, historically speaking, preceded functionalism. The identity theory of mind holds that each and every mental state is identical with some state in the brain. Some functionalists regard functionalism as replacing the identity theory. We hold, however, that functionalism puts the identity theory on a firmer footing. This is why we reverse the more usual order of presentation which treats the identity theory first, and come to it now after an initial treatment of functionalism.

According to the identity theory, your desire for ice-cream, your pangs of hunger, and your believing that the lights have turned green are all states of your brain. The view is sometimes described as the view that the mind is the brain, but this can be misleading. The view is not that the mind and the brain are literally one and the same thing. For, first, it is recognized that most brain states are not mental states, and, secondly, the view is not about the mind as such. It is a view about the *states* of the mind. The relationship between the mind and its states is a separate question. The same goes in fact for all the theories of mind that concern us in this book. They are theories of mental states, not of the mind itself. However, there is general agreement among philosophers of mind nowadays that the mind is not an entity that exists independently of its states; it is some kind of aggregation of mental states unified into 'one' mind, perhaps by a common relationship to a continuing material entity – namely, a certain body – or maybe a certain brain, or perhaps by links of psychological continuity in which memory plays a major role, or by some combination of these factors. The details are controversial and fall under the heading of the problem of personal identity, a topic which we won't be covering.

The inspiration for the identity theory is the way in which science expresses many of its discoveries in terms of identity. A simple

Origins of the theory

example is lightning. Science does not tell us that lightning and electrical discharges between clouds are lawfully correlated. It tells us that they are one and the same thing. Lightning *is* an electrical discharge between clouds. Again, heat in gases is not something that varies directly with molecular kinetic energy: it is molecular kinetic energy. Similarly, science has discovered not merely that wherever there is water there is H_2O; it has discovered that water is H_2O.

Occam's razor   In some early presentations the story was given an Occamist flavour. The picture was that science has discovered that whenever there is lightning, there is an electrical discharge of a certain intensity between clouds, and that this is a lawful correlation. Ontological economy – Occam's razor – then suggests making an identification. We should believe that there is one phenomenon described in two different ways. Likewise, went the story, we will discover that whenever someone is in pain, they have, say, C fibres firing, and that this is a lawful correlation. Occamist considerations then suggest that we identify pain with C fibres firing, holding that we have one phenomenon describable in both the language of neuroscience and the language of psychology.

This was a mistake. Take the case of lightning. Lightning is what we *see* in the sky during thunderstorms. But to see something is *inter alia* to respond to it causally, to be in a perceptual state as a result of the thing seen's causal action on one. Now, what science discovered is that it is an electrical discharge that causally acts on us when we see the familiar yellow flash in the sky. It was thus not an option to suppose that lightning is correlated with, but distinct from, the electrical discharge. For if it were distinct from, though correlated with, the electrical discharge, it could not be what causes our perceptual response, hence it could not be what is seen. It would be invisible!

The same goes for pain. We associate pain with a certain causal role, roughly, being caused by bodily damage and resulting in withdrawal behaviour. Hence the question of what pain is becomes simply the question of what plays that causal role. The essential structure of the situation can be set out thus:

1   Pain = occupant of causal role R (accepted fact).
2   Occupant of causal role R = brain state B (empirical discovery).
3   Pain = brain state B (transitivity of identity).

The identification follows by the transitivity of identity, without any need to appeal to Occam's razor.

The identity theory and functionalism

On this picture, the identity theory is a natural offshoot of functionalism, although historically it preceded it. Different versions of functionalism differ about the functional-cum-causal roles they give centre stage to in their theory of mind and the status they assign these roles, as we saw, but on any version of functionalism mental states occupy distinctive functional roles. The mind–brain identity theory is the very plausible empirical hypothesis that what will turn out to occupy the various roles will in each case be some state or other of the brain. The reason it is so plausible that the states that occupy the distinctive roles are states of the brain, rather than of the liver or the foot, or of the objects around us, is that we know that the creatures whose complex behavioural interactions with the environment lead us to ascribe a mental life to them are those that have highly complex brains, and that only these brains are complex enough to have states that fill the roles in question. There is simply not enough going on in my liver or in the desk in front of me for it to be at all plausible that the requisite states will be found in my liver or the desk. *Functionalism, physicalism, identity theory*

On this picture, the essential contention that commits us to a physicalist theory of mind is the claim that what plays the distinctive role of the various mental states is a purely physical state – namely, a state of the brain. It is this contention that supports the physicalists' supervenience of the psychological on the physical. For if it is correct, any minimal physical duplicate of our world will have exactly the same functional roles occupied and so be, according to the theory, psychologically exactly like our world.

In this context it is interesting to note that Descartes, perhaps the most famous anti-materialist philosopher of mind, was in part a dualist for *a posteriori* reasons. He believed that no purely physical state could play the required roles. He held that certain of our mental states associated especially with intelligence, rationality and free action display a flexibility and sophistication incompatible with a purely material aetiology. Descartes's position was reasonable given the science of his day, but given what we now know – *Descartes* in particular, concerning the role of computers in enlarging our conception of the behavioural flexibility and sophistication compatible with a purely material aetiology – it is overwhelmingly likely that it is purely physical states of our brains that play the required roles.

Some early objections to the identity theory

When the identity theory was first advanced, it met a barrage of objections, and was widely dismissed as resting on one or another confusion. We will briefly survey some of these objections.

One was that if mental states are identical with brain states, how had this fact eluded attention for so long? Identity theorists replied by citing the kind of identities listed already: lightning is identical with an electrical discharge, and temperature in gases is mean molecular kinetic energy, yet these facts took a good deal of establishing. The identity of mental states with brain states is, they urged, of a piece with scientific identities in general, and hence not something that should be expected to be obvious or particularly easy to establish.

Scientifically established identities also afforded a reply to the objection that we are not aware of mental states *as* being brain states. Water, lightning and temperature do not present themselves to us *as* H_2O, electrical discharge and mean molecular kinetic energy, respectively, but that, nevertheless, is what they are.

First-person third-person asymmetry   Identity theorists were also challenged to account for the asymmetry between first-and third-person access to mental states. My relation to my current itch is patently different in kind from my relation to your current itch; the way I know about my belief that it is about to rain is different from the way I know about your belief that it is about to rain. Here identity theorists pointed out that such an asymmetry is to be expected if mental states are internal brain states. Setting aside telepathy and invasive brain surgery, how else could I discover anything about the nature of your brain states other than by going by their 'surface' manifestations, by the way they control your reactions to environmental stimuli, lead you to utter various sentences, and the like? On the other hand, it makes good evolutionary sense that subjects should have special access to the nature of their own internal states, that they should have self-monitoring devices that generate beliefs about what is going on in their own brains by a kind of internal scanning process. Of course, this self-scanning process does not reveal them in their guise as states of the brain. According to identity theorists, what we are aware of when we are aware of our own mental states – that is, are aware of certain states of our brains – are highly relational, 'topic-neutral' features of them, features that are silent about the intrinsic nature of that which they are features of. We are aware that something is going on that plays a certain functional role – roughly, in the case of pain, that something is going on in us that is typically caused by bodily damage, that typically causes behaviour that tends to minimize that damage, and that typically causes the desire that it itself cease. Thus, functionalism is both a path to the identity theory and a way of handling the objection from introspection to the identity theory.

Some objected that mental states have properties that no brain state has, or even could have, and that brain states have properties that no mental state has, or even could have. Hence, by the principle known as Leibniz's law, that if $x = y$, then x and y share all properties, mental states could not *be* brain states, though they might be correlated with them. Thus, it was argued, an after-image is, say, yellow and two feet in front of your face, and a pain is in, say, your foot, but no brain state of yours is yellow and two feet in front of your face, nor is there a brain state in your foot. Conversely, any brain state of yours will be at a certain temperature and will be located so many inches inside your skull, but your belief that the Earth is (roughly) round is not at a certain temperature and is not so many inches inside your skull – indeed, your belief, it seems, is not of the right category to have such properties.

Leibniz's law

Identity theorists responded by drawing a distinction between mental states and **mental objects**, and proceeded to deny the existence of the latter, a position that has become widely accepted in the philosophy of mind independently of the debate over the identity theory and physicalism. In English we say 'I have a pain', a sentence that has the same syntactic structure as 'I have a hat'. This suggests that it has the same logical structure, in that both sentences assert a relation to obtain between a person and an object – a pain in one case, a hat in the other. Identity theorists pointed out, however, that the object in the case of 'I have a pain' is a strange sort of object, for it cannot exist independently of being experienced. A pain is necessarily someone's pain. They urged that we should view 'I have a pain' in the way we view 'I have a limp'. Just as limps are not things we have when we limp,

The denial of mental objects

so pains are not things we have when we are in pain. From a logical point of view, it would be better to say 'I pain' or, more naturally, 'I am in pain', just as we can say 'I limp', instead of 'I have a limp'. When we appear to attribute properties to the pain and the limp, we are really attributing properties to the pain experience and the limping. Someone with a bad limp limps badly; likewise, someone with a pain in their foot has a certain kind of pain experience, but does not literally have a thing called a pain in their foot. Similarly, according to identity theorists, there are no after-images to be yellow and two feet in front of your face; instead, there are experiences of having after-images, which are neither yellow nor two feet in front of your face, and it is these experiencings that are identical with brain states.

The case of belief is a little different. Here the identity theorists replied by distinguishing, on the one hand, the state of believing, the state which might be invoked in a causal explanation of why someone acted as they did, from, on the other hand, what is believed, the *proposition* believed, as it is often put. We will be saying a great deal more about this notion later when we discuss content in chapters 10 and 11; for now it is enough to note that we distinguish your belief that the coffee is near, thought of as what leads you, say, to reach for the coffee, from *what* you accept when you believe that the coffee is near. The proposition believed is what you accept. It is not a mental state, is not a cause of behaviour, and does not fall within the ambit of the identity theory. But it is only the proposition that it would be absurd to hold is warm or so many inches inside your head.

The major question for the identity theory in recent discussions is whether it should be thought of as a type–type or a token–token identity theory, and we now turn to a consideration of this issue.

Token–token versus type–type identity theories

The type/token distinction Individual things can typically be classified into kinds or types or classes in various ways. Thus, a particular table might be each of: a table, a brown thing, something in this building, and something chosen as an illustrative example. Often, especially in discussions in the philosophy of mind, the distinction between, on the one hand, individuals or particulars, and on the other, kinds, properties or classes of similar things is marked by calling the first 'tokens' and the second 'types'. Thus, the table is a token of the types: table, brown, in this building and so on, whereas being brown is a type with tokens: the table, a rotten apple and most soil. The terminology has its history in the need to distinguish in discussions of language the sense in which the line below contains one letter and that in which it contains two letters.

a   a

It contains two tokens of the one letter type.

When identity theorists identify mental states with brain states, should they be thought of as identifying types or tokens? Are they asserting that each type of mental state is some type of brain state? Or are they asserting that each token mental state is some token brain state? The first is the stronger doctrine. If each mental state type is identical with some brain state type, then each mental state token is identical with some brain state token. Illustrative analogy: it follows from the fact that blue is the colour of the sky, that every token of blue – that is, every blue thing – is a token of something with the colour of the sky.

The early identity theorists were not always explicit about whether they had in mind the stronger or the weaker thesis, but the way they introduced their theory in terms of the identities established by science certainly suggests that they had in mind the stronger, type–type thesis, for these scientific identities are all type–type. Water, that natural *kind*, is H_2O; heat in gases is a property, a kind in nature, so the identity between it and molecular kinetic energy is a type–type identity; the contention that lightning is an electrical discharge is not merely the contention that some instance or token of lightning is an instance of an electrical discharge, but rather the stronger claim that the one kind of phenomenon is one and the same as the other; and so on and so forth. And, of course, the use of the word 'state' in formulating the identity claim (mental states are states of the brain) suggests that a type–type identity is what is being urged, for 'state' is typically a word for kinds. For instance, when we talk of the *state* of the economy, we are talking of its *nature*, a nature that it may or may not share with other economies or with itself at other times; we are talking, that is, of the type – improving, bad or whatever – that it falls under.

Scientific identities are type–type

Moreover, the path to the identity theory via functionalism supports a type–type identity theory. The concept of an antibiotic is transparently a functional-cum-causal one, and what we find when

Functionalism and type–type identities

we look up lists of antibiotics are lists of chemical *compounds* – that is, lists of types of substances. Thus, the functional-cum-causal story that defines what an antibiotic is yields a type–type identity, or, more precisely, a whole set of them: the best antibiotic for lung infections is . . . , the most widely prescribed antibiotic for . . . is . . . , and so on, where the ellipses are filled in with names of compounds like 'tetracycline'. Again, the discovery that the most insidious poison known to us is curare is the discovery of the type that plays the role of being the most insidious poison, and it enables us to affirm the following type–type identity: 'curare = the most insidious poison'. Of course, as we have already noted, the type–type identity claim implies a token–token identity claim. Each and every token of curare is a token of the most insidious poison. The point is not that token–token identity claims are false, but that we can and do say more.

Examples abound. Typically, when we find what plays a certain functional role, we find the type that plays that role: the maximum safe level of exposure to ultraviolet radiation, the most reliable method of contraception, the easiest way to solve quadratic equations, the level of rental vacancies that best balances the interests of tenants and landlords, and so on. And each places us in a position to affirm a type–type identity. For instance, we might suppose that the level of rental vacancies that best balances the interests of tenants and landlords is a vacancy level between 2 per cent and 3 per cent.

Multiple realizability and type–type identity   Thus, a functionalist approach to the mind leads to the stronger variety of mind–brain identity theory, a type–type one. Or so it seems to us; but we should emphasize that many philosophers of mind draw the opposite conclusion. They hold that functionalism, with its lesson about the possibility of multiple realizability, shows that the type–type identity theory is false. The problem is that different types of state might occupy, say, the pain role in different creatures. Perhaps, as we traditionally pretend for the purposes of illustration, it is C fibres firing in humans but D fibres firing in dolphins. But dolphins with their D fibres firing would then be just as much in pain as we are when our C fibres are firing. According to functionalism, it is the role occupied, not the occupier, that matters for being in pain, and, as we noted in the discussion of functionalism, the point is plausible independently. For instance, we feel sorry for dolphins that exhibit all the signs of pain, despite not knowing in any detail how intrinsically like ours their brains are. But the identity theorist cannot allow both that pain =

C fibres firing and pain = D fibres firing. That would, by the transitivity of identity, lead to the false contention that C fibres firing = D fibres firing. Hence it is argued that identity theorists should retreat from a type–type identity theory to a token–token identity theory. Each and every token or instance of mental state M is some token brain state, but mental types are not brain types, being instead functional types. Or, to put the contention in terms of the pain example, each token of pain in humans is a token brain state, an instance of C fibres firing, as we supposed, and each token of pain in dolphins is an instance of D fibres firing; but the psychological type, pain, is neither C fibres firing nor D fibres firing. The psychological type is instead the functional, second-order property of being in the state (whatever that state may be in the organism in question) that plays the pain role. The lesson of functionalism for the identity theory is, it is urged, that psychological types are functional types, not brain or neurological types.

There is, however, a better way to respond to the multiple realizability point. It is to retain a type–type mind–brain identity theory but allow that the identities between mental types and brain types may – indeed, most likely will – need to be restricted. Money is a functionally specified notion, and, accordingly, different types of things are money in different societies. Nevertheless, we can make true identity claims about the types of things that are money in different societies: namely, money in our society = notes and coins produced by the mint, whereas money in early Polynesian society = cowrie shells (or whatever). Or consider the functional concept of assent. We can make true type–type identity statements about the (kind of) gesture that is the (bodily) sign of assent in Western societies, and the (kind of) gesture that is the sign of assent in certain Asian societies, despite the fact that the gestures are different. In the West, nodding the head = the gesture of assent, whereas a different side-to-side head motion – call it wiggling – is used in parts of Asia. So wiggling the head = the gesture of assent in parts of Asia. Similarly, the most effective antibiotic has changed with time, but that does not mean that we cannot identify the (kind of) chemical compound that is the most effective antibiotic at some particular time; what it means is that the identity statements need to include an explicit temporal restriction. In the same way, if indeed it is C fibres in us, but D fibres in dolphins, that play the pain role, then identity theorists must restrict themselves to saying: 'Pain in humans = C fibres firing' and 'Pain in dolphins = D fibres firing'. Similarly, if it turns out that the neurological state

Restricted identities

that plays the belief-that-one's-hand-is-behind-one's-back role in left-handed people is different from the state that plays the role in right-handed people, the identity theorist will need to distinguish the kind of state that is the belief that one's hand is behind one's back for lefties from the kind of state that is that belief for righties. Here's an analogy: the most popular kind of plant differs from place to place, and indeed from gardener to gardener. Nevertheless, for each gardener there is a most popular kind of plant. The 'multiple realizability' of being the most popular plant simply means that true identity claims about the most popular plant will have to contain clauses like 'for gardeners brought up in the English tradition', 'for gardeners who like Australian plants', and 'for Jones'.

Mental types are causes   The reason why this is a better response than abandoning the type–type identity theory in favour of the view that pain, the type, is the second-order, functional property of having a state playing the pain role in one is that it allows pain to *cause* the behaviour that we associate with pain. Just as it is penicillin that kills bugs, so it is the pain caused by contact with a hot kettle that causes you to withdraw your hand. True, it will be an instance, or token, of penicillin that does the causing; but we distinguish the relevant from the irrelevant properties of the token for the causing that it does, and it is its being penicillin that is causally relevant. In the same way, we want the fact that the token of pain is a *pain* to be causally relevant to your hand's withdrawal. But in both cases the causally relevant properties are *not* the second-order functional properties. What kills the bugs is not the fact that the penicillin is of a bug-killing type – it is the type itself that does the work. What causes your arm muscles to contract is not the fact that you have a brain state of the type that typically causes your arm muscles to contract – it is the brain state type itself. The point here is the same as might be made by observing that the properties of a stone throwing responsible for its breaking a window will be properties like velocity and mass, *not* its having properties that are so responsible. The consequence of refusing to identify psychological properties with neurological properties is that the psychological properties become causally impotent.

Role state versus realizer state   A piece of jargon can be helpful here. For any functional role we can distinguish the realizer state from the role state. The realizer state is the (kind of) state that occupies, or realizes, the functional role. The role state is the second-order state of having the functional role occupied. When you are poisoned, the realizer state is the kind of substance that is making you sick, and the role state is the state of having in you a substance that is making you sick. Thus, if you are poisoned on two different occasions by being fed different poisons, the realizer states on the two occasions are different, whereas the role state is one and the same (and, of course, what makes you sick on the two occasions is different, hence it is the realizer states that do the causing). Thus, from a functionalist perspective, there are two options concerning the metaphysics of psychological properties. Functionalism says that x is in pain iff x is in a state playing the pain role, but this thesis about truth conditions for being in pain is compatible with holding, *qua* metaphysical thesis, either that pain is the realizer state or that it is the role state. The mind–brain type–type identity theory takes the option of identifying psychological properties with realizer states (possibly different ones in different organisms or in the one organism on different occasions), not role states, and does so in order to preserve the causal efficacy of psychological properties.

*Essentialism about psychological states

A functionalist version of identity theory is thus compatible with a type–type style of identity theory. But it is not compatible with essentialism about psychological states. Functionalism plus the identity theory implies that it is not an essential feature of a mental state that it is the mental state that it is. This follows from the fact that it is not an essential feature of a brain state that it occupies the functional role that it does. Suppose that the state that occupies the pain role in humans is invariably C fibres firing; then, according to the functionalism-inspired identity theorist, 'Pain in humans = C fibres firing' is true. Nevertheless, it is only contingently true. C fibres firing might not have occupied the pain role in humans, just as arsenic might not have occupied the poison role in humans. If our neurophysiology had been different in various ways, arsenic would not be harmful to us. The suggestion is not, of course, that pain might have failed to be self-identical: everything is necessarily self-identical. The suggestion is that that which is pain the way things actually are, that which is pain in the actual world, is not pain in some non-actual possible world, just as the stuff – curare, as we supposed earlier – that is the most insidious poison the way things actually are is not the most insidious poison in some non-actual possible world.

Contingent
identities   There is thus an important difference between the identities
postulated by the mind–brain identity theory between mental states
and brain states, and the scientific identities used to introduce the
identity theory. The latter are not contingent, and they plausibly
capture essences. When we discovered that water is H_2O, we discovered its essential nature, and, as we saw in our discussion of the
causal theory of reference in chapter 4, it is plausible that it is
necessarily true that water is H_2O, notwithstanding its *a posteriori*
status. When the identity theory was first put forward, it was
widely believed that the *a posteriori* nature of 'Water = H_2O' and
similar natural kind identities showed them to be contingent. Now
that we know better, the best examples to use as a model for
understanding the mind–brain identity theory are contingent (and
a posteriori) type–type identity statements like the ones mentioned
above: 'The most insidious poison = curare', 'The sign of assent in
Western societies = nodding', and so on and so forth. What are
contingent here are the *statements* of identity.[4] Early presentations
of the identity theory sometimes talked of contingent identity as if
it were a special, contingent kind of identity that held between, for
instance, pain and C fibres firing, and curare and the most insidious poison. But, of course, in each case there is just *one* thing, and
it is necessarily self-identical.

Some have objected to the anti-essentialist nature of the mind–
brain identity theory. They have insisted that mental states are the
kind of mental states they are essentially. Pain could not have been
anything other than pain; belief that snow is white could not have
been anything other than belief that snow is white. However, provided that we hold to the position that mental states play distinctive causal roles, causal roles that figure centrally in determining
the kind of mental state they are, essentialism about mental states
is hard to sustain. What a state does is *not* an essential property of

---

[4] Warning: some philosophers are unhappy with describing statements like 'The
most insidious poison = curare' as *identity* statements, on the ground that 'the most
insidious poison' (and definite descriptions in general) are not properly speaking
singular terms, and identity statements are formed by flanking the identity sign
with singular terms. Moreover, they hold that singular terms are rigid designators.
Thus for them, all identity statements are automatically necessarily true. This can
look like a substantive disagreement with what we are saying, but in fact it is a
terminological one. The important point is that statements like 'The most insidious poison = curare' are contingent, as are the corresponding statements about
mental states if the mind–brain identity theory is true. It is not important whether
we call these statements identity statements, though those who refuse to do so will,
of course, think that the identity theory has an unfortunate name.

it. Physicalists sympathetic to functionalism have a choice to make here. In the terms introduced above, only if they hold that mental states are realizer states, not role states, can they give them their intuitively plausible causal roles; but then mental states are not the mental states they are essentially.

Annotated Reading

The classic article-length presentation of the identity theory is J. J. C. Smart, 'Sensations and Brain Processes'. The classic book-length presentation is D. M. Armstrong, *A Materialist Theory of the Mind*. Although both these works are directed to fellow professionals, they are written in a very direct, clear way that makes them highly accessible. A paper which is very clear about the irrelevance of Occam's razor and is explicitly a defence of the type–type version of the theory is David Lewis, 'An Argument for the Identity Theory'. The advantages of the type–type version over the token–token version are spelt out in a little detail in Frank Jackson, Robert Pargetter and Elizabeth Prior, 'Functionalism and Type–Type Identity Theories'. More elementary presentations of the identity theory can be found in most philosophy of mind texts, though typically, as we have said, the theory is presented before functionalism, and especially in American texts, as a view superseded by functionalism. Recent discussions of whether essentialist considerations make trouble for the identity theory date from lecture 3 in Saul Kripke, *Naming and Necessity*.

7

Three Challenges to Functionalism

If functionalism is true, then anything that is functionally like us in the relevant respects is psychologically like us. This chapter is concerned with three well-known examples of things that are, in one way or another, and to one extent or another, functionally like us and yet which intuitively are very unlike us psychologically. We will consider in turn the challenge posed to functionalism by the China brain, the Chinese room, and Blockhead. For each example we consider (a) whether the example really is, on reflection, of a creature that is very unlike us psychologically, and (b) to the extent that it is, we ask whether the example shows that functionalism is false, or does it instead teach us something important about *which* functional roles are crucial. We will suggest that to the extent that the examples are indeed of entities that are psychologically unlike us, they are examples of entities that do not have the right functional similarities to us, and so tell us not that functionalism is false, but rather about the functional roles that functionalists need to include in their story about psychological nature. In our discussion of the three examples, we will need to advert at various points to the fact that functionalism comes in many flavours. Fortunately, however, the examples raise many rather general issues about functionalism, and this means that we will often be able think in terms of a fairly undifferentiated version that captures general features common to most versions.

The China brain

The China brain is a putative counter-example to functionalism, due originally to Ned Block. Here is a slightly updated version of it. Imagine that artificial intelligence has advanced to the point where a program can be written which will allow an android with a 'brain' consisting of a computer running the program to behave actually and counterfactually much as a normal human does. It does not matter for the example how this programming is done; to avoid confusion about the nature of the program (which we will discuss in a later example), let us suppose that the program mimics the operation of a human brain at a neuron by neuron level. Neurones are essentially input–output devices made from organic matter, the overall input–output characteristics of the brain being determined by how the primitive neuronal devices are assembled. Hence, this supposition amounts to having the program reflect precisely the input–output nature of each neuron and how the neurons are connected one to another.

The next step in the process of constructing the example is to note that it won't matter, or anyway can hardly matter from a functionalist perspective, if the computer running this program is outside the android's body, connected by a two-way radio link to it. The final step gives us the China brain. Suppose that instead of the program being run on an external computer made of silicon chips, the entire population of China is enlisted to run the simulation. As the program mimics the way the brain operates at the neuronal level, this can be done by assigning each Chinese citizen the job of just one neuron. They have, let's suppose, the kind of phones that tell you what number has called you. When certain numbers or combinations of numbers ring in, they have to dial specified other numbers. Each citizen is given a precise set of instructions about what to do that ensures that what each does exactly models what their assigned neuron does, and the inputs to and outputs from their phones are connected up so as to run the program. Also, the initial inputs to the China brain come from the environment in much the same way as the inputs to us do, and the final outputs go to the limbs and head of the android via the radio link in such a way that its actual and counterfactual behaviour is much as ours is. Thus, the android will behave in the various situations that confront it very much as we do, despite the fact that the processing of the environmental inputs into final behavioural outputs goes via a highly organized set of Chinese citizens rather than a brain.

This is certainly not a realistic fantasy. The population of China is not large enough; the whole process could never take place fast enough; the citizens would get bored and careless; and anyway the program used to construct the example does not exist and never will (working at the neuronal level is ridiculously fine-grained). All the same, it does seem clearly intelligible, and if it is intelligible, it is fair to ask for an answer to the question of whether the system consisting of the robot plus the population of China in the imagined case has mental states like ours. Many have a strong intuition that it does not. If they are right, functionalism of just about any variety must be false. For the system is functionally very like us. Not only is it like us in all the functional roles seen as crucial by the common-sense functionalist, it is like us in just about every functional respect. Functionally, it *is* us; the difference lies in the dramatic difference in how the functional roles are realized, and that difference counts for nothing as far as mental nature is concerned, according to functionalists.

Denying the intuition

We think, however, that the functionalist can reasonably deny the intuition. The source of the intuition that the system consisting of robot plus China brain lacks mental states like ours seems to be the fact that it would be so *very* much bigger than we are. We cannot imagine 'seeing' it as a cohesive parcel of matter. We cannot see, that is to say, the forest for the trees. A highly intelligent microbe-sized being moving through our flesh-and-blood brains might have the same problem. It would see a whole mass of widely spaced entities interacting with each other in a way that made no sense to it, that formed no intelligible overall pattern from its perspective. The philosophers among these tiny beings might maintain with some vigour that there could be no intelligence here. All that is happening is an inscrutable sending back and forth of simple signals. They would be wrong. We think that the functionalist can fairly say that those who deny mentality in the China brain example are making the same mistake.

Consciousness

Before we leave the China brain example, we should note two important points about its role in the literature. First, it is sometimes directed simply to the question of whether functionalism can account for consciousness. In this manifestation it is granted that the China brain has beliefs and desires (after all, the robot will move in various ways in response to the environment, and thereby make changes to it of just the kind we associate with purposive, informed behaviour), but it is insisted that it is absurd to hold that it *feels* anything. We discuss the difficult question of feeling and consciousness in the next chapter. Our concern in this chapter is restricted to challenges for functionalism about mental states like belief and desire and mental traits like being intelligent.

Secondly, sometimes the example is given in a version that omits *Connection to* the robot. But then the population of China is emulating, in some *the environment* purely abstract way, the program in someone's brain with no obvious right way to connect the overall inputs and outputs with the environment. The case becomes essentially the same as the one we discussed when we considered the charge of excessive liberalism against certain machine versions of functionalism in chapter 5. There we argued that merely crunching numbers – or, more generally, inputs and outputs that have no natural or obvious connection to the environment that our mental states are about – is *mere* number (or whatever) crunching. If this is right, then the China brain example in the version that omits the appropriate robotic connection to the environment is of something that lacks a mental life, or anyway a mental life at all like ours. But in this version it is not an objection to functionalisms that include, in one form or another, the right sort of connection to the environment. These functionalisms might be called 'arm's length' functionalisms. Common-sense functionalism is an 'arm's length' doctrine in this sense.

The Chinese room

John Searle's Chinese room is one of the most famous examples in the philosophy of mind. We will present a variation on the original example. We suppose that someone called Tex, who understands English but not Chinese, is locked in a room that has an in-chute, an out-chute and a book full of instructions in English concerning the manipulation of Chinese characters. Stories in Chinese accompanied by questions in Chinese about the stories come in through the in-chute. Tex follows the instructions in the book as they apply to the stories and the questions, which in due course tell him which sentences in Chinese to copy on to pieces of paper and place in the out-chute. Tex does not understand the stories, the questions or the sentences he puts in the out-chute. As far as he is concerned, he is simply operating with squiggles. He is mechanically following some rules in English for manipulating symbols which are in various ways derived from the squiggles, and which conclude with his writing down some more squiggles on the paper that goes into the out-chute. We can make the example more up to date (and facilitate later variations on it that we will discuss) by supposing that the stories and questions in Chinese are typed into a computer outside the room and appear on its screen. Tex has a monitor in his room on which what is typed is also displayed in Chinese. He types in answers to the questions at a separate keyboard in the room, following the book's instructions religiously. His answers appear both on his monitor and on the monitor screen outside the room. We will conduct the discussion in terms of this version of the example.

Searle in effect points out that the book might well be such that Tex will consistently deliver Chinese sentences that, to someone who understands Chinese, count as sensible, intelligent answers to the questions in Chinese about the stories in Chinese that Tex receives. What appear on the screen are good answers in Chinese to questions in Chinese about stories in Chinese. Nevertheless, it would be quite wrong to infer from this that Tex understands Chinese. All he is doing is manipulating symbols according to formal rules without any understanding of what the various symbols stand for or mean.

It is clear that Tex does not understand Chinese, for he does not himself have the ability to answer the questions. It is Tex together with the book that has the ability. So the issue that needs to be addressed is whether the *system* consisting of Tex plus the book understands Chinese. What abilities are distinctively associated with understanding a language? It is plausible that being able to answer comprehension questions about a range of stories is part of what is required, but it is very much less than all that is required. One thing we need to add is the ability to extemporize, embellish and generally display the inventiveness and flexibility of a natural language speaker. If we *always* get back the same answer – accurate and intelligent though it may seem – in response to a story together with a question, we might well start to think that we are interacting with an automaton rather than a thinker and understander.

The example embellished We can embellish the original example, though, by supposing that Tex plus room has all these capacities. We can suppose that the book Tex is following does not always deliver the same answer in Chinese to a given question in Chinese. The book takes account of whether or not a question has been asked before. It contains instructions in English about what to do when a given sequence of squiggles (as Tex thinks of them) appears on the computer screen, that takes into account whether and how often that sequence of Chinese characters has appeared before. Obviously, by making Tex's book of instructions sufficiently complex (it will have to include instructions on how to modify the book itself in response to input, even if only by leaving different pages open), we can ensure that the answers Tex generates on the screen are exactly those that would come back from an intelligent Chinese speaker. That is, Tex plus the room passes what is known as the **Turing test**: to pass the Turing test is to respond to questions with all the signs of intelligence and thought distinctive of thinkers like us.

But at this point many people's intuition that we are dealing with something that does not understand Chinese starts to fade. It is still, of course, true that Tex does not understand Chinese, but an awful lot of processing is being done by Tex *plus* the book, and many argue that it is enough for the system to count as understanding Chinese.

For our part, though, we think that even after this embellishment, the system does not understand Chinese. In order to count as understanding Chinese, we need, among other things, the kinds of abilities distinctive of understanding what Chinese sentences and their parts *stand for*. The system does not even understand what the word 'book' stands for, because it cannot respond in the appropriate way to a book. It only ever responds to *sentences*, not to what they or their parts stand for.

We can put this point in terms of the distinction between semantics and syntax. Syntax has to do with questions of grammatical propriety, sentential structure, whether a word is a verb or a noun, and so on. Semantics has to do with the interpretations that attach to words and sentences; it relates to what words and sentences mean. It is by virtue of having a semantics that words and sentences in a language can serve to make claims about how things are, ask questions, issue commands and so on. Understanding a language is a matter of mastering its semantics. Tex has mastered the semantics of English and in fact uses this mastery to follow the book's instructions. But as far as Chinese is concerned, all Tex has are certain syntactic abilities. He can match up Chinese characters on a screen with those in the book and type them into a keyboard, but he has no idea what they stand for or mean. In this terminology, the question we face at this stage is whether, in the embellished example, the system of Tex plus the book has a grasp of the semantics of Chinese. Our claim is that it does not, for it does not understand what Chinese words stand for. This is manifested by the fact that it cannot respond appropriately to what Chinese words stand for. The system can respond only to words as they appear on a computer screen, not to what they stand for.

A further
embellishment
We could, of course, further embellish the example. Imagine a robot which sends information about the inputs through its eyes and ears and surfaces by radio in digital form to the Chinese room. Tex is still inside, and responds by writing it down, sifting through the book, and following its directions as before. After much (*even* quicker than before!) calculation, he goes to the console and types a response which is relayed to the robot. This makes the robot move through and respond to its environment much as we do. We can suppose that the book is detailed enough to constitute a program for the mind of a Cantonese-speaking adult woman. Thus, the robot will interact with its environment, including answering questions, in the very same way she would.

A system that
does understand
Chinese
But now the intuition that we are dealing with something that does not understand Chinese has faded completely, or so it seems to us. It is still the case that Tex does not understand Chinese, but there is an entity – call her Lin – that does understand Chinese. Lin is composed of the book that contains the all-important program, parts of Tex's brain, the robot and the radio. Lin, whose robot body is entering Kowloon, might believe she was entering Kowloon. Tex, in a laboratory in Dallas, might not even know that Kowloon exists, let alone believe he or anyone else is entering it.

We should say something quickly about a response Searle might make to replies like this. He might think that it depends crucially on there being a system bigger than Tex that does much of the work. This, he thinks, is what makes it seem plausible that the system is distinct from Tex, and can thus understand something that Tex doesn't. He might ask us instead to imagine that Tex memorizes the book, and stores all the changing data in his head. We are supposed to think that in this case there is no plausible distinctness between Tex and Lin, so if one fails to understand Chinese, so does the other. Tex doesn't understand Chinese, so nor does Lin.

We do not think that this variation makes an important difference. What we would have here are two entities who share a brain. The idea that distinct individuals might share a brain is not enormously different from that which we have grown used to from discussions of multiple personality disorder, although there is some difference, in that Lin relies on Tex to do the calculations that constitute her mental states (so if he gets bored or ill, it's very bad news for her indeed).

A computer
analogy
It may seem puzzling that Tex does all these calculations without knowing what it is he is doing. But in fact something like this

is commonplace in computer science. When one computer does calculations that emulate the behaviour of a different machine, the emulated computer is said to be a **virtual machine**. You may have seen an Apple™ Macintosh™ computer which has a window which has the look and feel of a machine running Microsoft™ Windows™. In fact, this is done by the Macintosh™ operating system directing that calculations be done at the binary level that emulate the behaviour of the Intel™ chip on which Windows™ runs. If you ask the Macintosh™ operating system what menus appear in its windows, it will be able to tell you. But if you ask it what menus appear in the Microsoft™ Windows™ look-alike window that it is supporting by emulating the Intel™ chip, it won't be able to tell you. It doesn't have information about the process at that level of abstraction. If you interrogate Windows™, however, it can tell you about its windows. This is roughly analogous to asking Tex about Kowloon directly, and drawing a blank, but getting an answer when you interrogate Lin.

In sum, the Chinese room example starts out as one where both intuition and any plausible functionalism agree that there is no understanding of Chinese. We can add to the example to get one where plausible versions of functionalism will have to say that there is understanding of Chinese (by the relevant entity, not Tex); but in doing so, we turn the example into one where intuition also says that there is understanding of Chinese.

Blockhead

We noted in chapter 5 that the most popular version of empirical functionalism is exposed to the charge of chauvinism. It insists on an excessive degree of internal similarity to us before something counts as having a mind; beings might fail to have minds by virtue of having internal processors which are better than ours! Would it be right to take the extra step of holding that *all* that matters for having a mind is being such as to ensure the right connection between external inputs and outputs? Something is an amplifier if it is such as to secure the right relationship between inputs and correspondingly bigger outputs, no matter how the job is done internally. What is done, not how it is done, is what counts. Should we say the same about the mind? Such a position can insist on specifying the inputs and outputs in arm's length terms, as is done

Input–output functionalism

in common-sense functionalism, and that what goes on inside matters to the extent that the job of appropriately mediating between the environmental inputs and behavioural outputs must be done by what is inside – as we noted in chapter 3, we do not want to count an appropriately manipulated puppet as having a mind. But that would be the extent of the constraints. Such a view might be called **input–output** or **stimulus–response functionalism**. It takes on board what is right about behaviourism – that behaviour in situations is crucial – but remedies at least part of what is wrong with it. Mental states are internal, causally efficacious states, *pace* behaviourism, but internal states that can be characterized fully as far as their psychological nature is concerned in terms of the behaviour that they do and would typically produce, or do or would produce if linked up in some natural way to the body. Input–output functionalism can be distinguished from **supervenient behaviourism** by the fact that the input–output functionalist insists that (most of) the states causally responsible for the behavioural profile must be internal. Suppose that Jane's normal-seeming behavioural profile is caused by puppeteers acting at a distance. The supervenient behaviourist might think she had mental states like ours; the input–output functionalist would not.

Input–output functionalism is false. A now famous example due to Ned Block shows that the way the job is done does matter. There are substantial internal constraints on being a thinker. The remainder of this chapter will be concerned with describing his example – the Blockhead example – and what is to be learnt from it. We approach the example, following his lead, via some remarks about chess.

Good chess versus being good at chess

Copy-cat chess   It is possible to play good chess without being any good at chess. Do what expert chess-players tell you to do! Your good chess will then be a sign of the ability to follow instructions and perhaps the ability to identify chess experts, but not of ability at chess. Alternatively, we can imagine that instead of turning to the experts for advice, you turn to a chart or *look-up tree* prepared by experts. Here is how the table could be constructed for when you are playing Black. At the beginning of a game there are only finitely many moves allowed by the rules. The chess experts nominate the best response to each possible move. We obtain a little table like

Figure 4 Look-up tree for the start of a chess game. The boxes represent the possible opening moves by White; the circles the responses to each nominated by experts.

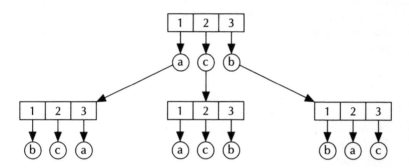

Figure 5 A more extended look-up tree for chess. Again, the boxes represent moves by White; the circles represent possible responses by Black as nominated by experts.

figure 4; the boxes represent the possible opening moves by White, and the circles the responses to each nominated by the experts. Now for each response by you as Black to White's opening move, there will be only finitely many legal responses by White. So we can extend the table by asking the experts to nominate their best response to each possible response by White (see figure 5); again, the boxes represent White's possible moves and the circles the responses to each as nominated by the experts. It is easy to see that this sort of diagram can *in principle* be extended as much as you like, and that anyone who owned such a diagram – perhaps prepared by Grand Masters over thousands of years – would be able to play very good chess without necessarily being any good at chess.

Anyone playing chess with a diagram like this is very vulnerable to changes in the rules: change one rule, and the diagram may become completely useless. But we can imagine tree diagrams which make allowance for various possible rule changes at any stage. Each row of boxes would be supplemented by additional boxes representing the possible moves under various rule changes, and below each box would be the circle representing the best response for that move, given that rule change, according to the experts. This would make an already *huge* tree even bigger, but does not introduce any new point of principle. In practice, of course, there is an insuperable problem with this plan for playing good chess. At each stage of a game of chess there are a large number of legal moves, and for each of these legal moves there are many legal responses. Writing out the look-up tree would in consequence involve what is known as a **combinatorial explosion**. Giving more than a line or two of the tree would require more distinct states than there are particles in the universe.

The game of life

Look-up trees *for life*   We are now ready to describe what has come to be known as the **Blockhead** example. At any point in a game of chess, there are only finitely many legal moves and countermoves. It is this fact that makes the chess look-up tree just described possible in principle. Likewise, at any point in a creature's life there are only finitely many discriminably distinct possible inputs and outputs at its periphery. Indeed, given quantum theory, there are probably only finitely many nomologically possible inputs and outputs; but in any case we know that there is a limit to how finely we distinguish different impacts on our surfaces and to how many different movements and responses our bodies can make. This means that in principle there could be a 'game-of-life' look-up tree written for any one of us – for Jones, say.

We list all the different possible combinations of pressure, light, gravity and so on impacting on the surface of Jones's body at the first moment of his life. This would be the first row of the game-of-life look-up tree modelled on Jones. It would correspond to the row of boxes in the chess tree above. The second row would give the behavioural response that Jones would make (in a wide sense that includes any relevant peripheral change) to each possible input. It corresponds to the first row of circles in the chess tree. The third row would give all the possible peripheral inputs for each of the various behavioural responses, and the fourth row would give Jones's behavioural responses to each of these. And so on and so forth for the whole of Jones's life. Of course, how long Jones lives depends in large part on which of the various possible inputs actually comes about, but we may suppose that a fail-safe strategy is employed – the look-up tree covers, say, one hundred and fifty years worth of possible inputs.

Jones's Blockhead twin is then defined as a creature that is *Blockhead* superficially like Jones but has inside it a chip on which Jones's game-of-life look-up tree is inscribed, and this chip controls Jones's Blockhead twin's every response to the environment. In the same way we can define a Blockhead twin for each and every one of us. The objection to input–output functionalism can now be stated very simply. It is that (a) Jones and Jones's Blockhead twin behave exactly alike, not only in how they respond to each and every situation, but in how they would respond to each and every possible situation; (b) Jones's Blockhead twin is not a puppet – the connection between its inputs and outputs is largely a consequence of how it is, not of how some puppeteer is; yet (c) though Jones is, we may suppose, intelligent and has a normal psychology, his Blockhead twin is no more intelligent than a toaster (as Block puts it) and has no mental life at all. It really is the kind of automaton that dualists (wrongly) hold that physicalism would reduce us to.

What is particularly interesting about the Blockhed example is *Blockhead's* that it tackles input–output functionalism on its favoured ground. *challenge to us* Many find input–output functionalism implausible when applied *all* to mental states in general, but it is at its most appealing applied to intelligence. There is no special 'feel' associated with intelligence, and it is intelligence that intuitively connects most closely with behavioural performance: the be-all and end-all of intelligence does seem to be certain capacities to deliver answers to problems set by questioners or by the environment. Yet the clearest intuition about Blockhead is precisely that it completely lacks intelligence and understanding. Indeed, given the intuitive appeal of an essentially behavioural approach to intelligence – while insisting, of course, that traditional behaviourism was wrong to refuse to see explanations in terms of intelligence as genuinely causal ones proceeding by appeal to internal nature – we should all try and say something sensible about why Blockhead is not intelligent. It is not enough to say 'It is fortunate I am not an input–output functionalist', or 'I hereby renounce input–output functionalism'. We all need to say *why* Blockhead is not intelligent.

Before we give our answer to this question, we note what seem *Some wrong* to us to be some wrong turns. You might say that the reason *turns* Blockhead is not intelligent is that everything it does or would do is determined in advance. It thus lacks the flexibility that is part of being intelligent and being rational. But of course if determinism is true, everything anyone ever does is determined from the very beginning of time. Some have inferred from this that determinism is incompatible with intelligence and especially with rational decision making, and have accordingly taken comfort in the fact that modern quantum theory is indeterministic. But this seems to us a pretty desperate position. It is hard to see how throwing in some random fluctuations would make what would otherwise be irrational rational.

You might object that the look-up tree could never be written down because it requires knowing all the possibilities for inputs at any given time and all the outputs that someone – Jones, as we imagined – would make to each and every input, and such knowledge is impossible. But what matters for the argument is that the story that the look-up tree tells exists, not whether we could know it. For each and everyone of us there is a huge story about what we would do in response to each and every possible input and sequence of inputs, so we can make sense of the idea that the story is written on a chip inside a Blockhead.

You might object that we *cannot* make sense of the idea that the story in the form of a huge look-up tree is contained inside Blockhead. The look-up tree could not exist because it would involve a combinatorial explosion. As we noted above, the look-up tree for a short game of chess, let alone the game of life, would take more particles than there are in the whole universe. This reply seems to us to misunderstand the role of thought-experiments.

The fact that Blockhead is practically, and perhaps even nomologically, impossible seems to us no more to the point than the fact that Twin Earth is practically, and perhaps also nomologically, impossible. The point of a thought-experiment is to test a conceptual claim, typically a claim about the relation between two concepts. In the case of Twin Earth, we test the hypothesis that being watery and being water necessarily go together. We come up with the answer that they do not necessarily go together by making clear sense of the possibility – Twin Earth – where water is not watery, and what is watery is not water. In the case of Blockhead we test the hypothesis that being behaviourally exactly alike someone intelligent is sufficient for being intelligent, and come up with the answer that it is not, by describing a possibility we understand and comprehend (while realizing that in practice it is quite impossible) – a Blockhead twin of an intelligent Jones – where what is behaviourally exactly alike someone intelligent has no intelligence (and indeed no thoughts) at all.

Finally, you might object that although it is missing the point to complain that the Blockhead example is impossible either in practice or perhaps even nomologically, it is right to be suspicious of intuitions about cases *that* far removed from what is possible in any but the most abstract sense. Perhaps, in particular, we should resist the intuition that Jones's Blockhead twin lacks intelligence. The trouble with this objection is that Blockhead is *so* like all the cases where we feel that someone lacks understanding: someone who cannot play chess except by asking an expert what to do at every stage is someone who does not understand the game, and someone who cannot give you the square root of a number other than by looking up a table of square roots is someone who does not fully understand what a square root is. The intuition that Blockhead lacks intelligence is simply a natural extension of what we learn from these simple, familiar cases. Moreover, we can give a reason why Blockhead lacks understanding and intelligence – a reason that, we will argue, makes sense of our strong intuition that Blockhead is deficient, and so explains and justifies the intuition.

Why Blockhead is not a thinker

A message of much recent philosophy has been the importance of *causal connections* of the right kind. You do not count as seeing something unless your perceptual state is caused by that thing. Part of what justifies thinking of an object – the chair in front of me or the White House – as a persisting material thing is the way early states of the object are causally responsible for later states of it. The identity through time of a person is in part a matter of their psychology being causally connected over time. Likewise, causal connections of the right kind are central to being intelligent, to rationality and to belief.

It is not irrational *per se* to believe that the Earth is flat. It is irrational *given* what else you believe and given your history. Rationality is in part a matter of your beliefs evolving in the right way from your earlier beliefs and sensory data. We should all believe that the Earth is round (or oblate, to be more precise) because that is the right belief to have caused in us by our pasts. Likewise, being intelligent centrally involves having trains of thought that evolve in the right way. Later thoughts have to be

Rationality and causal history

caused in the right way by earlier ones. If a brain scientist inserts a probe into your brain that causes the crucial thought that enables you to announce the proof of Goldbach's conjecture, this is not a sign of your intelligence or rationality. It is either a fluke or a sign of the intelligence of the brain scientist, depending on the causal origins of her action in inserting the probe. Moreover, it is part of being a belief of a certain kind that it tends to have certain results. Part of what makes something the belief that if P, then Q, is that, combined with the belief that P, it tends to cause the belief that Q. (We enlarge on the importance of tending to evolve rationally to being a belief when we discuss the intentional stance in chapter 9.)

Simple input–output devices exhibit massive causal dependencies between early and late stages. The state of a sundial or an amplifier or a carburettor that is responsible for its capacity to generate the appropriate outputs on Monday is typically a major causal factor in its capacity do the job on Tuesday. The situation with much more complex structures like human beings is correspondingly more complex. How we respond to stimuli on Tuesday depends on all sorts of factors in addition to how we are on Monday, including what has impacted on us between the two days and what we have thought about in the interim. This is part of what confers on us the flexibility of response that makes us intelligent. Nevertheless, causal dependencies between earlier and later thoughts are crucial. It is just that how we respond in the future depends on a much more diverse range of factors than simply how we have been in the past – what we have thought about and what has happened to us in the interim also enter the equation.

Blockhead's causal peculiarity   The trouble with devices that work by a look-up tree is that they lack the appropriate causal dependencies. The state that governs the responses to inputs early on plays no role in causing the state that governs the responses later on. It couldn't, for the look-up tree is written down in advance. The state that will govern the later responses already exists at the earlier time. The input–output profile of the look-up tree at any given time – any complete row of squares followed by circles – does not generate the profile at any later time. If on Monday you make a sundial or Frankenstein makes a person, you do not need to do anything extra to handle how what you have made will respond to various inputs on, say, Tuesday. What you made on Monday plus what happens in the meantime does that for you, and this is crucial to the way the Tuesday responses depend on the Monday ones.

By contrast, the only causal dependency manifested in the look-

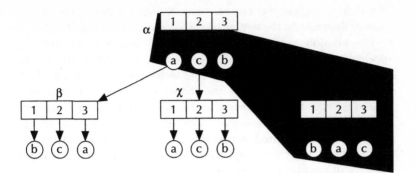

Figure 6   The Blockhead example – a look-up tree that simulates living an intelligent life. What actually happens lies within the shaded area.

up tree is in which element of the tree's input–output profile at some time is the actual input and output at that time. That depends not on the profiles at earlier times, but on which elements of those earlier profiles are themselves actual. It is like a recipe for roast duck that tells you at the end to go to another recipe for the sauce. Although what is in the first recipe plays a role in what you do subsequently, the content of the second recipe is, we may suppose, quite independent of the content of the first. This means that there is minimal dependency of the later input–output nature of Blockhead on its earlier input–output nature: the state that governs the later input–output nature does not depend for its existence or its nature on the earlier state (as we have already noted), but the output of the earlier state does settle that it is this state instead of some other one that determines the later input–output nature. But thinking is not like that; the content of what we think at a time typically depends in part on the content of what we thought at various earlier times, and that is crucial for it to count as thought and as rational thought.

In sum, Blockhead's input–output profile at any given time does not depend in the right way on its input–output profiles at earlier times for Blockhead to count as a thinker, or even as something displaying rationality and intelligence. The input–output nature of the state that controls Blockhead's behavioural response at time t is not caused by the input–output nature of what controls Blockhead's behavioural response at any earlier time $t - n$. Figure 6 helps make the point. In the figure the shaded area represents what actually happens. The point is that as you progress through the shaded region you are *not* progressing through states whose nature depends on the nature of earlier states in the shaded region.

One possible confusion: let's call the various sets of pre-recorded possible inputs together with appropriate outputs *nodes*; at any given time, a Blockhead can be said to have a certain node which is *active*. The active node is the one which will be searched until the input that has been given to the Blockhead is found, and the pre-recorded output produced. Now let's suppose that the Blockhead partly represented in figure 6 has node γ currently active. So if we give it input 1, we will get output *b*; and if we give it input 3, we will get output *c,* and so on.

Now it is true that *the fact that it is node γ that is currently active* does indeed depend on the past nature of the Blockhead. Indeed, it depends on the nature of node α, together with the fact that node α received input 3. But the nature of node γ itself does not depend on the nature of node α, or indeed on anything else about what has happened to it since its initial creation; and this is what is objectionable, in the sense of disqualifying it from being a thinker.

Common-sense functionalism and Blockhead

The argument to the conclusion that Blockhead is not a thinker rests on a constraint on belief and intelligence that is supposed to be part of folklore. The way belief evolves over time, the importance for rationality of belief evolving causally in the right way, and the fact that what is believed depends on what was believed and what happens to a subject are plausibly common knowledge – implicit or explicit – and part of our ordinary conception of belief. This means that Blockhead is not an objection to common-sense functionalism. Blockhead shows that input–output functionalism is false. How things are inside matters for our mental nature over and above how our insides manifest themselves in determining our environmental input–output connections. But Blockhead does not show that common-sense functionalism is false. Indeed, we could have seen this straight off. It is *intuition* that delivers the answer that Blockhead has not a thought in its head. We did not describe an experiment that shows that Blockhead is unintelligent. We followed Block in supposing that once the case was described, the answer was intuitively clear – and common-sense functionalism is the version of functionalism most concerned to honour clear intuitions about the mind.

Annotated Reading

The Chinese nation example is presented in Ned Block, 'Troubles with Functionalism'. John Searle's Chinese room case has been very widely discussed (at times, with some heat). Perhaps the best place to start is John Searle, 'Minds, Brains, and Programs'. A more informal presentation, combined with replies to the many objections that have been raised, is his 'Is the Brain's Mind a Computer Program?' Among the many replies he considers are those he christens the 'systems reply' and the 'robot reply'. The systems reply is the first one we expounded. The reply we eventually settled on is a combination of the systems and robot reply. A good recent discussion is in chapter 6 of Jack Copeland, *Artificial Intelligence*. The classic source for Blockhead is Ned Block, 'Psychologism and Behaviourism.'

8

Phenomenal Qualities and Consciousness

Mental states and 'feels' An itch feels different from an ache. A stabbing pain feels different from a burning one. But the belief that two is the smallest prime does not feel different from the belief that the Earth is oblate. Beliefs don't have 'feels'. Again, seeing something that looks red is a different experience from seeing something that looks green, but hoping that the drought will break is not a different experience from hoping that a cheque will not bounce. Hoping is not an experience, though it is sometimes associated with various experiences – of relief when the cheque does not bounce, of joy when the rain arrives. In what has become a common way of putting the difference, we distinguish psychological states for which there is *something it is like to be in them* from those for which the notion seems to make no sense.

Bodily sensations and perceptual experiences are prime examples of states for which there is something it is like to be in them. They have a **phenomenal feel**, a phenomenology, or, in a term sometimes used in psychology, are raw feels. Cognitive states are prime examples of states for which there is *not* something it is like to be in them, states that lack a phenomenology. These terms – 'phenomenal feel', 'having a phenomenology', 'there being something it is like to be in them', 'raw feels' – are not exactly transparent. They are ways of getting you to identify the distinction we have in mind on the presumption that you are already familiar with it. If you are not already familiar from your own mental life with the distinction between mental states that have a distinctive feel and those that do not, no words of ours will help you grasp it. Our words are intended not to inform you of a distinction you were previously ignorant of, but to identify for you the distinction this chapter is concerned with.

There is debate about which states fall into which category.

What about desires and emotions? Desires, particularly desires for food and sex, are often intimately associated with various sensations, but it is arguable that the desires themselves fall into the same class as cognitive states. The desire for food based on the belief that you will die unless you eat is exactly the same *desire* as the desire for food based on pangs of hunger. The desire *per se* has no special feel or phenomenology. Likewise, it is plausible that emotions are associated with, but not constituted by, the feelings – pangs of jealousy, swellings with pride, and the like – that are notoriously linked with them. In any case, we will not be concerned with which psychological states precisely fit which category. We will be concerned almost exclusively with the prime example of phenomenal mental states afforded by colour experiences, though similar points could be made about smells, pains and the like.

Colour experiences, then, will be our main examples of psychological states for which there is something it is like to be in them, of states with a phenomenology. Traditionally, phenomenal states have been seen as raising a general problem for physicalism, a problem that is not local to one or another form of it. The idea is that physicalism's general picture is too impoverished to have a place for phenomenal qualities. More recently, phenomenal states have been prominent in a discussion *within* physicalism about the adequacy of any functionalist theory of mind. Here the argument has been that functionalism is essentially a relational approach to mental states, an account of mental states in terms of the causal relations they enter into. What differs from one version of functionalism to another is which causal relations are crucial, and how the crucial ones are identified. Phenomenal qualities have been alleged to show that any purely relational account of mental states is inadequate.

Physicalism and phenomenal states

The question of qualia

This dual role for phenomenal qualities has led to an unfortunate dual role for the technical term **qualia** (singular: quale). Some use the term to name phenomenal qualities conceived as a matter of definition as falling outside the physicalists' picture, so that to believe in qualia is to espouse a non-physicalist theory of mind – such philosophers are sometimes called qualia freaks. On this usage,

The use of the term 'qualia'

to deny qualia is to deny that phenomenal qualities fall outside the physicalists' picture of the mind.

Others use the term 'qualia' to name phenomenal qualities conceived by definition as involving some relatively intrinsic feature, some feature not capturable functionally, of our mental states. On this construal, to believe in qualia is simply to deny functionalism; it is not necessarily to deny physicalism. And to repudiate qualia is to hold that the full account of the perceived redness of a sunset or the hurtfulness of a pain requires no more than the full story about the functional roles of certain internal states. Moreover, functionalism of one variety or another is widely accepted as an account of the intentional states or propositional attitudes – the mental states that we typically characterize in terms of 'that' clauses: your belief that snow is white and your desire that you eat sometime today are examples. (We discuss these states and how they come to be characterizable in terms of 'that' clauses in chapters 10 and 11.) Hence the issue about qualia in this second sense often comes down to the issue of whether or not all psychological states reduce in some way or another to intentional states. Does the hurtfulness of a pain supervene on being disposed to *believe* that damage has occurred, *desiring* that the disposition to *believe* that damage has occurred cease by virtue of the damage ceasing, and the like?

In what follows we will keep separate the two issues: the qualia objection to physicalism that the phenomenal side of psychology eludes the physicalist, and the qualia objection to functionalism – the claim that there is more to phenomenal mental nature than functional role. We will start by addressing the second issue.

The spectrum inversion objection to functionalism

Intuitively, phenomenal nature is **intrinsic**. The perceived redness of a sunset is a feature of how the experience is here and now; you cannot capture its nature fully by talking of its similarities and differences, of what causes it, and of what it causes. It is as intrinsic as squareness. But then perceived redness in particular, and colour experience in general, cannot be captured in functional terms, in terms of causal relations. The spectrum inversion objection is an attempt to make precise this intuitive objection to functionalism.

Colour inverts   It takes off from a speculation that has occurred at some time or other to almost everyone. How do you know that your colour experiences are the same as someone else's? If you differ in which things you see as being the same colour and which things you see as being different in colour, this difference will show up in your respective behaviour. The two of you will differ in what you classify together and what you classify apart. But suppose that your experiences of sameness and difference in colour are the same as the other person's. Then you will both make the same classifications. But surely, runs the speculation, you could agree about what looks the same and about what looks different in colour, while differing radically about which individual colours things look to have. More precisely, the following seems possible. Don has a colour invert, call him 'Nod'. The situations that cause Don to experience red cause Nod to experience green. The situations that cause Don to experience yellow cause Nod to experience blue. Things that look black to Don look white to Nod. In general, when Don has the experience of some colour, Nod has the experience of a colour opposite it on the colour wheel. Nevertheless, the responses in the various situations arising from Don's and Nod's very different colour experience are the same. For they have each been taught to call the colour experience caused by the sight of blood, geranium petals and certain sunsets 'red'. The fact that Don's experiences are very different from Nod's does not affect this. Likewise, both will use 'green' in the same situations – on seeing watered grass, for the experience caused by the light that indicates 'Go' at traffic lights, and so on – despite the difference in their experiences. Corresponding to the inversion of colour experiences will be a 'masking' inversion of colour-term usage. Similarly, when they are asked to discriminate on the basis of colour or to group things together on the basis of colour, what they do will be the same. What is prompting them will be very different – the similarity Don sees among the things he calls 'red' will be very different from the similarity Nod sees among the things *he* calls 'red' – but the net effect will be the same: both put the tomatoes in with the geranium petals, and separate them out from the cornflowers.

The objection to functionalism is that Don and Nod are functionally alike, while having radically different colour experiences. When Don has an internal state typically caused by seeing blood, which typically elicits the word 'red' from him and causes him to group what he sees with blood and ripe tomatoes, so does Nod, and conversely. But their colour experiences are totally different. Therefore, functional role does not exhaust phenomenal nature. There is more to the phenomenal nature of colour experiences than their functional role.

Is Nod
possible?

One response to this argument is to deny the possibility of the case of Nod. Don and Nod might be functionally similar, but could not be functionally exactly alike. There is a vibrancy about red that distinguishes it from green – the vibrancy that leads most people not to paint their house red, but leads some to choose a red sports car. But this means that things that look red catch the eye more than things that look green, and is not *catching* the eye conceptually connected to behaviour. Could something that caught the eye *more* be *harder* to pick out? Again, there is a coolness about blue that distinguishes it from its more prominent complement on the colour wheel, yellow, and this coolness–prominence difference is reflected in choices about which colours to surround oneself with and which colours to paint safety zones in. And so on and so forth. This response argues that if you consider the matter carefully and in detail, you will see that Don and Nod would not behave exactly alike in all possible situations. If this is right, colour experience supervenes on functional role, and there is no objection to functionalism from phenomenal qualities.

Modifying
functionalism

The second standard response to the argument grants that Don and Nod would not be functionally exactly alike, but insists that there is more to say about the case. For suppose that we discovered that people divide into two classes when it comes to decisions about internal decorating schemes, paintings and the like. The division is perhaps rather like the familiar one between introverts and extroverts, or between type A and type B personalities, except that it pertains to aesthetic decisions broadly construed. When we investigate the neurophysiological differences between the two groups, we find that although they have states inside them playing roughly the same functional roles – they are functionally similar, though not of course exactly the same (they choose different paintings to hang in their bedrooms, for instance) – the states that realize these similar roles are systematically reversed. What is caused by the sight of blood in the first class is caused by the sight of grass in the second, and vice versa; what is caused by the sight of the sky in the first class is caused by the sight of sunflowers in the second, and vice versa; and so on round the colour wheel. The claim is that it would be very plausible to hold that the two groups had very different colour experiences, that the sight of blood caused in the first group an experience rather similar to that caused by the sight of grass in the second, for instance, and that part of the reason why this would be a plausible hypothesis derives from the discovery about internal realization.

On this view it is *both* functional role and nature of neuro-physiological realization that determines nature of experience. The plausibility of the position rests on the plausibility of the claim that if we discovered these substantial differences in what realizes the key functional roles associated with colour experience, sub-stantial differences that explain differences in what we think of as the more marginal functional roles associated with one or another colour experience (how restful or discordant various colours are, what colours go well together, and the like), it would be right to say that colour experiences differ from person to person more dramatically than we have hitherto realized (we know already from differences in performance on tests for colour-blindness that there is a good deal of variation).

This view seems to us the more attractive physicalist response to the argument from spectrum inversion. It seeks to do justice to the sense that functional role leaves out something when we come to consider the phenomenal side of psychology, but does so with-out invoking spooky properties. It is neurophysiology, perhaps combined with some aspects of functional role, that provides the missing bit, not something spooky. The argument from spectrum inversion is, on this view, an argument for qualia in the sense of making plausible the view that more than functional role plays a part in fixing phenomenal nature, but it is not an argument for qualia in the sense of an argument that the phenomenal side of psychology falls outside the physicalistic picture. We now turn to perhaps the best-known argument designed to establish the stronger conclusion.

The knowledge argument challenge to physicalism

It is not in dispute that we are in part physical things. We have physical bodies and are located in a physical world. The issue is whether we are entirely physical, whether the physical story about us is the complete story about us. The knowledge argument seeks to show that the material or physical story about us is not the com-plete story about us, because it leaves out the sensory part, the 'redness of reds' part.

We are invited to consider the situation of Mary, a brilliant physicist and neuroscientist. She is confined to a black and white room, a room in which she and her surroundings look just the way a black and white film looks. She has a black and white television

Mary

and a huge black and white library, and through them access to all
there is to know about physics and neuroscience, and in fact all
there is to know about the physical nature of our world and the
creatures, humans included, in it. (We may pretend that she is
living sometime in the future when all the outstanding problems
in the physical sciences have been solved, and that she has a pro-
digious memory and ability to make sense of the huge body of
physical information at her disposal.) She will then know everything there is to know about the physical nature of our world and
of us, and consequently about the functional roles the various
physical states play in us. In short, she will know everything there
is to know about the nature of our world, about us and about our
place in it, according to physicalism. If physicalism is true, there
is nothing she does not know.

However, it seems clear that there is something she does not
know. She does not know what it is like to see red, and in general
to have colour experiences other than those of black, white and
shades of grey. She will know, of course, that should she be released from the room, she would on seeing blood utter the words
'That is red' (assuming she chose to speak English). For she will
know the way that the light from blood impinging on English-
speaking perceivers affects their brains in such a way that those
words come out of their mouths. But should she be released, she
would discover something else: the distinctive nature of the experience that typically accompanies those words.

The point can be put by contrasting her knowledge of motor
cars with her knowledge of us. Although there are no motor cars
inside her room, she will know from her library and television all
there is to know about them: just how they work and why they
move as they do. She will also know how we work and what causes
us to move as we do (assuming that dualist interactionism is false).
But she will not know all there is to know about us, and this fact
will become manifest to her on her release. She will realize, through
her own experience of colour, that her previous conception of
what we humans are like was seriously impoverished. But if her
previous conception was seriously impoverished, then, because it
included everything in the physicalists' story, that story is seriously impoverished. It leaves out the special nature of colour experience. And, more generally, it leaves out the phenomenal side
of psychology. For clearly the same line of argument could be
developed to show that the hurtfulness of pain or the itchiness of
an itch is left out of the physicalists' story. Suppose that Mary has

never had an itch or a pain. She knows that the people she sees on her television scratch and wince, as well as the full physical story of what causes them to do so. Won't she nevertheless *learn* something the first time she has an itch or feels pain?

Replies to the knowledge argument

The knowledge argument has attracted a great deal of discussion and a very large number of replies. We will discuss some of the most interesting ones. Each of these replies deserves much more discussion than we can give it here. In the annotated reading section we give details of where to find fuller discussions of the issues.

We express what we know and believe using sentences (a point we will discuss in some detail when we address the internal sentence view of belief in chapters 10 and 11). And you may know one way of saying what you know without knowing another way of saying it. This is what happens when you can say what you know in English but cannot say it in Japanese. You can express your knowledge that snow is white in English, but cannot express it in Japanese. This is Mary's situation, runs this reply. In the room she knows how to express her knowledge of the world and of us in a language that draws on the terms of the physical sciences, expressions for functional roles, terms for shades of grey, and so on, but not in terms of the colour vocabulary. When she gets out of the room, she learns how to express her knowledge in terms of the colour vocabulary. She does not learn anything new about us or our world, only something about the words that can be used to express what she already knew. Her vocabulary expands but not her conception of what the world and we are like; hence, it is fallacious to infer that her conception of the world and us was impoverished before her release.

The language reply

The trouble with this reply is that it seems that she *does* learn more than something about language. She will not say, 'Now I know a new way of saying what I knew all along' – what one says on learning how to say 'Snow is white' in Japanese. Something much more substantial than that has happened to her. Moreover, before her release she knew a great deal about the conditions under which colour terms like 'red' are used. Her situation with respect to colour words in English is not at all like the situation of non-Japanese speakers with respect to Japanese. They do not know when it is right to use the various Japanese words. By contrast, if physicalism is true, Mary already knew all there was to know about the circumstances in which the various colour words are used by competent English speakers.

The opacity of knowledge reply

Cicero denounced Catiline. Cicero and the most famous orator in Rome were one and the same person. Hence, the most famous orator in Rome denounced Catiline. Indeed, Cicero's denouncing Catiline is the very same fact as the most famous orator's doing so (on some ways of counting facts). Nevertheless, you might know that Cicero denounced Catiline without knowing that the most famous orator in Rome did. This illustrates the famous opacity of knowledge: from '$a = b$' and 'S knows that a is F' it does not follow that S knows that b is F.[5] The knowledge argument overlooks the opacity of knowledge, runs this reply. While in the room, Mary knows that Jones outside is in a certain neurological state N playing a certain role R. This state is his sensing red, and his sensing red is the very same fact as his being in N playing R. The opacity of knowledge tells us that this physicalist position is quite consistent with Mary not knowing that Jones is sensing red, or at least not knowing this until her release.

Different modes of acquaintance with the same facts

A similar reply draws on the fact that one phenomenon can present itself under different descriptions or in different guises. The same war presents itself very differently to participants, journalists and readers of press reports, but it is still the one war. Why cannot we reply to the knowledge argument by insisting that sensing red is one phenomenon, which presents itself differently to someone experiencing it as opposed to someone, Mary, say, investigating it *qua* neuroscientist. We have one way of being acquainted with a neurological state, Mary has another; but it is fallacious to infer that we and Mary are acquainted with different facts.

The trouble with the opacity of knowledge reply is that the best explanation of the opacity of knowledge turns on the possibility of knowing some of a thing's properties without knowing all of them. The person who knows that Cicero denounced Catiline but does not know that the most famous orator in Rome denounced Catiline does not know something about Cicero: namely, that as well as

---

[5] In our illustration we use a name and a definite description for 'a' and 'b', respectively. Cicero also went under the name 'Tully', and often the opacity of knowledge is illustrated with 'Tully denounced Catiline' in place of 'The most famous orator in ancient Rome denounced Catiline'. However, the claim that it is possible to know that Cicero denounced Catiline without knowing that Tully did is controversial for reasons that are here irrelevant.

going under the name 'Cicero', he was the most famous orator in Rome. But Mary is precisely *not* in this kind of situation if physicalism is true: she knows all the properties of our internal workings that there are to know.

A similar point applies to the version of the reply to the knowledge argument that appeals to the fact that one phenomenon can be known under different descriptions or guises or modes of acquaintance. This is the explanation of Mary's ignorance that is available to dual attribute theorists, not the explanation available to physicalists. If Jones's sensing red is a neurological state with a special non-physical property, then some descriptions that pick it out will do so via this special property, and it will be known to some experiencers *qua* bearer of this special property, under this guise. But there are no such properties to underpin this style of explanation of Mary's failure to be able to move from the one mode of acquaintance to the other if physicalism is true.

There is an important distinction between knowing that and knowing how. Knowing that is propositional knowledge concerning how things are. Knowing how is an ability, like knowing how to ride a bicycle. Of course, knowing how to ride a bicycle involves a good deal of knowledge that – you will not get far on a bicycle if you do not know that the end with the handlebars is the front. But you can know all the facts there are to know about riding a bicycle – be able, for instance, to give an outstanding talk or write the perfect handbook on the subject – and yet not know how to ride a bicycle. Now consider someone who is currently not sensing red but knows what it is like to sense red; something has looked red to them in the past, and they remember what it was like, or perhaps a false 'memory' of sensing red has been planted in their brain (thus, it cannot be maintained that it is *impossible* to know what it is like to sense red unless one has in fact sensed red). In what does their knowledge of what it is like to sense red consist? Answer: in their possession of certain abilities. They can imagine sensing red, and they are able to recognize simply by looking that something is red on being presented with it in daylight. According to this reply, it is these abilities, not knowledge that, that Mary lacks when she is in her room and which she will acquire on sensing red.

The knowing how reply

The trouble with this reply is that although Mary will acquire certain abilities when she first senses red, it is hard to believe that that is *all* she will acquire. It seems to many that she learns something important about what life and the world are *like*, and that is knowledge that.

You can know P and know Q, yet fail to know everything that the conjunction of P with Q entails; for you may fail to put the two together aright. Indeed, the articulation of proofs in logic and mathematics can be seen as the process of putting the pieces together aright (think of the hints on finding proofs in logic texts). Mary's situation while inside the room is that she has all the ingredients she needs to work out what it is like to sense red; however, there is too much detail for her to get it together aright. According to this reply, she cannot integrate her knowledge into one coherent body of information. She is like someone who knows the location and size of every dot on a piece of paper but cannot see the patterns – the swirls and lines – until they step back a bit from the paper. The patterns are there in the information they had at the beginning, and in principle could have been worked out beforehand, but in practice the task is beyond them.

The trouble with this reply is that what Mary learns seems to be different in *kind* from what she knew beforehand. When you step back from the paper and see patterns that you missed beforehand, at the very same time as you see the patterns, you apprehend that they were 'there' all along. It really does seem to be putting together what was already available. But what Mary will learn seems to be something quite new about how things are.

Water is nothing but H_2O, and it has no properties that are not fully explicable as properties of H_2O: water is not H_2O with special extra properties distinct from those it has *qua* H_2O that make the H_2O count as water. In sum, what we might call H_2O-ism about water – by analogy with physicalism about the mind – is true. Nevertheless, you cannot deduce everything about water from full knowledge about H_2O. This follows from the famous *a posteriori* status of 'Water = H_2O' which we discussed in chapter 4. You might, for instance, know that there is H_2O hereabouts, without knowing that there is water hereabouts. We should, runs this reply, think of the relationship between the physical way the world is and the psychological way it is, including of course the phenomenal way it is, as like the relationship between the H_2O way the world is and the water way it is. The relation is one of metaphysical necessity without *a priori* deducibility. No wonder Mary cannot deduce the full nature of the world from full knowledge of the physical way it is: the physical way it is necessitates, without enabling the deduction of, the psychological way it is.

The first trouble with this reply is that it runs afoul of the most attractive way of understanding the necessary *a posteriori*, the way we articulated earlier, in our discussion of the causal theory of reference in chapter 4.

Our understanding of 'water' is as a rigid designator whose reference is fixed by 'the stuff that fills the water role', where the water role is spelt out in terms of, say, satisfying most of the following: being an odourless and colourless liquid, falling from the sky, being called 'water' by our experts, being necessary to life on the planet, filling the oceans, and so on. The combination of the fact that 'water' and 'H_2O' are rigid designators with its being *a posteriori* that H_2O fills the water role explains why sentences like 'Water is H_2O' and 'If H_2O covers most of the planet, water covers most of the planet' are necessary *a posteriori*. At the same time, the fact that we understand 'water' as being a rigid designator of that which fills the water role means that the sentence 'Water = the stuff that fills the water role (is the watery stuff)' is (contingent) *a priori*. But then it follows that a *rich enough* story about the H_2O way things are enables the *a priori* deduction of the water way things are. True, we cannot deduce where the water is from where the H_2O is, but we can deduce it from where the H_2O is along with the information about H_2O filling the water role. One who knows both where the H_2O is *and* that H_2O falls from the sky, is odourless and colourless, and so on – that is, is the watery stuff – can deduce where the water is.

The second trouble with this reply is that the thesis that the physical way the world is necessitates, without enabling the deduction of, the psychological way it is involves a mysterious kind of emergence when viewed from a physicalist standpoint.

It is implausible that there are facts about very simple organisms that cannot be deduced *a priori* from enough information about their physical nature and how they interact with their environments, physically described. The physical story about amoebae and their interactions with their environment is the whole story about amoebae. Mary would not lack any knowledge about them. But, according to physicalism, we differ from amoebae essentially only in complexity of ingredients and their arrangement. It is hard to see how that kind of difference could generate important facts about us that in principle defy our powers of deduction, and the fact that we have a phenomenal psychology is certainly an important fact about us. Think of the charts in biology classrooms showing the evolutionary progression from single-celled creatures on the far left to the higher apes and humans on the far right: where in that progression can the physicalist plausibly claim that failure of *a priori* deducibility of important facts about us *emerges*? Or, if it comes to that, where in the development of each and every one of us from a zygote could the physicalist plausibly locate the place where there emerge important facts about us that cannot be deduced from the physical story about us?

The 'There must be a reply' reply
If certain mental states have qualia in the sense of properties that fall outside the physicalists' picture, these qualia must be epiphenomenal. This follows from the considerations concerning causal closure discussed in chapter 1. But then beliefs and memories cannot be regarded as responses to the existence of qualia. The exposition by qualia freaks of the knowledge argument can in no sense be the *outcome* of the instantiation of qualia. Moreover, these expositors must allow that Mary's discovery, as they insist it must be described, of something important and new about what things are like is in no sense due to the properties, the qualia, whose alleged instantiation constituted the inadequacy of her previous picture of the world: they cannot say that she comes to realize that her previous picture is inadequate *because* it is inadequate.

Sometimes this reply is allied with an unduly strong view about the connection between knowledge and causation: we can only know about what impinges somehow or other on us. This is a mistake. We know about the future, and our knowledge extends beyond the light cone (we know, for instance, that it is not plum jam from there on). Nevertheless, when we identify some particular happening as what leads us to revise our conception of how things are, typically it is important that this happening can be seen as caused by something that justifies our change of mind. It is hard to see how what causally impacts on Mary when she leaves the room could justify belief in qualia. We know enough about how the world works to be entitled to hold that what would happen to her when she leaves her room could be fully accounted for in physical terms; and how could these physical facts justify belief in qualia?

This reply does not tell us what is wrong with the knowledge argument. It seeks to show that there must be something wrong with it somewhere. What we know about the way the world works tells us that when she leaves the room Mary *cannot* acquire knowledge of how things are that outruns the physical story she knew beforehand – despite the fact that it certainly seems that she does! It seems to us to be the most powerful reply to the knowledge argument. It is what makes the phenomenal side of psychology such a hard problem. We have a good argument – the knowledge argument – that the physicalist picture is inadequate; yet we have a good argument – from causal considerations – that it must be adequate!

This situation has led some philosophers to hold that the whole problem has somehow been misconceived. We need a new start. We need to examine the very terms in which the problem has been set up. It seems to us, however, that recent attempts to put forward views of this kind are deeply obscure. You must judge for yourselves.

Consciousness

We now come to an even more controversial issue, that of consciousness.

What is consciousness? A traditional view, one that is arguably to be found in Descartes, sees consciousness as an extra ingredient in our mental life over and above what we feel, believe, desire, hope, perceive, and so on and so forth. Consciousness is thought of as a kind of stream in which the various mental states inhere. This view has few adherents these days. The obvious objection to it is that consciousness is always and necessarily consciousness of something – of what one is feeling, believing, hoping or whatever. We cannot separate consciousness from the various mental states. Today, most philosophers of mind take the view that we must seek an account of consciousness in terms of the mental states themselves. Consciousness is to be found somewhere *in* the complex story about what we feel, believe, hope, perceive and so on. This does not mean that any creature with a mental life is conscious; that, as we will shortly see, is a further question. But it does mean that any creature with *our* range of mental states is conscious. The problem, then, is where conscious is to be found in the complex story about mental lives like ours.

There are many views about where to look. One major division *Modest views* is between those who accept our (fairly standard but far from universal) way of introducing qualia in the sense that is neutral in the debate between physicalism and anti-physicalism, in the sense in which the term is a synonym for 'phenomenal qualities', and those who reject that way of introducing the notion. We said that perceptions and sensations are mental states with a phenomenal feel; we said that the 'What is it like to be in them?' question has an answer in their case. The contrast, as we saw the matter, is with states like beliefs and desires that lack a phenomenal feel or quale. Of course, qualia sometimes come along with various beliefs and desires, but they are the qualia of feelings or perceptions distinct from the beliefs or desires themselves. We can call views of this kind *modest*: they limit the number of states that display qualia. The most popular view of consciousness among those in the modest camp insists that having states with qualia is essential for being conscious. Its appeal rests on the naturalness of using the same kind of language that we used in characterizing qualia in characterizing consciousness. In both cases we seek to convey what we have in mind by talking of an inner mental life and of what it is like to have experiences of one or another kind.

It is important to bear in mind that 'qualia' here simply stands for the features distinctive of sensations and perceptions. So the doctrine just described amounts to the view (plausible to our minds) that having perceptions or sensations is essential to being conscious. Those, but only those, who are convinced that qualia do not figure in the physicalist scheme will see this account of consciousness as an anti-physicalist one.

A special version   Some holders of this account of consciousness maintain that having states with qualia is sufficient, as well as necessary, for being conscious; but more plausible versions of modest theories insist that for subjects to count as conscious they must have beliefs and desires, especially beliefs and desires about their sensational states: part of being conscious is having cognitive and conative *attitudes* towards one's sensational states. Finally, there is a rather different kind of modest view. It is modest in granting that only sensations and perceptions have qualia, but it downplays the importance of these states with qualia for being conscious. On this view, the essential feature of conscious beings is that they have mental states directed towards other mental states. Although there could be beings that had beliefs and desires but lacked beliefs and desires concerning their beliefs and desires, they would, of necessity, live totally unreflective lives, and, runs the view, the essence of consciousness is the ability to reflect on one's mental states. These beings would have minds but not be conscious.

Qualia for belief and desire?   The second class of views of consciousness starts by challenging the way we introduced qualia or phenomenal qualities. On these views, there *is* something it is like to have a belief or desire of a certain kind. It is false that only sensations and perceptions have phenomenal character. Such views are immodest, as we will put it, in that they expand the class of phenomenal qualities. Sometimes the view is that it is impossible to have a belief or desire without the distinctive feel. Sometimes it is that it is impossible to have a belief or desire without the *possibility* of the distinctive feel – the 'feel' is there to be experienced by any subject who directs their attention towards what they believe and desire. Sometimes the view is merely that, as a matter of fact, beliefs and desires are sometimes or always associated with distinctive feels. This last view is not a covert return to the modest view of phenomenal qualities; for, though the phenomenal qualities are only contingently associated with beliefs and desires, they are *distinctive* of them. They are *not* the qualia of sensations and perceptions that may accompany the beliefs and desires. As immodest views essentially reject any special place for sensations and perceptions in respect to, as we might put it, 'feeliness', the accounts of consciousness they offer typically accord no special place for sensations and perceptions.

It is time to look at some of these positions in more detail.

According to the modest view of consciousness, consciousness is nothing more than qualia coupled with propositional attitudes. There is nothing distinctively qualitative about the attitudes: the nature of belief and desire is given exhaustively by some other properties, usually functional ones. This is not as strange as it might seem. Everyone agrees that there is a distinction between **occurrent** and non-occurrent **beliefs** and desires. Occurrent ones are somehow at the forefront of the mind; and if there is a special qualitative aspect to belief, then it attaches only to these. But most of our beliefs and desires are non-occurrent; and the very beliefs and desires which guide our behaviour are overwhelmingly non-occurrent. When we go to the refrigerator to get a bottle of mineral water, beliefs about the spatial layout of the kitchen, desires to minimize the effort involved in covering the distance, and countless others are all contributing to the process. Yet none of these has a special qualitative aspect, and this does not impair their capacity to govern our actions.

What of occurrent beliefs? Proponents of the modest view think that there is nothing special going on here either. It is true that sometimes beliefs or desires may be involved in processes of deliberation. But this may be cashed out in terms of there being second-order beliefs and desires: beliefs about the beliefs we have, or about the appropriateness of them, and desires about what desires we have, as when you judge that you desire not to desire ice-cream, or

Modesty about consciousness

deliberate as to whether your belief that water is H_2O serves you well. The modest view may well contain an analysis of consciousness in terms of the kinds of special beliefs or desires required for consciousness (such as the desire to believe truly, or the candidates above), but this is meant to be an explication of what is meant by consciousness, and is thus *a priori*. When these sorts of claims are made by proponents of the modest view, the claim is not a metaphysical conjecture. The claim is not that if you have these special sorts of beliefs and desires, then other things being equal, this will result in your having the extra property of consciousness; it is rather the claim that, on careful reflection, nothing more is meant by the claim that a being is conscious than that they have these special sorts of beliefs and desires.

In addition, sometimes beliefs appear to 'run through the mind' while these deliberations go on; but perhaps this consists only in either the sentences that express the belief or desire running through the mind or a pictorial image that depicts the believed state of affairs coming to mind. Sometimes you may say to yourself, 'I really do love wattle trees' and have a quale as of hearing the sentence, or summon up a visual image of the layout of your garden. No doubt these things happen in conjunction with our beliefs from time to time, but the modest view of consciousness takes them to be qualitative experiences which are separable from the beliefs themselves. Perhaps, as a matter of analysis, to be conscious requires both the special sorts of beliefs and desires and sometimes having some accompanying qualia, but in that case we count a view as still modest if it allows that fully fledged beliefs and desires can exist without consciousness or some connection to it.

The immodest view about consciousness
The immodest view holds that belief and desire have distinctive phenomenologies over and above any quasi-pictorial or auditory qualia that may sometimes accompany active beliefs or desires. The non-occurrent nature of most of our beliefs and desires poses a real challenge for such a position. Are we to say that we do not believe most of what we normally take ourselves to believe? All those beliefs we acquired at school about Shakespeare, world pressure belts, and the valences of various elements: do we believe them only as we explicitly recall them? That would be absurd, especially as we have seen that a belief can be actively action-guiding without being occurrent in the way that is required for consciousness. One possibility, associated with John Searle, is the view that beliefs and desires which are not occurrent are genuine beliefs and desires only insofar as they can become occurrent. But

here the special role of the alleged phenomenology of belief and desire becomes very strained. Such a view must admit that most of our beliefs and desires do not have a distinctive phenomenology, yet insist that it is only because they can acquire such a phenomenology that they are genuine. It is hard to see what role the phenomenology is supposed to play. It isn't claimed that beliefs and desires have this phenomenology at all times as part of their nature. Nor is this phenomenology required for the beliefs and desires to play their causal roles in regulating action (even internal actions such as non-conscious inference). What can be so important about the capacity to become occurrent? Imagine that there is some belief which guides Arthur throughout his life, which never becomes occurrent. There are, however, some circumstances (which never occurred in Arthur's life) under which it would have become occurrent. Imagine that Arthur has a twin; the latter's behaviour has been guided by a state just like Arthur's, except that this state would never become occurrent (perhaps something about the state would self-destruct on the path to occurrence). What reason have do we for accepting that Arthur's state is a genuine belief, and thus about the world in some respect, whereas his twin's state is a mere causal engine, not about anything?

Searle's is not the only way in which some connection with consciousness might be deemed essential to genuine beliefs and desires. You might think that, regardless of whether a belief is ever occurrent or has the capacity to become occurrent, it needs to be connected to a conscious state in some other way. Perhaps a genuine belief has to be caused by conscious perceptual experience, or has to have an effect on perceptual experience. To develop such a view, there would have to be a very careful spelling out of exactly what the required connection must be. Presumably not any connection between belief and occurrent experience would be enough to convert a mere dispositional state into their preferred kind of belief. Suppose you have some belief about the size of Norway that will never become occurrent, but that does have an impact on the nature of your qualitative experience of green things. It would seem very *ad hoc* to think that this makes a difference. But other candidates, more closely tied to experiences that might be associated with the causes or effects of the belief, still strike us as fairly arbitrary. Why stipulate, for example, that a genuine belief or desire must be caused by a conscious state? This would make subliminal advertising a conceptual impossibility, inasmuch as it works by unconsciously affecting the beliefs and desires of the public. At least Searle's proposal draws a principled line on the connection between consciousness and propositional attitudes. For him there is something that it is like to have beliefs and desires (or perhaps there is something distinct which it is like to have each and every belief and desire), and nothing is a true belief or desire unless the state has the power to make its possessor have the appropriate experience. We do not think that there is anything which it is like to have a belief; and nor do we think that if sometimes there were something that it is like to have a belief, that it would be required for that state to be a genuine belief. But with the weaker connections between propositional attitudes and consciousness it is even hard to see why, for any particular proposal, it would even *prima facie* be a requirement for someone's having a genuine belief or desire.

Consciousness and physicalism
On the modest view, consciousness does not pose any more of a problem for physicalism than phenomenal experience already does. The physicalistic theory of your choice about beliefs and desires can remain in place, with the question of consciousness being a question of what, if anything, one has to add to that picture by way of special beliefs and desires or qualia to get a combination of states that deserves to be called conscious.

On the immodest view, however, the problem is not so simple. One style of immodest view holds that beliefs and desires have, contingently, a conscious aspect. There is something that it is like to have a belief and desire, but you can have a belief or a desire in its absence. On this view what it is to be conscious, or part of what it is to be conscious, is to have a belief or desire with the associated phenomenology. Proponents of this view need to give an account of phenomenal qualities of intentional states as well as of 'raw feels'. They have no special problem about reconciling beliefs and desires as such with physicalism, however. The possibly problematic qualitative aspect which is necessary for consciousness is not necessary for believing, desiring and so on.

Things are more difficult for the styles of immodest view that insist that the qualitative aspect is necessary for genuine belief and desire. For these views to count as physicalist views of belief and desire, there must be available a physicalist account of the qualitative aspect they see as integral to consciousness.

Some philosophers have just such accounts. There are at least as many physicalist accounts of consciousness as there are brands of functionalism. For it is always possible to speculate that consciousness supervenes on some level of functional organization. You could be a common-sense functionalist about consciousness, holding that being organized in the way which common-sense functionalism says is sufficient for beliefs and desires is itself sufficient for consciousness. Or you could be an empirical functionalist about consciousness, holding the view that sharing whatever internal architecture of the brain cognitive science will discover best explains our capacities is what it takes to be conscious. Or you might think, with Searle, that what it takes to be conscious is at a more basic physical level – a physical neuro-chemistry like ours, for instance.

We will conclude by distinguishing two very different approaches to the problem of consciousness that physicalists can take. Physicalists must identify consciousness with some part of the physicalist account of us – perhaps with the having of certain beliefs and desires, including beliefs and desires about beliefs and desires, combined on some views with certain qualitative experiences, all conceived of in physicalistically acceptable terms. We have just been reviewing some of the possible positions. Along one dimension of variation we find different physicalistically acceptable ingredients identified with consciousness. Along a second dimension of variation we find different kinds of argument for the favoured identification. Some see the identification as arising out of an *a priori* conceptual claim about consciousness allied with the relevant empirical information; others see the matter entirely as a piece of metaphysical speculation that leads to an *a posteriori* necessary identification of consciousness. On the first approach, we are to interrogate what we understand by consciousness, finding, let's say, that it comes to nothing more than the having of certain beliefs and desires which are then analysed functionally; we then make a plausible empirical claim that the relevant functional organization supervenes on physical nature, and proceed to the desired physicalist identification. On the second, the story is entirely *a posteriori*. It is of a kind, runs the argument, with the way we made the necessary *a posteriori* identification of water with H_2O. Obviously, the first approach is that of common-sense functionalism; the second that of empirical functionalism.

We think, as you might expect given our common-sense functionalist sympathies, that the physicalist should go down the first path, and that the analogy with the identification of water with H_2O does not support going down the second. The identification of water with H_2O has an *a priori* component. It is part of what we have always meant by 'water' that the stuff which has the same

A priori *versus* a posteriori *physicalist approaches*

chemical properties as the stuff of our acquaintance which actually falls from the sky, is potable and so forth, is water. This is how we identify water. We then discover the chemical structure of that which we have so identified, and it is a conceptual truth that all and only the stuff with that structure is properly called 'water'. This delivers the essential property and the famous necessary *a posteriori* identification. The key point here is similar to the one we made against the 'H_2O-ism' reply to the knowledge argument. We should not accept the necessary *a posteriori* identifications by metaphysical fiat, but rather as flowing out of a piece of conceptual analysis combined with the relevant empirical information. We thus agree with those physicalists who see it as a prime task to provide a suitable analysis of consciousness as an essential preliminary to making the physicalist identification they seek. Part of what makes the problem of consciousness so hard is that there is as yet no analysis that comes close to holding the field. There is no analogue available to physicalistic theories of consciousness of the reference-fixing formula that water is what actually fills rivers and so on; we can only gesture introspectively. Being unable to get a fix on consciousness in this way it is hard to do anything which is the analogue of examining it to determine its structure.

Annotated Reading

The challenge presented to physicalism by the 'feely' side of psychology is discussed in virtually every text in the philosophy of mind. A good, simple, but none the worse for that, evocation of the sense that the yellowness of yellows and the hurtfulness of pains is left out by physicalism is to be found in Keith Campbell, *Body and Mind*, chapter 5; for a full scale defence of this position, see David Chalmers, *The Conscious Mind*. Recent presentations of the other side are Owen Flanagan, *Consciousness Reconsidered*, and Daniel Dennett, *Consciousness Explained*. Both these books are positive contributions to a physicalist treatment of consciousness as well as containing replies to arguments that consciousness and raw feels are left out by physicalism. They are research monographs but ones written in a lively, accessible style. A detailed, important contribution to the issues raised by the inverted spectrum argument (and the related 'absent qualia argument' which we do not discuss) is to be found in the exchange between Ned Block and Jerry Fodor, 'What Psychological States are Not', and Sydney Shoemaker, 'Functionalism and Qualia'. A recent attack on the idea that we should believe in qualia in *either* of the senses we distinguished is to be found in Michael Tye, *The Imagery Debate*, chapter 7.

The knowledge argument has a long history in one form or another. Recent interest in it arises particularly from Thomas Nagel, 'What is it Like to be a Bat?' and Frank Jackson, 'Epiphenomenal Qualia' and 'What Mary Didn't Know'. A very useful consideration of the many issues raised by the argument and a presentation of the 'knowing how' reply to it is David Lewis, 'What Experience Teaches'. The view that belief requires consciousness is particularly associated with John Searle, *Intentionality*. A clear, early presentation of the idea that consciousness is belief about mental states is to be found in D. M. Armstrong, *A Materialist Theory of the Mind*. The view that qualia and, by association, consciousness by their very nature defy understanding is mentioned near the end of Jackson's 'Epiphenomenal Qualia' (though, for the record, he is now inclined to the 'there must be a reply' position on qualia), and defended at length in Colin McGinn, *The Problem of Consciousness*. A good, thoroughly up-to-date collection is Martin Davies and Glyn W. Humphreys, eds, *Consciousness*.

9

Instrumentalism and Interpretationism

Instrumentalism

Metaphysical and anti-metaphysical views of mind

Functionalism and the identity theory view mental states as inner, causally efficacious states of persons. They are literally inside us, and they do some causing. Behaviourism denies that mental states are inner, causally efficacious states, but nevertheless has a view about their nature: namely, that they are behavioural dispositions. These theories are thus metaphysical views of mind; they advance views about what mental states *are*. This chapter is concerned with an anti-metaphysical theory of mind, the theory known as instrumentalism. It does not offer a view about what mental states are, but instead offers a view about when ascriptions of mental states to subjects are true: roughly, they are true when they serve their purpose. Before we can give a more precise account of the doctrine, we need to discuss what the purpose of ascribing mental states is according to instrumentalism in a little detail, and this is the burden of the first part of the chapter.

Intentional states

The focus will be on **intentional states** or **propositional attitudes**, those mental states we characterize using indicative sentences in 'that' clauses and which we distinguished in the previous chapter from the more phenomenal mental states like pains and colour experiences. We will have a good deal to say about the class of intentional states in chapters 10 and 11. For now it is enough that beliefs and desires are central examples of intentional states and the ones we will be concerned with in this chapter.

In a brief final section we will consider the relation between this theory of mind and a doctrine sometimes known as **interpretationism**, according to which the question of what mental state a person is in is more like the question as to whether a joke is funny or whether something is red than one might have thought.

Stances and intentional systems

We have noted a number of times that we could, given that the phys- *The physical*
ical world is causally closed, predict in detail a person's behaviour *stance*
in terms of their physical make-up and that of their surroundings.
Some of these predictions will be irreducibly probabilistic – or at
least, they will be if current physics is right about indeterminacy.
Such a prediction is called a prediction from the **physical stance**.
Predictability from the physical stance is in very many cases only
predictability in principle. Interesting predictions from the physical
stance of a person's behaviour are rarely possible in practice. We
can predict from the physical stance that someone will rise in the
air from information about their weight, the nature of the rope
running over a pulley that they are attached to, and the weight on
the other end of the pulley; but we cannot predict that someone
will step around a hole in the ground, or enter a taxi, or play a
sonata, or serve to the backhand, from the physical stance. And
the same goes for complex machines in general. We often cannot
predict what our computers or our cars will do from what we
know of their physical make-up: we do not know enough of the
physical detail, and even if we did, the task of putting the mass of
detail together to get a prediction would defeat us.

Nevertheless, we can make successful predictions about the be- *Prediction from*
haviour of complex machines, and in particular about the behav- *behavioural*
iour of those complex machines we call 'people'. We make them *patterns*
by noting patterns in behavioural response, patterns that we can
latch on to independently of knowing in detail what is going on
inside the complex machines. A very simple example is our ability
to predict that a computer will turn on when we press a certain
switch. Most of us know little about the internal wiring, but all we
need to know to make the prediction is the regularity that we can
observe 'from the outside'.

In the case of people often the best way of capturing the behav- *The intentional*
ioural patterns is by adopting the **intentional stance** towards *stance*
them. We view people as having beliefs and desires, and predict
that they will behave in a way that would satisfy their desires were
their beliefs true. That is, we, ascribe what is called **practical
rationality** to them. In an alternative terminology, we apply belief–
desire psychology to them. Your prediction that Jones will step
around the hole in the ground is based, say, on your belief that he
believes that there is a hole in the ground in front of him and that

continuing in a straight line will lead to his falling into the hole, combined with your belief that he does not want to fall into the hole. Mary predicts that Ivan will mail the cheque after he receives the letter of demand, because she believes that he believes that mailing the cheque will halt the impending court proceedings, and she believes that he desires to halt those proceedings.

The suggestion is not, of course, that we explicitly construct and run through little arguments from hypotheses about beliefs and desires every time we predict someone's behaviour. We predict that people will drive off when the lights turn green. But we would not live very long if while driving we consciously went through the argument: that person believes that the lights have turned green, that person believes that it is safe to drive off when the lights turn green, that person wants to drive off provided it is safe to do so, therefore, that person will drive off. Most of the time we form expectations about people's behaviour quite automatically. Nevertheless, our expectations are typically caused by views about what they believe and desire, and though the beliefs and desires are not explicitly before us when we act, we could, would and do cite them as being what make our expectations rational. We could not get across a crowded room, play a game of tennis or negotiate a roundabout unless we interpreted others as believers and desirers exhibiting practical rationality.

Practical rationality is, however, only part of the story about the intentional stance. It is the easy part of the story, which tells us (in the sense of making explicit – it is hardly news to us) how we predict behaviour *given* belief and desire. It is a story we have already come across in our discussion of behaviourism. It needs to be supplemented by an account of how we form the needed hypotheses concerning what people believe and desire in the first place: how, as it is often put, we find the right **interpretation** of subjects' behaviour. The story also needs to be supplemented by an account of the constraints that govern the way we revise our hypotheses concerning what is believed and desired in the face of new behaviour, and the way we take belief and desire to evolve as circumstances change. The details are controversial, but there is a fair measure of agreement about the overall picture.

Charity as a starting place　First, we start by supposing that people believe what they ought to believe given the situation they are in. We take it that persons looking in the direction of, say, a chair typically believe that there is a chair in front of them. Sometimes the emphasis is on the subjects' beliefs being largely true, sometimes on their beliefs being largely true by our, the interpreters', lights. For the only way an interpreter can implement the policy of supposing, as a good starting hypothesis, that the subject's beliefs are largely true is by supposing that they are largely the same as the interpreter's. In either guise, this starting assumption is known as the **principle of charity.** Part of the rationale for it lies in the appeal of the doctrine that belief is a state designed to fit the world. The contrast is with desire, which seeks to fit the world to it, and fantasy, which does neither. Thus, your belief that the furniture in your room is arranged in a certain way is a response to the furniture's arrangement; it is a state that seeks to conform itself to how the furniture is arranged. By contrast, your desire that the furniture in your room be arranged in a certain way is a state that seeks to conform the furniture to it. But if belief is designed to fit the world, then it must tend to fit it if all goes well, and what it is for a belief to fit the world is for it to be true. The other part of the rationale for the principle of charity is that we interpreters have to start somewhere, and it is better to start from somewhere we find plausible than from somewhere we find implausible, and plausibility here must in some way come back to the interpreter's own perspective on matters. We inevitably regard what we ourselves think as not hopelessly implausible – otherwise we would not think it.

In some discussions the principle of charity is replaced by a **principle of humanity**. Here the emphasis is on starting by supposing that subjects have the beliefs that we would have *in their situation.* If someone is wearing a blindfold, do not start by attributing to them the beliefs we have, but instead attribute to them the beliefs we would have were we blindfolded. But the common theme in the midst of the diversity is the idea that we interpreters start by taking subjects' beliefs to be the beliefs they ought to have; the differences are over how best to capture this basic insight: in terms of truth, of similarity to us, or of similarity to us moderated by difference in situation.

Humanity as a starting place

Secondly, if we start by attributing to others the beliefs and desires recommended by the principles of charity or humanity, and the predictions we get by the principle of practical rationality turn out to be seriously flawed, obviously we must revise our hypotheses about what is believed and desired. This much is common ground. There is controversy, however, over how far we can revise and still be treating the subject whose behaviour we are predicting as a believer and desirer, and in general a subject of intentional states. Some say that we could end up with the view that a subject's beliefs are almost entirely mistaken, and in any case completely different from ours. Some say that of necessity most of a subject's beliefs are true, or anyway similar to ours, and that we cannot depart too far from charity. We will return to this issue later (in chapter 12), noting that there are reasons (based on the principle of humanity) for allowing that in suitably bizarre circumstances, someone's beliefs could be largely false.

The rational evolution of belief

Finally, there is broad agreement about the role of theoretical rationality. By and large, we expect people's beliefs to evolve under the impact of new information and reflection on what is already before them in the way that they ought to evolve. Suppose you believe that if it rains, then the match will be cancelled. This commits you to believing that the match will be cancelled should you learn that it will rain. This is an example of the requirement of that aspect of theoretical rationality known as deductive rationality; but equally there are requirements of inductive rationality. Someone who refuses to accept the evidence that smoking is bad for them exhibits inductive irrationality. Although there is no deductive proof from the available evidence to smoking being bad for you, it is overwhelmingly probable on the evidence that it is bad for you. It is of course a commonplace that people are not ideally rational – people commit the gambler's fallacy (and worse – see the extensive psychological literature referred to in the annotated reading section) – but there are limits to how far we can allow them to depart from theoretical rationality and still count as believers. There is a difference between belief and fantasy, as we noted above, and part of what makes the difference is the way belief evolves: belief evolves in the right and proper way for belief (whereas the evolution of fantasy is largely unconstrained), and evolving in the right and proper way is evolving in a more or less rational way.

Intentional systems theory

The issues just canvassed are commonly referred to under the heading of intentional systems theory or principles of interpretation. The task of intentional systems theory is to articulate the principles governing the forming and revising of the belief–desire hypotheses that underlie our ability to predict successfully, to form true expectations about, what subjects will do. We have noted that it has three parts. One part is concerned with finding starting hypotheses; this is the part concerned with the principles of charity and humanity. Another part is concerned with the connection between the hypotheses accepted at any given stage and behaviour; this is the non-controversial (by the standards of the philosophy of mind) part relating to practical reason. And finally there is a part concerned with the evolution of belief under constraints of theoretical rationality. More detail on intentional systems theory can be found in the reading recomended at the end of the chapter.

Intentional systems theory is the key to understanding instrumentalism. But it is not unique to instrumentalism. Other theories of mind can and should give a prominent place to intentional systems theory. It is, for instance, part of common-sense functionalism. The common-sense functionalist can and should think of the tenets of intentional systems theory as a core part of our understanding of mental concepts, and so as something to be incorporated into the common-sense functionalist story. For instance, the common-sense functionalist should hold that part of what makes a state belief is that it evolves by and large rationally, and so should include this in the functional role definitive of belief. This follows from the idea that belief is a state designed to fit the world, and that is part of our folk or common-sense conception of belief. Likewise, the axiom of belief–desire psychology that figures so centrally in intentional systems theory is equally part of common-sense about the mind and so part of common-sense functionalism. What is distinctive about instrumentalism is its *relationship* to intentional systems theory, as we will now see.

Instrumentalism and intentional systems theory

Instrumentalism is the doctrine that the predictive role of beliefs and desires is the whole story about them. There is nothing more to being a believer and a desirer, a thing with beliefs and desires, than being a being whose behaviour is well predicted by the principles of the correct version of intentional systems (or of interpretation) theory, whatever precisely the correct version is. Questions about the true nature of belief states and desire states are idle questions. All there is to say about belief and desire is encapsulated in the story about when ascriptions of belief and desire are true: '*S* believes *P* and desires *Q*' is true iff (a) the behaviour of *S* is well predicted by intentional systems theory, and (b) the best belief and desire hypotheses for predicting *S*'s behaviour according to the principles of intentional systems theory are that *S* believes *P* and desires *Q*.

The essential motivation for instrumentalism comes from the conviction that our understanding of belief and desire, and intentional

Instrumentalism defined

states generally, is conceptually linked to the way we predict behaviour in terms of them, combined with the conviction that speculation about what goes on inside us plays no role in our capacity to predict the behaviour of others in terms of belief and desire. We simply do not know enough for it to play a role. Even more obviously, the ancient Greeks and Goths did not know enough, and yet they predicted behaviour successfully from the intentional stance. Hence, runs the argument, in philosophizing about belief and desire we should restrict ourselves to what can be said quite independently of speculation about internal workings, and that means that we should restrict ourselves to giving accounts of belief and desire at the level of their role in capturing patterns in behaviour – exactly as instrumentalism does. Although there are, of course, internal and in particular neuroscientific explanations of our behaviour, they are no part of the *philosophy* of mind, as the point is sometimes put.

Instrumentalism and outside control

There is an immediate difficulty for instrumentalism arising from Christopher Peacocke's Martian marionette example. The Martian marionette, M, is a 'person' whose every movement is controlled by radio waves sent from Mars. It does not have a brain. Instead it has a device that receives the signals from Mars and then sends out signals to its limbs. We can imagine that it moves just as smoothly as we do, and 'behaves' just as intelligently as we do. For instance, its movements might be copied from the movements of Jones. The Martian controller records what Jones does in each situation, and then sends the appropriate signal to make the marionette do the same. It follows that the intentional stance will be just as successful in predicting the behaviour of the marionette as it is in predicting the behaviour of Jones. But sentences of the form 'M believes P' and 'M desires Q' are all false. M behaves as if it believes and desires, but in fact it is the controller that has all the beliefs and desires.[6] The obvious way for instrumentalists to handle this case is by insisting that to count as a believer and desirer, the causation of the relevant behaviour must lie *inside the subject*: S believes P and desires Q iff S behaves as if S believes P and desires Q as a result of *the way S is*. After all, the instrumentalist might observe, we don't count something as fragile unless *its*

---

[6] You might think, depending on the details of the story, that by analogy with our story about Lin in chapter 7, there could be some wider system including the marionette and some aspects of the controllers and the machines they use which as a whole has beliefs and desires. But that is compatible with the claim that the marionette M does not have beliefs and desires.

nature is responsible for its being such as to break on dropping. The instrumentalist might appeal to this idea, and apply it to psychology. Doing this involves a small departure from the policy of refusing to say anything about what goes on inside subjects when giving an account of what makes them believers and desirers, but it is obviously a small departure.

Instrumentalism shares with its close cousin, analytical behaviourism, the implausibility of the denial that mental states are inner causes. But it avoids the major difficulty for behaviourism concerning the identification of individual mental states with behavioural dispositions, the difficulty that the behavioural dispositions do not match up with individual mental states. Instrumentalism is a story in the first instance about what it is to have a huge rich array of mental states, and only derivatively about what it is to be in one or another mental state. The reason for this is the point we noted when discussing behaviourism. Behaviour cannot be predicted from a sparse story about what someone believes and desires. Too many totally disparate behaviours are compatible with a sparse story. Accordingly, intentional systems theory uses a rich story about what S believes and desires to predict S's behaviour. More precisely, intentional systems theory needs the notion of a system of belief that works in terms of a notion of belief that comes in degrees. When we predict what someone will do, we need not only to know a lot about what that person believes, we also need to discriminate between various strengths of belief. This is particularly obvious when we predict behaviour on a racecourse. People very often do *not* bet on the horse they think will win. They bet on the horse whose chances of winning by their lights are better than the odds being offered. Similarly, intentional systems theory needs the notion of a system of desire that discriminates between how much we want various outcomes. In order to predict that people will go to the dentist, we need to know that they care *more* about having good teeth than they do about avoiding discomfort. Our illustrations were thus misleading in proceeding in terms of very incomplete fragments of what is involved by way of belief and desire hypotheses in predicting behaviour and in suppressing the complications consequent on the fact that belief and desire come in degrees. But we had no choice; a properly inclusive story would take far too long to write down.

What all this means is that instrumentalism does not identify individual beliefs and desires with behavioural dispositions. All it has to say about individual beliefs and desires is that S believes, say, that snow is white if and only if that follows from the complete

Instrumentalism and behaviourism

The primacy of systems of belief and desire for instrumentalism

story about what S believes; and what makes it true that S desires not to fall is that this follows from the complete story of what S desires. One question about instrumentalism, therefore, is whether this way of deriving individual beliefs and desires from systems of belief and desire is satisfactory. Can it, for instance, account for the way we discriminate among a person's beliefs and desires, seeing them as playing distinctive roles in their own right, in explaining action and in the formation of new belief? Another, particularly pressing question is whether it can explain failures of deductive rationality. If the only sense in which someone believes that the triangle in front of them is equilateral is that it follows from their total system of belief, then they cannot believe that the triangle is equilateral without believing that it is equiangular, for the latter follows from anything the former follows from. But couldn't someone suffer a failure of deductive rationality and believe that the triangle is equilateral without believing that it is equiangular? After all, it took a bit of work to prove that an equilateral triangle is necessarily an equiangular one. We will return to these important matters in the discussion of content and representation in chapter 11, for they arise independently of issues concerning instrumentalism in particular.

Are mental states in part determined by how things are with others?

A common objection to instrumentalism is that it makes the question of which intentional states a subject is in too much a matter of how things are with *others*. The fact that your behaviour can be predicted from the intentional stance is a fact about you. It is also a fact about a potential predictor. It might therefore seem that instrumentalism is committed to the view that what you believe and desire is in part a fact about others. Just as what makes something funny or red is in part a matter of how it interacts with those who find it funny or red, so part of what makes it true that you believe that snow is white is the fact that another's supposing that you so believe enables them to predict your behaviour. But in fact instrumentalism is not committed to the view that how it is with others is part of what makes it true that you believe and desire as you do. When instrumentalists say, as we put it above, that 'S believes P and desires Q' is true iff (a) the behaviour of S is well predicted by intentional systems theory, and (b) the best belief and desire hypotheses according to the principles of intentional systems theory for predicting S's behaviour are that S believes P and desires Q, 'the best belief and desire hypotheses' means those hypotheses that would be arrived at by *perfect users of intentional systems theory who had all the relevant information*. It would be very implausible to hold that what you believe and desire is determined, for instance, by what works best for someone who knows very little about you and in any case has a bad memory! And the fact that according to instrumentalism you believe P if and only if perfect users of intentional systems theory who had all the relevant information would say that you believe P no more makes your believing P in part a fact about that interpreter than the fact that ideal followers of the right procedure for getting square roots obtain 4 when they apply it to 16 makes the fact that the square root of 16 is 4 a fact about the persons following the procedure. What *ideal* users of a procedure arrive at is determined by the *procedure* itself.

The major problem for instrumentalism (apart from the fact that it must, like behaviourism, deny a causal role to the mental, and the problem about failures of deductive rationality mentioned above as a topic for discussion in chapter 11) is the Blockhead example. The Blockhead example shows, as we noted in chapter 7, that it matters how the trick is turned inside – that supervenient behaviourism is false. It is true both of me and my Blockhead input–output duplicate that we behave in a way well predicted in terms of the intentional stance, and in both cases it is because of how things are inside that our behaviour is well predicted in terms of the intentional stance. It follows that the instrumentalist's account of the semantics of belief and desire ascriptions is mistaken. We require more for the truth of an ascription of belief and desire than that it does well in predicting a subject's behaviour from the intentional stance, and does so because of what is going on inside the subject. The Blockhead example shows that the instrumentalist's claim about when we count belief and desire ascriptions as true is simply false.

The Blockhead objection to instrumentalism

The obvious response to this failure is to abandon the semantic part of instrumentalism and move to an eliminativist version of instrumentalism, best called **fictionalism**. This view is that pretending that there are beliefs and desires enables us to make predictions that we would otherwise find impossibly difficult, but it abandons any claim that what we mean by ascriptions of belief and desire is that such 'pretences' work. Belief and desire ascriptions as ordinarily understood are all false. Beliefs and desires are 'convenient fictions' that aid – indeed, are often indispensable for – the prediction of behaviour in circumstances.

Fictionalism

How can 'things' that do not exist help in prediction? An illustration that is often used concerns centres of gravity. We predict

Centres of gravity

various aspects of the movement of a system of bodies in mechanics in terms of its centre of gravity; but strictly speaking, runs the suggestion, there is no such thing. There are the various bodies, and that is all. This analogy can be misleading. For any system of particles with masses m_i, and position vectors $\mathbf{r}_i$, there *is* a point whose position vector is given by $\Sigma m_i.\mathbf{r}_i/\Sigma m_i$, but there is *not* in general a particle at that point with mass Σm_i. Or, to use a simple illustration, if the system consists of a particle of mass 4 gm at point A and another of mass 8 gm at point B, then there *is* a point on the line between A and B, two-thirds of the way towards B, but there is *not* a mass of 12 gm at that point. Now, certain properties of the system of particles can be predicted by supposing that the system is a single particle with the combined mass of the particles located at the centre of gravity (a single 12 gm particle on the line between A and B, two-thirds of the way towards B, in our illustration). The fiction is that there is a particle at the centre of gravity with the combined mass of the particles, but the centre of gravity – the place the particle is said to be at – is not a fiction. The analogy the fictionalist wants is not with centres of gravity *per se*, but with what we sometimes pretend is located at centres of gravity for the predictive purposes at hand.

Should we accept fictionalism? We postpone this question to the discussion of eliminativism in chapter 13. For now, we note the point that instrumentalism is no longer the comfortably uncommitted doctrine it presented itself as: a cautious refusal to traffic in speculation about what goes on inside us. The only viable version turns out to be a version of the radical thesis that all ascriptions of belief and desire are false.

Interpretationism

Instrumentalism and interpretationism

There is a final issue that we should note before leaving instrumentalism. It concerns the relationship between instrumentalism and interpretationism. Interpretationism is the view that part of what makes it true that a subject has certain intentional states is the fact that they would be interpreted as having them by a suitably placed expert interpreter: to be in mental state M is to be such that you would be assigned M by a suitably placed expert. What makes someone a suitably placed expert? Clearly, someone who is convinced that red-headed people all have a short fuse, and so assigns 'has a short fuse' to anyone with red hair, does *not* count as a suitably placed expert. Saying that red-haired people have a short fuse is one thing; their in fact having a short fuse is another. A suitably placed expert is, as we put it above, a perfect user of intentional systems theory who has all the relevant information. Thus the view is that to be in M is to be such that you would be assigned M by perfect users of intentional systems theory who have all the relevant information. Thus interpretationism is essentially an instrumentalism that makes explicit reference to the views of especially well-placed persons making use of the instrumental value of the assignment of mental states.

The point of giving an explicit role to a third party, the expert interpreter, lies in what is sometimes called the uncodifiability of rationality. Logic textbooks typically contain sections on what is and what is not rational, both in the deductive sense and in the inductive sense distinguished above, and lay down various rules governing rationality – for instance, that it is rational to infer Q from (P and Q), and that it is irrational to believe (P and Q) with more conviction than Q. But the fact remains that there are large gaps in the theory of rationality. There is no accepted, complete theory, and many hold that as a matter of principle rationality cannot be fully codified. But this means that intentional systems theory, with its heavy reliance on the notion of rationality, cannot be made explicit; of necessity we must rely on the capacities of certain people – the expert interpreters (and most of us who do not suffer from autism are, to one degree or another, potential experts if we know enough about the behaviour of those we seek to interpret) – to deploy intentional systems theory to good effect. We rely on an *ability*, not a codified or codifiable theory, is the suggestion. Hence, the talk of prediction in instrumentalism must be understood not as prediction following a set of rules, but prediction exercising an ability possessed by some perhaps idealized predictor. Interpretationism is then simply a version of instrumentalism that makes this fact desirably explicit.

The uncodifiability of rationality

The uncodifiability of rationality is sometimes used to argue against the possibility of strict laws connecting the physical and the psychological. There are, of course, plenty of laws in a perfectly respectable sense of 'law' connecting physical facts with mental ones: 'People hit hard on the head lose consciousness' and 'Ingesting large amounts of alcohol adversely affects memory recall' are examples familiar to the person on the St Kilda tram; and there are

Psychophysical laws and rationality

many, more sophisticated, examples from neuroscience concerning, for instance, connections between brain functions and various mental abilities, memories, perceptions and the like. The claim, though, is that there can be no strict, exceptionless laws in the sense aimed for in the 'hard' physical sciences, and the reason given for this claim is the uncodifiability of rationality. If rationality plays an essential role in the ascription of mental states but cannot be codified, how could the complete physical story about a subject settle in each and every case what mental state they are in? There will, runs the suggestion, always be the possibility of some leeway in deciding what mental state a subject is in that is created by the lack of hard and fast rules for what is rational. Or to put the matter the other way around: if the physical story always settled in principle any subject's mental states, it would settle what is rational and what is irrational for any subject in each and every case, and that violates the uncodifiability of rationality.

Abilities are not miracles　　There is a major problem for this argument, or so it seems to us. Interpretationists grant that we have the ability to divide the rational from the irrational; indeed, this ability is a central plank in their theory. But abilities are not possessed by magic. We are finite beings whose abilities and capacities can in principle be explained. In particular, when we exercise our ability to divide the rational from the irrational, we must be responding to some relevant feature or features of the examples. We cannot here and now *say* in full detail what the feature or features are; we cannot, that is, tell the full story about rationality. But there must be a full story to be told. The point is similar to the one made earlier in our discussion of common-sense functionalism concerning our grasp of what is grammatical. We cannot write down in full detail the rules we follow in judging that something is grammatical, but there must be rules that we are following (in part implicitly, which is why we cannot write them down in full) when we make these judgements. The alternative is the incredible one that we make the judgements by miracle. Thus, although it may be true that all that is possible for us here and now is a partial codifying of rationality, there is a full codifying to be had (whether we will ever find out what it is in the sense of writing it down is another question). Thus, it is false that rationality is uncodifiable in principle in any strong sense of 'in principle', and that is enough to blunt the argument that there *cannot* be strict laws connecting the physical and the psychological, while leaving open the possibility that we will never be able to *say exactly* what they are.

Interpretationism, like instrumentalism, is vulnerable to a Blockhead objection – as you would expect, given the close connection
between the two theories. Expert interpreters would assign the
very same mental states to your Blockhead input–output duplicate
as they in fact do to you. Confronted not by you behaving in
various ways in various situations but by your input–output Blockhead duplicate, they would say the same about it as they say about
you, because it would move and make the very same noises as you
in each situation. But if being assigned mental states by an expert
interpreter is what it *is* to be in mental states, then it follows that
your Blockhead input–output duplicate has the very same mental
states as you have – whereas in fact it has not a thought in its head.

*The Blockhead
objection to
interpretationism*

   Interpretationists can avoid this objection by modifying their
doctrine to allow expert interpreters to take into account what
goes on inside. Told how the Blockhead works, expect interpreters
would no doubt withdraw their attribution of mentality to it. But
this marks a big change in doctrine. No longer is interpretationism
a theory of mind that follows instrumentalism in resolutely turning its back on questions of what goes on inside a creature (provided, of course, that what goes on inside is doing enough of the
work to prevent the creature from counting as a puppet). Indeed,
it will, it seems, have turned into some variety or other of functionalism – most likely a kind of common-sense functionalism,
given the prominent role of intentional systems theory in interpretationism, and given that intentional systems theory is itself part
of common-sense functionalism.

Annotated Reading

The classic source for the intentional stance is Daniel Dennett, *The Intentional Stance*. Although this is a book for fellow professionals, it is written
in a very engaging, accessible style. You should be aware, though, that it
is not always completely clear where Dennett stands on instrumentalism
versus functionalism versus behaviourism. The most influential presentations of the role of the principle of charity in the interpretation of behaviour and of the thesis that strict laws connecting the psychological with
the physical are impossible are to be found in various writings of Donald
Davidson, usefully collected in *Inquiries into Truth and Interpretation* and
Essays on Actions and Events. Some of these papers can be hard going the
first time around, and you may find William Child, *Causality, Interpretation,
and the Mind* a help here. If you want to look further into the principles
of charity and humanity, Richard Grandy, 'Reference, Meaning and Belief',

and Colin McGinn, 'Charity, Interpretation, and Belief' are good but not easy. The Martian marionette example comes from Christopher Peacocke, *Sense and Content*.

The psychological literature on human irrationality is extensive, but some of the crucial cases are clearly and succinctly described in Stephen Stich, *The Fragmentation of Reason*, chapter 1. He uses the cases to show that one could not reasonably require that for a subject to be a believer, he or she must be *ideally* rational. We are not sure that anyone has ever held this extreme doctrine, but if they have, the cases certainly refute it. Good places to enter the psychological literature are R. Nisbet and L. Ross, *Human Inference: Strategies and Shortcomings of Social Judgment*, and Daniel Kahneman, Paul Slovic and Amos Tversky, *Judgment under Uncertainty: Heuristics and Biases*.

Part III
About Content

10

The Language of Thought

If mental states are internal states, neurophysiological states in fact, what can we say about their structure? Obviously a full answer to this question a waits developments in neuroscience, but according to Jerry Fodor's famous language of thought hypothesis, we can here and now say something rather general about the nature of a certain class of mental states, those variously known as intentional states, states with **content**, or propositional attitudes – namely, that they are sentence-like. Before we say more about what this amounts to, we need to indicate the relevant class of mental states.

Some mental states can be described using indicative sentences or statements in 'that' clauses – for example, Fred's belief *that snow is white* and his desire *that the Tories win the next election*. The sentences in these 'that' clauses are truth-valued, so can be regarded as expressing a proposition, the proposition that is true iff the sentence expressing it is true. Fred's belief that snow is white is thought of as Fred's having the attitude of believing the proposition that snow is white, as opposed to having the attitude of hoping that snow is white, desiring that snow is white, or whatever. Thus these mental states are commonly called 'propositional attitudes', for they involve taking an attitude of believing, hoping or whatever to a proposition.

Propositional attitudes

Theorists vary in the ontological seriousness with which they view the propositional objects of the attitudes. But it is clear that we need a way of talking about what someone believes and desires (for instance) that abstracts away from the particular language we and the subject may happen to use to say what they believe and desire. You may agree with a Japanese speaker that snow is white and on the desirability of peace, despite the fact that the sentences you and the Japanese speaker would use to capture what you believe

and desire are very different. One way to express this fact is to say
that the two of you believe and desire the same propositions. Likewise, we need a way to talk about the conditions under which a
belief is true, a desire is satisfied, a fear is realized, and so on and
so forth. The language of propositional objects does this for us.
How metaphysically seriously we take the talk of propositions is
an issue in fundamental ontology that we set aside here.

Intentional
states and
content

Propositional attitudes are also commonly referred to as 'intentional states'. The term comes from the fact that a propositional
attitude is *about* what the relevant proposition is about. If you
desire that it rain soon, your desire is about what the proposition
expressed by the sentence 'It will rain soon' is about: namely, rain
in the near future. Moreover, its 'aboutness' does not depend on
the existence of what it is about. There may be no rain in the near
future; nevertheless, that is what you desire. Your desire counts as
being about future rain in that only future rain would make the
proposition that you desire true, and so satisfy your desire. Again,
some believe in the Devil but that is not a matter of their being in
the belief relation to the Devil; there is no such thing to be related
to. Rather, they believe that the Devil exists, and their belief counts
as being 'about' the Devil only in the sense that the proposition
they believe could not be true unless the Devil exists. Finally,
propositional attitudes are said to have content: their content is the
proposition towards which they are directed – what is believed,
desired, feared or whatever. Thus, propositional attitudes are commonly called 'contentful states'. (There is a variant usage according to which a distinction is drawn between the content and the
propositional object of an attitude; we discuss this and the general
issue of content in the next chapter.)

According to the language of thought hypothesis, not only do
certain sentences serve to give the propositional objects of beliefs,
desires and thoughts in general, but in addition, the thoughts are
themselves sentence-like. What Fodor proposes is that these mental states have constituent structure much as sentences do. A sentence may be viewed as made up of syntactically significant parts
– the parts we recognize when we parse it by identifying subject,
verb and so on – put together according to certain rules. In the
same general way, according to Fodor, thoughts have parts put
together in certain ways.

The idea is not, of course, that thoughts *look* like sentences, that
if we dive into someone's head, we will see states that look like
writing in grey matter, as opposed to writing in ink on paper, or

that look like the patterns of sound waves that are spoken sentences. It is that thoughts have a sentence-like structure in that, for instance, the thought that snow is white and the thought that snow is cold may share a part – and this does not mean merely that the sentences used to report them share a part, but that the thoughts themselves do – and it is by virtue of sharing this part that both get to be thoughts about the very same stuff: namely, snow.

In this chapter we will start by saying more about what the language of thought hypothesis is, and why we are supposed to believe it. Then we will proceed in a more sceptical vein. We will describe an alternative hypothesis – that what is inside our heads should be thought of as more like maps than sentences – and argue that the map hypothesis explains the phenomena that language of thought theorists correctly insist need to be explained.

The language of thought hypothesis

The hypothesis comes in two parts. The first concerns how a mental state gets to express a certain proposition; the second tells you what attitude is being taken to that proposition – whether it is believed, hoped, feared, desired, entertained or whatever.

The story about how a mental state gets to express a certain proposition is that it is made up in a combinatorial way from atomic components which themselves have representational or semantic properties – that is, they stand for things, properties and relations, much as the parts of a natural language sentence do, and thereby get to have meanings. Words are the atoms of natural language. In English 'biscuit' represents biscuits,[7] and 'crisp' represents some property of biscuits which makes them crack satisfyingly when chewed. But these atoms don't express propositions by themselves; we must combine them in various ways to make claims capable of being true or false about the world. Thus, 'Biscuits are crisp' makes a claim about the world which is true (or, equivalently, expresses a proposition that is true) just if the things 'biscuit' stands for have the property 'crisp' stands for.

So it is supposed to be with thoughts. Completed cognitive science will identify physical properties of brain states which will allow us to reidentify syntactic tokens of the same type; to let us

Atomic and molecular representations

[7]   Except in the United States, where it represents scones.

reidentify some brain state α at different times and be sure that it always names the same thing, type of thing, or property. Let's suppose, then, that brain state α represents a biscuit, and brain state β represents the property of being crisp. The idea is that there is some purely syntactic operation in the brain (albeit at a fairly abstract level) which combines these two representations in a way which is analogous to predication (what we did when we put 'are crisp' after 'biscuits') to form a subject–predicate 'sentence' in **mentalese**, as it is commonly called. We can look into someone's head and see that an instance of state α is connected to an instance of state β in a way which creates an instance of crispness being predicated of the biscuit: $\beta(\alpha)$. We now have a representation which is not atomic, but rather structurally molecular, and which expresses a proposition because it has a truth condition: it is true just if what α stands for has the property β stands for – which, in our example, will be the case just if biscuits are crisp. An important question, obviously, is how the states in the brain that are atomic components – the 'words' of mentalese – get to stand for what they stand for; and the same question arises for the parts of a natural language, of course. The account we have just rehearsed is about how, on the language of thought hypothesis, to derive the representational content of a molecule from the representational contents of its atomic parts. It says nothing about the problem of what determines the representational contents of the atoms – that is, the semantics of the atoms. We will postpone a discussion of this question until the next chapter, which is on content. For the purposes of the present chapter, we will simply assume that it can, somehow or other, be solved.

Belief boxes and desire boxes

The second part of the story tells us what makes it true that one or another *attitude* is being taken to the proposition: do we believe that beer is near, do we desire that beer is near, do we hope that beer is near, and so on? On the language of thought hypothesis, what attitude you take to a proposition depends on the causal-functional role of the sentence token in the head that encodes it – $\beta(\alpha)$ in our example. Very crudely, if the encoding sentence token that expresses the proposition that biscuits are crisp is connected up in your brain so as to make you behave as though biscuits are crisp (given your desires), then you *believe* that they are crisp. If, on the other hand, the token is connected up so as to make you try to bring it about that they are crisp (perhaps by putting them in the oven), you *desire* biscuits to be crisp. Often this is encapsulated in the metaphor of the belief box and the desire box. A token which is functionally connected so as to cause an agent to behave as though the proposition it expresses were true is said to be in the belief box, whereas one which is connected so as to cause the agent to make it true (other things being equal) is said to be in the desire box.

Thus we have a two-part theory. What proposition a token of mentalese expresses depends on the semantic or representational properties of the syntactic or structural constituents and on the way they are put together. Our future cognitive scientist examines some structure in the head, and wonders what mental state the structure is. She breaks it down in to its syntactic components – two states structurally combined in the relation of predication, as it might be. She then looks at her favourite theory of the semantics of atomic representations, and discovers that one state represents chocolate, the other nearness. So the proposition represented by the state is that chocolate is near. End of part one. Part two requires that she find out whether this token is located in the belief box or the desire box. If it plays the role that means that it belongs in the belief box, then the subject *believes* that chocolate is near, whereas if its role places it in the desire box, then she *wants* chocolate to be near.

This theory is importantly different from common-sense functionalism (or indeed functionalism in general). According to functionalism, the role played determines the propositional object (how so, we discuss in chapter 11). But according to the language of thought account, functional role primarily settles whether the state is a belief or a desire, not what its propositional object is. Nevertheless, a state's propositional object is supposed to play a role in explaining behaviour. If the syntactic token of the proposition that chocolate is nearby is in, say, the desire box, then the very physical properties which allow us to identify it as a token which represents that proposition will, together with the fact of being in the desire box, serve to explain the chocolate-seeking behaviour of the agent. However, the direction of explanation is the reverse of that which obtains in the case of functionalism. The desire for chocolate is not the desire for chocolate because, roughly, it (typically) causes chocolate-seeking behaviour. For Fodor, the state causes chocolate-seeking behaviour because it is a desire for chocolate. The contrast is sometimes expressed in terms of a contrast between 'inside-out' and 'outside-in' stories. The language of thought theorist advances an inside-out story that identifies the propositional object independently of the functional role, and sees the sentence of mentalese

The contrast with functionalism

that encodes the proposition as in part determining the functional role. Functionalism, by contrast, is an outside-in story that sees the functional role as determining the propositional object.

Why are we supposed to believe in the language of thought?

So that is the elegant story about intentional states that is the language of thought hypothesis. Why should we believe it? The answer on offer is that only it can explain what needs to be explained. A number of features of thought are identified, and it is argued that the language of thought hypothesis is the best explanation of them. The features that have been seen as particularly supportive of the hypothesis have varied somewhat over time, and from one presentation of the 'case for it' to another. We will focus on three features of thought that we take to be central: (a) **systematicity** and **productivity**, (b) the similarities in behaviour arising from different thoughts, and (c) the way thought evolves causally.

Systematicity   Language is systematic. Both 'Jill loves Mary' and 'Mary loves Jill' are meaningful sentences of English, and in general, if '*aRb*' is a meaningful sentence, then so is '*bRa*'. What is more, this is no accident. It falls out of the combinatorial structure of our language, from the fact that it is made of parts that we can rearrange to express different propositions which are systematically related one to another.

So with thought. If you can think that Jill loves Mary, then you can think that Mary loves Jill, and in general, if you can think that *aRb*, then you can think that *bRa*. Indeed, all the patterns of systematicity that we see in language are mirrored in thought. But if the physical tokens in the brain that encode propositions had no internal structure, if the structure that encodes the proposition expressed by the sentence '*aRb*' had no systematic relationship with the structure that encodes the proposition expressed by the sentence '*bRa*', it is hard to see why this should be so. On the other hand, if the representational properties of physical tokens in the brain depend on their structure in the same kind of way that the representational properties of sentences do, if brain states have a syntax, if mentalese exists, we have a relatively straightforward explanation of the systematicity of thought. The fact that if you can think that *aRb*, then you can think that *bRa*, is explained by the fact that the state that encodes the former is a rearrangement of the parts of the state that encodes the latter. And, of course, this explanation generalizes to explain more complex cases.

A very similar argument can be made, appealing to productivity. Language is productive. We can build new sentences out of the parts of old sentences to form sentences that we may never have encountered before. Nevertheless, we understand these new sentences. Part of what is involved in mastering a language is acquiring the ability to generate and understand new sentences as the occasion demands. This ability is tied to the way the meaning of sentences depends on their structure – to the compositionality of meaning, as it is often put. The ability depends, that is, on our grasp of how the meanings, and in particular the representational properties, of the wholes depend on those of their parts and on how the parts are put together. Thought is also productive. We can think quite new thoughts, and there is no upper limit to the new thoughts that we can think except that imposed on us by our status as finite beings. Supporters of the language of thought hypothesis point out that if thought is like language in having a syntax, then we can explain the productivity of thought in the same way as we explain the productivity of language.

Productivity

Thirdly, although different thoughts have different effects, they are often not that different. The thought that Fred is happy and at the party has rather similar effects to the thought that Fred is at the party. The first typically causes the utterance 'Fred is happy and at the party', the second the utterance 'Fred is at the party' – effects with an obvious common element. Again, the thought that coffee is there will typically have a different effect from the thought that coffee is here, but the effects will have the obvious similarity of being directed towards coffee. It is, urge supporters of the language of thought hypothesis, good methodology to posit similar causes of similar effects, and their hypothesis does exactly that. For instance, the thought that coffee is there will share with the thought that coffee is here the bit that represents the coffee.

Causes and effects

Finally, thoughts evolve causally over time. One thought leads to another by causing it. Suppose Jones believes that if there is snow outside, it is cold outside. He then learns that there is snow outside. His thought that if there is snow outside, it is cold outside, then combines with his new belief that there is snow outside to lead him to believe that it is cold outside. Moreover, this causal evolution over time is driven by the propositional objects of the thoughts in question. It is because one thought is a *that if there is snow outside it is cold outside* thought and the other is a

Evolution of thought

that there is snow outside thought that the new thought is a *that it is cold outside* thought. The language of thought hypothesis has an attractive explanation of this. The relevant propositions are encoded in syntactically structured states in Jones's head, and it is the natures of these structures that regulate the way one thought gives rise to another. Moreover, we know that a story of this kind can be made to work. Computers store information in structures with a syntax, and the causal transactions between these structures are governed by the syntactic nature of the structures. Supporters of the language of thought hypothesis are fond of pointing out, reasonably enough, that their picture of the mind and its workings parallels the picture that applies to computers. It cannot be accused of being an untested bit of armchair theorizing.

The map alternative

The case just outlined for the language of thought hypothesis is an argument to the best explanation. There are some phenomena that need to be explained, and, argue its supporters, their view is the best explanation of them. We agree that the phenomena need explaining. However, there is another explanation possible of these phenomena, the so-called map story. In this story mental maps play the role given to mental sentences in the language of thought hypothesis. The rest of this chapter will be concerned with giving the map alternative to the language of thought.

Representation is structured   First we need to note a point that is, or should be, common ground among all theorists, or at least all theorists who allow that thoughts are states in the head that represent reality as being one or another way, that encode propositions, that have content – to mention just some of the unfortunately many ways of putting essentially the same idea. These states must be structured, and this structure must play a central role in determining their representational content. It is unbelievable that internal representation is unstructured. Why is this the case?

Suppose that Jones's head has states S_1, S_2, . . . that represent things around her as being, respectively, R_1, R_2, ... Thus, S_2 might be A fibres in the C region of the brain firing, or a certain kind of overall pattern of activity distributed through the central nervous system, and R_2 might be that there is coffee over there. What is unbelievable is that similarities between the various R_i

should in *no way* correspond to similarities among the S_i; it must be the case that enough information about a finite set of S_i giving which R_i each represents enables in principle the working out, for some new S_i, which R_i it would represent. What it means to say that the way the R's serve to represent the S's is structured is that at some level of abstraction the similarities and differences between the R's correspond to similarities and differences among the S's, and it is this fact that underlies our ability to grasp for some new R which S it represents.

The point here is a general one about systems of representation, about structures that in one way or another stand for things. Consider the familiar arabic system we use to pick out numbers. We have ten distinct physical shapes: '0', '1', . . . '9', and we have to *memorize* which number each stands for. But we do not have to memorize for *each and every* shape which number it stands for, and it would be impossible to do so. Once we have done the memorizing job for the initial ten and have grasped the rules for putting together one or more of these ten shapes to name numbers, we can name any number we please precisely by exploiting the fact that relationships among the *namers* correspond to relationships among the *named*. There are other systems for picking out numbers, of course. The Roman system uses different primitives ('X', 'V', 'L' and so on) and different rules of combination of these primitives (less satisfactory ones, which is why the arabic system was a great advance). But it remains true that structure plays a vital role. Without it we could not master the system. All systems of representation that are in any significant sense openended, that do more than serve to represent some strictly circumscribed set of things or situations, must exploit structure; thus, numerals, house plans, street maps, sentences, words and graphs, precisely because they are open-ended systems of representation, must and do exploit structure. They are structured representations.

Now the brain's representational capacities are open-ended. That much we most certainly learn from the kinds of considerations that supporters of the language of thought hypothesis advance: productivity and systematicity are both aspects of this open-endedness. Thus the brain must somehow or other be able to construct an indefinitely large number of representations from a finite number of ingredients in such a way that what is represented is some systematic function of the nature of the ingredients and the way they are assembled. Brain representations must be structured representations, just as graphs, sentences, maps, pictures, house plans and so on are. This is the point that should be common ground in the debate, or so it seems to us.

Minimalism about the language of thought

Sometimes it seems that all the language of thought theorists wish to insist on is this fact that internal representation is structured. There is, however, an important issue that gets glossed over by this friendly conclusion. It concerns the difference between the way sentences represent and the way maps (and more generally *n*-dimensional arrays) represent. They are alike in being structured, but are nevertheless importantly different. The language of thought hypothesis is thus more than the undeniable claim that representation in the brain is structured. This means, if we are right, that it is unfortunate that its supporters often refer to their theory simply as the *representational* theory of mind. A theory can be representational without being a language of thought theory.

The way maps represent

Maps are informationally rich

The way maps, pictures, diagrams, graphs and the like represent differs in two important, connected respects from the way sentences represent. First, maps give some (putative) information by giving a lot of information. This is the point behind the saying that a picture is worth a thousand words. Take, for instance, the section of the map of the United States that gives information about how far apart New York and Boston are. We can identify the section of the map that is particularly relevant – the top right-hand part, say. But that part of the map does a great deal more than tell us how far apart New York and Boston are. It tells us that Boston is to the north of New York, that there are various towns on the railway line between them, that Boston is nearer the border with Canada, that New York is nearer Philadelphia, and so on and so forth. And this is no accident. There is no way of extracting just the physical bit that gives the information about how far apart Boston and New York are from the bits that give us the rest of the information. The same is true of tree-rings: they tell us how old a tree is and also which were the good seasons and which the bad (the wider apart two adjacent rings, the better the season), but we cannot dissect out the bit that tells us about the tree's age from the bit that tells us about the good seasons. By contrast, sentences can give discrete, small, isolated bits of information – the sentence 'Boston is north of New York' does exactly this.

Secondly, there is no natural way of dividing a map at its truth-assessable representational joints. Each part of a map contributes to the representational content of the whole map, in the sense that had that part of the map been different, the representational content of the whole would have been different. Change the bit of the map of the United States between New York and Boston, and you change systematically what the map says. This is part of what makes it true that the representation is structured. However, there is no preferred way of dividing the map into basic representational units. There are many jigsaw puzzles you might make out of the map, but no single one would have a claim to have pieces that were all and only the most basic units. The reason is that there is no natural *minimum* unit of truth-assessable representation in the case of maps. By contrast, there are natural ways of dividing up passages of prose at the representational joints. Suppose that a passage of prose contains the sentence 'Boston is north of New York'. This is a truth-assessable representational unit – it makes a (as it happens true) claim about how things are, but no bit of it, say, 'is north of New York', does. The phrase 'is north of New York' is neither true nor false. The same is true of representational units that are not truth-assessable but *stand for* particulars or objects. 'Boston' stands for a city, but 'Bosto' does not stand for anything (or if it does, it is a fluke, and has nothing to do with what 'Boston' stands for). By contrast, part of a map that stands for a city itself stands for part of that city. Passages of prose have minimum representational units, maps do not. Maps and sentences are alike, however, in that 'local' damage has a local effect on representational content. Blacking out part of a map or part of a passage of prose degrades especially the putative information given by that part. By contrast, damage to part of the structure that stores holograms in most storage systems degrades the resolution of the hologram as a whole. It gets fuzzier, rather than leading to a gap in the hologram.

Maps do not have representational atoms

Do maps explain the phenomena?

We can now state an alternative to the language of thought hypothesis. It is that intentional states are maps in the head, rather than sentences in the head. The suggestion is not, of course, that something that *looks* like a map is in the head, but rather, that the way head states represent is like the way maps represent, in being essentially rich (they say a lot if they say anything) and in lacking representational joints (there is no minimum truth-assessable unit of representation). This is important in connection with the suggestion commonly made by supporters of the language of thought hypothesis that maps are good for representing spatial matters – where rivers and mountains are, and the like – but are no good for representing the movement of the share index in New York or the fact that, on average, more goals are scored in the second half of World Cup matches than in the first half. This may be true of *some* maps, but it is not true of map-like representation in general. We can be certain that something map-like can serve to represent any empirical fact about our world. The world itself is map-like: it is a vast array in space-time, rather than a two-dimensional configuration on paper, but that difference is inessential to its map-like status. And, of course, the world itself makes true each and every fact about our world; it is a *perfect* representation of itself.

The issue between the language of thought hypothesis and its rival, the map theory, is a complex one that will not be settled in this book. In the next chapter on content we will canvass some of the considerations for and against the two theories, and suggest that the map theory is at least as attractive as its rival. All we will do here is note that the map theory explains the phenomena cited by supporters of the language of thought. This means that these phenomena do not favour the language of thought over the map theory of internal representation.

Systematicity   First, a map that represents Boston as being north of New York has the resources to represent New York as north of Boston, and a map that represented New York as north of Boston would be a kind of rearrangement of the map that represents Boston as north of New York. Again, a weather map that represents various facts about air pressure, rainfall and temperature gradients has the capacity to represent many 'rearrangements' of such facts. We introduce this example to emphasize that the representational content of maps is not especially linked to how things are spatially; an increase in air pressure is a matter of an increase in molecular momentum. Another example is the map-like representations in phase-state physics. Of course, the weather maps that appear in the daily papers also contain words and numbers, so we should not forget the possibility that internal representation works by a combination of dynamic mental maps and mentalese.

Productivity   Secondly, the conventions of cartography do not set an upper limit on the number of different possible distributions of cities, areas of high pressure and the like that a map framed within those conventions can represent. A map-maker can represent a quite new situation as easily as a word- or sentence-maker can.

Thirdly, different maps can be more or less similar to each other, and these similarities and differences show up in the similarities and differences of the effects that these maps may have – for example, on people giving verbal reports of what the maps say, or on those using the maps to navigate their way around or to help them decide what to wear when they go outside. *The causal argument*

Finally, maps are physical entities whose structure can govern the way they evolve over time. When cartographers update maps or put two maps together to make one that incorporates all the information in a single map, these operations are governed in part by the structures of the maps they are working on. And in order to find a target, rockets use a kind of internal map that gets continually updated as new information comes in. In these rockets, later maps are causal products of earlier maps plus what comes in via the rockets' sensors. Hence map theorists can tell an essentially similar story to language of thought theorists about how thoughts evolve over time as a function of their propositional objects. The difference is that in one case the propositional object is encoded in a sentence-like structure and in the other it is encoded in a map-like structure. In this context supporters of the language of thought sometimes stress the point we noted before that computers work on sentence-like internal representations. But there seems no particular reason to believe that the way evolution 'solved' the problem of internal information processing in flesh-and-blood machines should be similar to the way we flesh-and-blood machines solved the problem in metal and silicon machines. Moreover, there is an active research program devoted to developing computers that work on internal representations that are more like maps than sentences. *Evolution of thought*

It seems to us, therefore, that there is no choosing between the language of thought picture and the map picture as far as the considerations typically advanced in favour of the language of thought go.

Supporters of the language of thought sometimes object that the map alternative we have been describing is more the hope of an alternative than a genuine competitor. Of course, the features listed above – systematicity and all that – have some explanation or other. Almost no one thinks that miracles are happening. The issue is what sort of explanation they have, and the map theory *The objection from messiness* says nothing concrete about how the brain works. By contrast, the language of thought hypothesis says literally that our brains work in broadly the way computers work – namely, by manipulating reidentifiable symbols in a rule-governed way. This means that the language of thought provides an elegant structural explanation of how the brain works that explains systematicity and so on. It is consistent with the map theory, however, that the physical or neural organization of the brain that realizes the map could be very messy indeed. The proponents of the language of thought see this messiness as an objection: when there are a number of possible explanations of a range of phenomena, isn't it good methodology to favour elegance?

But the messiness may be no cost to the theory. Indeed, the fact that cognition is a product of evolution by natural selection suggests that messiness is to be expected. Evolution proceeds by patches, small changes that are of strictly local benefit. The language of thought model of cognition, by contrast, would be rather like an all-powerful programmer sitting down with a description of the desired result and coding it up, with nice neat isomorphisms between the topmost level of a description of the competencies required and the various levels at which they are implemented. But evolution, to the extent that it's like computing at all, is like the sort of *ad hoc* programming you get when a patch is added every time a new feature is required or an old one fails. The cheapest local fix which gives immediate benefits is what is required, and is likely to be selected.

It thus seems to us that the considerations commonly supposed to favour the language of thought hypothesis are completely neutral between it and map-like views of internal representation. The real debate, insofar as it is possible to conduct it ahead of what neuroscience reveals, turns on questions we discuss in the next chapter. The different pictures of internal representation are associated with different approaches to the problem of content.

Annotated Reading

The classic source for the language of thought hypothesis is Jerry Fodor, *The Language of Thought*. A short, more recent statement is the appendix to his *Psychosemantics*. Gilbert Harman, *Thought*, and Hartry Field, 'Mental Representation', provide alternative, helpful perspectives on and arguments for the view. David Braddon-Mitchell and John Fitzpatrick, 'Explanation and the Language of Thought', contains further criticism of the language of thought story. For a recent, clear and forceful approach, rather different from ours and very sympathetic to the language of thought, see Kim Sterelny, *The Representational Theory of Mind*.

An influential source of the map view is a brief remark by F. P. Ramsey, in 'General Propositions and Causality', and the idea is developed in detail in part 1 of D. M. Armstrong, *Belief, Truth and Knowledge*. See also Colin McGinn's discussion of mental models in the final chapter of *Mental Content*. David Lewis, 'Reduction of Mind', is most explicit about how the live issue between the language of thought and the map view is the nature of mental representation. Michael Tye, *The Imagery Debate*, defends a mixed view – a sort of 'maps with sentences written on them' – from a perspective that combines philosophical considerations with empirical findings in psychology.

11

Content

In the previous chapter we observed that there is a class of mental states that are variously described as intentional states, as propositional attitudes, and as having content or representational content. They are the mental states we typically describe using indicative sentences in 'that' clauses; and what they are about – their propositional objects, their contents or representational contents – correspond, respectively, to what the relevant sentences are about, the propositions they express, and their content. What we have here are many ways of describing essentially the same phenomenon. In this chapter we will follow the now common practice of talking principally in terms of content.

The subject of content is controversial, to put it mildly. There are bewilderingly many theories of content, and there is even dispute about what 'the problem of content' is. What issue is it that needs addressing? Our approach will be to describe what we take the problem of content to be; then, in the light of our account of what the problem is, we will describe the two most appealing and best-known strategies for solving it. They are very different, as you will see. One (the best-known) draws on the language of thought, the other on the map picture of internal representation, both of which we discussed in the previous chapter.

What is the problem of content?

How are truth conditions possible? The problem of content has two parts to it. First, the content of a belief is a property of it that is responsible for its being true or false. One-half of the problem of content is to explain how this is possible. What sort of property confers truth evaluability on certain psychological states? Moreover, while my belief that snow is white is like my belief that grass is green in having a truth-value (true), they differ in the conditions under which they are true. Our account of how certain psychological states get to be truth valued needs to be one that explains in addition how they get to have the *particular* truth conditions that they have.

A similar question arises for the other states with content. Although hopes and desires, for example, do not have truth conditions, they do have satisfaction or realization conditions, and these can be specified in terms of truth conditions. Fred's desire to become President in the year 2000 will be satisfied if it is *true* that Fred becomes President in 2000. Mary's hope that he will fail will be realized if it is true that he will fail. We will, however, focus on belief in the main in the interests of keeping things as simple as possible. *Satisfaction conditions*

It might seem easy to answer our question about truth conditions. Belief is, we have said, a propositional attitude. But if belief states are relations to propositions, they are automatically truth-evaluable. They are true just if the proposition that is their object is true. Moreover, a belief has the truth conditions that its propositional object has; thus the answer to how a belief gets to have the truth conditions it has is simply by having the propositional object that it has. But this is merely a restatement of the problem. For how do certain psychological states, and in particular beliefs, get to have propositional objects in the first place? And how does a given belief get to have one propositional object rather than another? *A non-answer*

We can highlight the problem by setting it in a materialistic context. How can a material state in the head be 'attached' to a proposition, and moreover one proposition rather than another? But in fact the problem is independent of the issue of physicalism. It is just as much a question how an arrangement of 'ghost stuff' could be assigned a proposition, and moreover one proposition rather than another. We noted in the previous chapter that philosophers of mind typically seek to steer clear of controversial issues in ontology concerning the nature of propositions. Proposition talk for them is a convenient way of talking about truth conditions while abstracting away from the particular language in which what is believed (or desired or . . .) is specified. The point here though is that even given some strongly realist view of propositions as 'abstract' or 'transcendent' entities outside space-time to which certain mental states (and, for that matter, certain sentences) have some special relationship, it would still be necessary to explain how the non-abstract mental states (and sentences) get to have the special relationship to one or another abstract or transcendent entity.

The causal problem   The other half of the problem of content arises from the role of content in explaining behaviour. The contents of belief and desire are causal-explanatory properties of them, as well as being the feature of them that allows beliefs to be true or false and desires to be satisfied or unsatisfied. Jones's running away is causally explained by the fact that she has a belief with the content that there is a tiger nearby, along with her having a desire with the content that she wishes to go on living. When we tell the story about how a belief gets to have truth conditions, and further the particular truth conditions that it does have, we must ensure that the story centrally involves a property of the belief that can serve to explain behaviour. The same goes for a desire and its satisfaction conditions, of course. We must, that is, respect and account for content's dual role in psychology. This point gives us another reason for not answering the truth conditions problem merely by reference to a special relationship to a proposition conceived as something outside space-time: it is completely obscure how a relation to something outside space-time could play a role in causal explanation.

Dual theories of content   Some have despaired of finding a single feature that can do both jobs – that of, on the one hand, being what determines a belief's truth conditions and a desire's satisfaction conditions, and that of, on the other, causally explaining the effects a belief and a desire have on behaviour. Accordingly, they have proposed *dual* theories of content. There is content for truth conditions and satisfaction conditions – semantic content, as it might be called in light of its connection with the propositional or representational aspect of belief and desire – and there is a separate notion of content for explaining behaviour.

This bifurcation of content is very unattractive. Jones's belief being that there is a tiger nearby explains her running away precisely because to believe that there is a tiger nearby is to believe that it is *true* that there is a tiger nearby. If she had believed that it was *false* that there was a tiger nearby, she would not be running. Again, the role of her desire in getting her to run is tied to her desiring that it be *true* that she goes on living. Moreover, the schema much adverted to already for explaining behaviour in terms of belief and desire presupposes that their contents are truth valued. For, recall, the schema is: subjects behave in a way that satisfies their desires (that is, makes *true* what they desire) if their beliefs are *true*. Content cannot do its causal-explanatory job unless it is truth-assessable. The way we use the schema depends on beliefs having truth conditions and desires having satisfaction conditions.

There are two different approaches to the problem of finding a unified theory of content, each drawing on a conspicuous feature of intentional states, and in particular belief – our focus here. One conspicuous fact about belief is the way it guides us around the world – what you believe determines what you will do to get what you desire. As it is sometimes put, following F. P. Ramsey, belief is a kind of map by which we steer. This is a functionalist approach to content; it is the functional role of a belief that determines its content. The other conspicuous fact about belief is the way we use sentences to capture what we believe. Further, when we contemplate what we believe, we at least sometimes seem to be involved in some kind of 'saying to ourselves'; so we might think of belief as a kind of inner assertion that may or may not issue in public assertion. The two approaches to the problem of content that will concern us in the rest of this chapter draw their inspiration from these two different sources. It will be obvious from our preliminary characterization of them that the first is the one linked to the map theory of internal representation of the previous chapter, the second to the language of thought. By the end of this chapter we will be in a position to honour our promise to catalogue the relative philosophical strengths and weaknesses of these two accounts of internal representation.

Two different paths to a unified theory of content

The map theory

Belief as a map by which we steer

We start by rehearsing some of the points about the notion of a representational state made in the previous chapter.

Representation revisited

There are many physical structures that can be thought of as representing how things are in some regard or other. The number of rings in a tree's cross-section represents how old the tree is. The reading on a gauge represents the level of petrol left in the tank. A map of Australia represents the layout of various cities, rivers, mountains and the like.

In each case we have a correspondence between various possible states of what is doing the representing and various possible states of what is being represented: for each possible number of rings in the tree there corresponds a possible age of the tree; the possible positions of the pointer correspond to the possible amounts of petrol in the tank; different possible arrangements of lines, shapes and colours on the map correspond to different possible locations of the various geographical features of Australia. It is the correspondence that determines the representational content. It is because the number of rings corresponds to the age of the tree that having five rings represents the tree as being five years old, having twenty rings represents the tree as being twenty years old, and so on. It is because of the way in which the position of the pointer corresponds to the level of fuel left in the tank that pointing far left corresponds to the tank being empty, pointing far right represents the tank as being full, and so on.

What determines the appropriate correspondence relation between states of the 'representor' and those of the 'representee' varies from case to case. In the simplest cases the correspondence is causal co-variance in normal circumstances: as a consequence of the way the rings in a tree are laid down, the number of rings normally co-varies with the age of the tree. Petrol gauges are slightly more complicated, because conventions of calibration come into the picture, and maps are distinctly more complicated, because the conventions of cartography are considerably more complex and detailed than those that govern fuel gauges. In the case of Identikit pictures, similarity comes into the picture – the representational content of an Identikit picture is in part a matter of the picture resembling the suspect.

Accuracy
versus
inaccuracy

In any case, correspondence, however analysed in any particular case, is enough to elucidate the notions of representational content, and of a representational content's being *accurate or inaccurate*. Let the states of the representor R be $R_1, \ldots,$ and the states of the representee S be $S_1, \ldots,$ and let R_i correspond (according to whatever is the right correspondence relation) to S_i; then R's being in R_i represents S as being in S_i, and R's being in R_i is accurate if and only if S is in S_i. For example, the various possible states of the petrol gauge in a typical car are: needle points far right, $\ldots,$ needle points far left, and the various possible states of the petrol tank are: full, $\ldots,$ empty. By the correspondence relation we are all familiar with – the one we need to know about if the gauge is to be any use to us – this means that the content of the needle pointing almost far right is that the tank is almost full, and this reading is accurate if and only if the tank is almost full.

The map theory of belief content exploits this basic idea. Belief is, according to it, an internal state (of the brain, as it happens) that represents the world as being a certain way, and so the content of belief is obtained by finding the right correspondence relation between the possible states of the head and the possible states of the world. A belief then counts as accurate, or *true* as we say when it is belief we are dealing with, if the possible state of the world corresponding to the head state is how the world actually is.

Clearly a crucial question for this theory is what the right correspondence relation for the case of belief might be. The map theorist's answer is in terms of how the belief controls behaviour. It is, that is, a functionalist answer. We can illustrate the essential idea with an example. Consider someone walking through a minefield. You will very quickly be able to say where he believes the mines are *not*. After a few more crossings of the minefield in different directions, you will be able to say pretty precisely where he believes the mines are. What you are doing here is matching where he takes the mines to be located with how he behaves. But how he behaves is determined by how his head is. Each different possible pattern of behaviour corresponds to a different state of his head, because same head state implies same behaviour in any given situation. So what you are doing is tantamount to matching head states with possible ways the world is according to what he believes. And the rule you are following is, of course, the axiom of belief–desire psychology we have adverted to so often already: subjects behave in a way that secures what they want if what they believe is true. You are applying this rule on the plausible assumption that he wants to live. Generalizing, the proposal is that we match the head states that are beliefs with possible states of the world by the rule that each state of the head gets assigned the possible state of the world which is such that if it were the way things actually are, the behaviour that head state causes would realize what the subject desires.

The right correspondence relation for belief

Although we folk are not in the habit of stating the axiom of belief–desire psychology in the terms just given, it is in fact familiar to us all. For we implicitly follow the axiom to go from behaviour to how subjects believe things to be virtually every day of our lives. What shows that Tom believes that BHP shares will rise? He bought BHP shares, and that behaviour will realize what he wants – a profit – precisely if BHP shares rising is the way things will be.

What shows that Mary believes that Harry has a weak backhand? She hits to Harry's backhand, and that behaviour will realize what she wants – to win the game of tennis – precisely if Harry has in fact a weak backhand. And so on and so forth. The map approach to the content of belief is thus an answer wholly congenial to common-sense functionalism, for it draws on part of our folk theory of the mind.

Content as a set of possible worlds

There are a number of points to note about this version of the map theory of belief. First, the content of belief according to it is a *set of possible worlds*. Although the theory as just sketched talks of 'the' possible state of the world assigned to each head state that is a belief, any specification of a way things might be that could plausibly be regarded as what a subject believes will leave an awful lot open, for there is an awful lot about which subjects have no opinion (whether there are an odd or an even number of molecules in the universe, who will win the next election, or whatever). So we should think of the content of a belief as the set of worlds that for all the subject believes could be actual. 'The' possibility that is the content of a belief on this theory is, then, really a set of possible worlds, each of which agrees with respect to 'the' possibility. Which of the various possible locations of the mines that our subject's behaviour revealed to us as being the way he took the mines to be located, and so to be the content of his belief about the mines' locations, will be a common thread running through all the worlds consistent with how he takes things to be. They will all agree in having the mines at those locations. Indeed, typically, our subject's opinion as to where the mines are will be to a certain extent indeterminate (not too indeterminate, we trust). He will have narrowed down their location to within, say, a centimetre, but for no mine will it be the case that he believes that it is at some absolutely precise location. After all, how many of us have an opinion as to *exactly* how tall we are? Thus, the set of worlds that represents how he takes things to be will vary not just as to whether there is an odd or an even number of molecules, but also in where *exactly* each mine is.

How content is causally relevant

Secondly, the theory meets the fundamental desideratum that it explains how a belief gets to have the truth conditions it does in a way that respects the causal-explanatory role of content. It is the causal role of certain head states that makes it true that they are beliefs with a certain set of worlds as their content. The set of worlds that is the content of belief is a way of describing the causal role of the head states: the head state produces behaviour which is such that were the way things actually are a member of the content set, the behaviour produced would tend to satisfy the subject's desires in the sense of bringing about a world that is the way the subject would like things to be. That is, on this theory, the content of belief is both a set of worlds *and* a functional role, for the set of worlds is a way of describing the functional role. The set of worlds does not do any causing, of course. The map theory steers clear of the mystery of having a relation to a set doing some causing. Rather, the set of worlds serves to describe the effect of the behaviour which is caused by what happens inside the head. At the same time, assigning belief a set of possible worlds as its content automatically makes belief truth-evaluable. The set of worlds in question is the set of all the ways in which things might be consistent with the belief. If one of those ways is the actual way things are, then the belief is true: to be a true belief is to be a belief that has as its content a set of possible worlds that includes the way things actually are.

Finally, it is clear how sentences can give the content of belief. We simply choose a suitable sentence that is true in each possible world in the set that is the content of the belief.

Next, there is the point that constitutes the second reason for calling the theory a map theory. One analogy between how we take things to be and a map is their shared role in steering us around the world. We use maps to find our way around. This lies behind the approach to content via behaviour. The second point of analogy lies in the fact that a map is like a picture in being worth a thousand words, in being, as we noted in the previous chapter, essentially representationally rich. Maps give small amounts of information by giving large amounts of information that include the small bits. A map of the world tells you which mountain is the highest mountain in the largest island but does this by telling you a great deal more. For it says which island is the largest by saying something about the size of all the islands, and it says something about the size of any particular island in the course of saying something about where it is and what shape it is. Likewise, it says which mountain is the highest in the course of saying where all the mountains in the largest island are and how high they are. The contrast is with sentences, which can give only small, isolated bits of information – the sentence 'Kosciusko is the highest mountain in the largest island' for instance.

Now the approach to content via behaviour is one that first yields the content of a rich system of belief, and then gives the

Steering is by systems of belief

content of individual beliefs only inasmuch as they are part of this rich system of belief. The reason is the point we noted in criticizing behaviourism. Individual beliefs grossly underdetermine behaviour. There is no behaviour that the belief that there is a mine near the tree as such points to. It is rather a rich system of belief to the effect, say, that there is a mine near the tree, that the mine is likely to be triggered by going near it, that moving one's legs in such-and-such a way will not bring one near the tree, that there is not a bigger mine that can be avoided only by going close to the tree, that triggering mines tends to cause death, and so on and so forth, along with the appropriate desires, that points to behaviour. When we described recovering the minefield walker's belief as to where the mines are located from his behaviour, we took for granted a great deal about what he believed (and about what he desired). That was fine. It was common knowledge. But the point remains that only the rich system (much of it being common knowledge in this case and the other cases we have discussed) has the required connection with behaviour to give a plausible path to content.

As a further example, think of what happens when you do something as simple as walking across the room to turn the radio on. Your behaviour is the product of an enormously detailed system of belief that is constantly updated as you move, as information floods in through your senses concerning where the objects in the room are, how to avoid them, where your body is, and what results various movements of your body will have. It is this system by which you steer. We don't of course consciously reflect on such beliefs, modifying our behaviour appropriately. If we did, we would walk a bit like puppets, and have our heads cluttered by reflections on what we believe, which would get in the way of the beliefs themselves doing their job. Indeed, had our ancestors spent too much time reflecting on what they believed rather than acting on it, they would not have survived long enough to produce us. The evolutionary advantage of having a great many beliefs that 'work in the background', as it is put in computer jargon, is obvious.

In sum, individual beliefs are not maps by which we steer. It is whole systems of belief by which we steer. For this reason we will from now on refer to the map-system theory of belief.

The problem of interpretation   Finally, we should note that there is an important topic that we have set to one side. We said that we can work out what a person believes from their behaviour, and we gave a couple of simple illustrations. A major question in the philosophy of mind concerns the articulation of the rules that we follow when we do this. The problem of interpretation is the problem of articulating and defending the rules we follow in going from behaviour to what subjects believe and desire. It is hard because in going from what a person does to what they believe, we make assumptions about what that person *desires*. We assumed that the person facing the minefield desired to live, for example. But how do we know what a person desires? We use what they do, given assumptions about what they *believe*; thus, movement in a certain direction is evidence of a desire for coffee only if the subject believes that there is coffee in that direction. How do we break out of this apparent circle: that the content of belief comes from behaviour plus the content of desire, but the content of desire comes from behaviour plus the content of belief? We discussed this question briefly along with other issues concerning interpretation in chapter 9, but much more could be said about this difficult question.

We now turn to the main rival to the map-system theory, the internal sentence theory. After we have presented it, we will be in a position to consider their relative merits.

The internal sentence theory

We can state this quickly as we have covered the essentials in the previous chapter on the language of thought. According to it, a belief is an internally inscribed sentence of mentalese, the language of thought. It gets to be a belief rather than, say, a desire or a hope because of what the internally inscribed sentence does. It gets to have the content it has by virtue of having a syntax that means it can be viewed as a representational molecule whose content is determined by the contents and arrangement of its representational atoms – in much the same way as happens with a sentence of a public language.

To interpret a public language is to assign objects, properties and relations to various parts of the language. This is what gives a language a semantics. It is what makes it more than a purely syntactical object; it is what gives the various bits of the language their meanings. This assignment is often called a 'lexicon'. We can then give the truth conditions for the sentences of the language in terms of the lexicon and an account of how to *parse* it – that is, of what the sentences of the language are, and how to classify the various parts in terms of whether they stand for objects, properties,

Semantics for public language

relations, and so on and so forth. To illustrate for the simplest possible case, suppose we are given that a sentence S is to be parsed as a simple subject–predicate sentence of the form 'a is F'. The truth conditions for S can then be given thus: S is true if and only if the object assigned to 'a' in the lexicon has the property assigned to 'F' in the lexicon.

Semantics for mentalese

Likewise, to interpret a sentence of mentalese we need a lexicon and a parsing. Suppose that the parsing tells us that some structure in the brain is a subject–predicate sentence of mentalese, and the lexicon assigns an object to the subject and a property to the predicate. Then the belief that is a relation to that sentence will be true if and only if the object has the property. This, of course, is only a schematic answer to the question of where the belief's content and so truth conditions come from. We put flesh on the bones of the theory by advancing one or another account of how to do the parsing and of how the words (atoms) of mentalese get their interpretations.

Why the sentences have to be inside the head

There are two reasons for having the sentences inside the head, rather than on paper or as sound-wave patterns in the air, as is typically the case with sentences in public languages. Dogs and gorillas, for example, have beliefs, and though dogs and gorillas arguably have rudimentary public languages, it is clear that these languages are not rich enough to provide enough contents. They believe things whose content we can and do give in our public languages but which could not be given in theirs. Therefore, if (any of) their beliefs are relations to sentences, they will have to be relations to sentences in their brains. Secondly, there is the need to give content the right kind of causal-explanatory role. Individual beliefs are internal states of the brain (though there could in theory be a dualist version of the internal sentence theory that has the sentences inscribed in ghost stuff) whose content is causally responsible for behaviour. Thus we want content to be a function of how certain parts of our brains are, and the sentences of mentalese are internal configurations of our brains, whereas the sentences of English are structures in books and patterns of sound waves.

There are, moreover, the causal connections among beliefs in virtue of content that we discussed in the previous chapter. Your belief that there is a tiger outside may get together with your belief that tigers are dangerous to cause you to believe that something dangerous is outside. Internal sentence theorists construe this kind of causal transaction in the head as determined by interactions of the relevant sentence-like or syntactic structures somewhat as the internal causal transactions that underlie those capacities of computers we naturally describe in psychological terms (while granting that the descriptions are not literally true) – accessing *memory*, *adding* numbers, *computing* the velocity of an incoming rocket and so on – are governed by syntactic structures.

Both the internal sentence theory and the map-system theory meet the two desiderata we outlined at the beginning: they explain how beliefs can have content and so truth conditions (and how desires can have satisfaction conditions, but we will continue the policy of focusing on belief), and they do so in a way that makes it clear how content can be causally explanatory. This is no mean achievement and explains why they hold the field. There are, however, various problems for the two theories. Supporters of the internal sentence theory like to tell us about the problems for the map-system theory; supporters of the map-system theory like to tell us about the problems of the internal sentence theory. As authors of a text, we are obliged to tell you both sides of the story (but we will not conceal our affection for the map-system theory).

Discussion of the map-system theory

According to the map-system theory, individual beliefs are derivative on systems of belief: Jones believes that P inasmuch as she has a system of belief according to which P. This follows from the way content is assigned to rich systems of belief (and desire), not primarily to individual beliefs (and desires). It is not denied, of course, that people have individual beliefs that differ one from another in various ways: in the behaviour they explain, in point of subject-matter, in how well supported they are, in whether they are true or false, and so on. The suggestion is that we should understand the properties of individual beliefs in terms of properties of the conceptually prior notion of a system of belief. Thus Jones's belief that P differs from her belief that Q in what it explains, in how well supported it is, and in being true, just if, respectively, her system of belief's property of holding that P differs from her system's holding that Q in what it explains, in how well supported a property of her system it is, and in whether it is something that her system gets right.

There are two advantages in taking the notion of a system of belief as fundamental. We will mention these before we address

Individual beliefs and systems of belief

the feature of the map-system theory that gives rise to the principal objection to it.

Beliefs do not come and go one at a time

The map-system theory explains nicely the *holistic* nature of belief. What would it be like to believe that there is milk in the refrigerator, and *nothing* else? It seems as impossible as having money without the social and economic circumstances that give sense to something being money. To believe that there is milk in the refrigerator, you have to have enough by way of belief to count as understanding what milk is, what a refrigerator is, and what it is for one thing to be inside another. It takes a lot of belief to be any amount of belief, and this is precisely what the map-system approach says. Similarly, change in belief ramifies. You cannot lose or acquire just one belief. If you learn that there is no milk in the refrigerator, you thereby learn too that your memory of having put some there last night is faulty, or perhaps that your house guest is a secret milk-drinker, that you will need to go out and buy some milk before you have people in for afternoon tea, that the refrigerator is not as well stocked as it should be, and so on and so forth. What happens, it seems, is rather like what happens when you change, say, how far apart the dots representing Boston and New York are on a map. That change automatically changes the represented relative positions of all the cities *vis-à-vis* those two cities.

Neurophysiological neutrality

Secondly, it means that the philosopher of belief can remain neutral on the neurophysiology of representation in the brain, on how our brains store information about how things are around us and use it to control the movement of our limbs. A number of cognitive scientists argue that the brain represents the environment in a radically holistic and distributed way, like a map, but more so. There is no part or process in the brain that 'says' that there is a desk in front of me, that stores that bit of information especially; there is instead a structure (known as a connectionist network) that represents a whole way things around me are, including that there is a desk in front of me. Such a view is obviously congenial to the view that regards a system of belief as the fundamental notion. Defenders of the language of thought think that they have powerful empirical reasons for internal representation being language-like, but we argued in the previous chapter that the phenomena they rightly point to as demanding an explanation require only the common ground position that internal representation is structured, not that its structure is language-like.

Some have seen a problem for the map-system theory here. Isn't it part of our common-sense view of the mind, they argue, that one belief rather than another may be especially involved in causing some bit of behaviour. Perhaps it is Jones's belief that there is beer in the refrigerator and not her belief that there is milk in the refrigerator, that causes her to move towards it. But then must it not be the case that there is some part of the brain especially associated with the belief that there is beer in the refrigerator, and some *other* part especially associated with the belief that there is milk in the refrigerator, in order that the first rather than the second can be especially involved in causing the bodily movement towards the refrigerator?

Must different beliefs have different locations in the head?

Consider, however, David Lewis's example of electrical and thermal conductivity in metals. The categorical basis of both dispositional properties is the same loose bonding of the outer electrons in the metal (roughly). Nevertheless, we can distinguish causal explanations in terms of electrical conductivity from those in terms of thermal conductivity. We make the distinction in terms of the nature of what gets produced. The lighting up of a bulb attached to metal wires consequent on the throwing of a switch is explained by the electrical conductivity of the wires, whereas the heating up of the handle of a metal poker placed in a fire is explained in terms of thermal conductivity. In both cases the identical underlying causal basis is involved in producing the result being explained; but if it is involved in the way distinctive of electrical conductivity, then that is the feature of the metal to cite as explanatory, whereas if the basis is involved in the way distinctive of thermal conductivity, then it is thermal conductivity that is to be cited. Similarly, if, according to Jones's system of belief, there is milk and there is beer in the refrigerator, an explanation of her behaviour that adverts to the belief about beer and not to the belief about milk can be made true not by there being something in her brain more especially associated with beer than milk, but by the kind of behaviour that gets caused, and by the stimulus that causes, or would cause, it. Beer-seeking behaviour is not the same as milk-seeking behaviour. Perhaps her moving towards the refrigerator counts as both, given that she believes both milk and beer are in the refrigerator, but once the door is open, or information comes in that undermines her view that the beer and the milk are in the same place, there will be a manifest difference in behaviour that will reveal which belief content really explains the behaviour.

We now come to the principal objection to the map-system theory. Suppose you believe that Mary and John are at a party, does it follow that you believe that Mary is at the party? Yes, it seems, and it might seem attractive to go further and advance the general principle that entailment preserves belief, that belief is closed under entailment, the principle

(E)   If S believes that P, and P entails Q, then S believes that Q.

The map-system theory of belief is committed to (E). According to it, to believe that P is to have a system of belief according to which P, and that in turn is the case just if every member of the set of worlds that gives the content of the system is a P-world. But if P entails Q, every P-world is a Q-world, and so any system of belief according to which P is also a system of belief according to which Q. At first blush this consequence seems exactly right. After all, we happily say that a map which represents Sydney as 900 km by road from Melbourne thereby represents Sydney as at least 700 km, under 1000 km, and so on and so forth, from Melbourne. Or think of how you would respond to a request to make a drawing that represented Tom as shorter than Dick and taller than Harry without representing Dick as taller than Harry! What *is* clearly fallacious is the principle

(D)   If S believes that P and S believes that Q, and $(P\&Q)$ entails R, then S believes that R.

It is a commonplace that subjects can fail to put different things they believe together aright. Jones may believe that Mary lives in New York, that Fred lives in Boston, and that Boston is north of New York, but fail to put all this together and form the belief that Mary will have to travel north to visit Fred. The map-system theory is not committed to (D), however. Jones may, consistently with the theory, have a system of belief according to which P and a *different* system of belief according to which Q, and so fail to believe that $P\&Q$ by virtue of not having a system of belief according to which $P\&Q$. Indeed, it makes good sense that subjects should have different systems of belief, just as travellers often have a number of maps which they use on their travels. The number can (does!) generate problems of co-ordination, but this is compensated for by the ease of using small, as opposed to big, maps.

It makes sense that the brain should do a certain amount of compartmentalizing of information storage and representation.

There are plausible counter-examples to (E), however. It was a discovery in geometry that every equiangular triangle is equilateral; it took some proving. But how could it have, if it is impossible to believe that a triangle is equiangular without believing that it is equilateral? Accordingly we must, it seems, distinguish the belief that A is an equiangular triangle from the belief that A is an equilateral triangle. Again, couldn't someone believe that Fred has two children without believing that the number of Fred's children is the smallest prime? Nevertheless, every possible world in which Fred has two children is a world in which the number of Fred's children is the smallest prime. The only too familiar phenomenon of necessary truths that are opaque, the phenomenon that makes logic and mathematics hard, goes against (E). For whenever it is opaque that P entails Q, it will surely be possible to believe that P without believing that Q – isn't that part of the point of saying that the entailment is opaque?

Counter-examples to (E)

Many draw a more general moral from the troubles for (E). They argue that any account of the content of belief, be it associated with the map-system theory or not, that treats the content of a belief as a set of worlds – the worlds consistent with how the belief represents things as being; that is, the set of worlds where the belief is true – is a mistake. They suggest that we need to distinguish the propositional object of a belief, conceived as a belief's truth conditions, from the content of a belief. The belief that A is equiangular and the belief that A is equilateral would thus have the same propositional object but different contents. The same idea in an alternative terminology distinguishes a coarse-grained notion of a proposition, according to which, for example, the proposition that A is equiangular and the proposition that A is equilateral are one and the same because they are true at the very same worlds, from a fine-grained notion of a proposition, according to which the proposition that A is equiangular and the proposition that A is equilateral differ because they involve, or are built up out of, different concepts, the role played by the concept of an angle in the first being played by the concept of a side in the second. In this terminology, the belief that A is equiangular and the belief that A is equilateral have the same coarse-grained propositional object, but different fine-grained propositional objects.

The objection to content as a set of worlds

There is no doubt that there is a serious issue here for the map-system theory of belief and the associated account of content in terms of sets of possible worlds. However, the situation does not seem to us to be as bad as it is commonly painted by internal sentence theorists. There are two points that the map-system theorist can make in reply.

The first is that *one* legitimate notion of content for belief is simply that of how things are according to a belief, of how the belief *represents things as being*, and the belief that A is an equiangular triangle and the belief that A is an equilateral triangle do *not* differ in this regard. There are not two different ways things might be – one being that A is an equiangular triangle and the other being that A is an equilateral triangle. 'They' are the very same way things might be. It is thus not an objection that the notion of content offered to us by the map-system theory delivers this answer. But the question remains as to what map-system theorists should say about the putative counter-examples to (E). Here, and this is the second point, they need to appeal to the important difference between what a person believes and their ability to capture or report what they believe in a sentence. Self-deception and difficulties in finding the right words to report what we believe ('What's the name of that colour?') are commonplaces. When Jones discovers that a triangle she already knew to be equiangular is also and necessarily equilateral, she does indeed discover something, but arguably not about how things are but about how it is that two different sentences constructed out of interestingly different materials represent the very same way things are.

Thus, map-system theorists can (and must) distinguish a notion of belief whose content is given by the set of worlds where the belief is true from a notion of belief tied to a subject's ability to report their belief in a sentence – a notion according to which, in order to believe that P, you must be able to produce P itself, or something close to P, or something that would count as a good translation of P into the language you speak (we do not want to deny that a Russian believes that snow is white even if he cannot produce the sentence 'Snow is white' as a sentence that captures what he believes). We suspect that the everyday notion of belief slides between a notion tied to the ability to report on how a subject takes things to be, and their so taking things whether or not they can report on the matter in language. This distinction is sometimes described in terms of a distinction between what is explicitly believed and what is implicitly believed. On the map-system view you implicitly believe everything that obtains according to the map by which you steer. Your explicit beliefs are those aspects you can report on with reasonable ease by means of sentences.

Internal sentence theorists avoid commitment to (E), because the mentalese sentence corresponding to '*A* is an equiangular triangle' may be stored in *S*'s head in the absence of the mentalese sentence corresponding to '*A* is an equilateral triangle', much as a book might have written in it one sentence in the absence of the other. However, there is a complication that needs to be noted. The internal sentence theory does *not* hold that Jones believes *P* if and only if the mentalese for *P* is stored in her head. She will have too many beliefs and not enough storage space. Rather, internal sentence theorists appeal to a notion of **core beliefs** – they are the ones actually encoded in the brain by being stored in the belief box – and distinguish them from **derived beliefs**. But what are derived beliefs on their view? The answers vary. Clearly, internal sentence theorists cannot say that a derived belief is any belief entailed by a subject's core beliefs. That would reinstate (E), something they very much want to avoid. Typically, they characterize derived beliefs in terms of the ease with which the appropriate sentences are internally generated and placed in the belief box. This distinction between derived beliefs and core beliefs might be supposed to capture a kind of implicit–explicit distinction, core beliefs being explicit, derived beliefs being implicit.

(E) and the internal sentence theory

Thus, both internal sentence theorists and map-system theorists in their discussion of (E) need to appeal to the ease or otherwise with which subjects generate certain sentences that serve to give the content of what they believe, with, of course, a major difference in respect to the location of the sentences. For the former the relevant sentences are inside us; for the latter they are potentially outside us.

There is an interesting difference between the ways the two theories treat the distinction between implicit and explicit belief. For the map theorist, reports on beliefs are reports on what is already there. Although the belief among Australians that Sydney is south of the only city in Australasia with a population of more than a million whose name begins with the letter 'B' will probably count as an implicit belief (until the matter is brought out into the open), because it takes a bit of 'processing' to generate the relevant (public) sentence as expressing something believed, the processing does not create the belief. What it creates is the sentential report of the belief. By contrast, according to internal sentence theorists, implicit beliefs aren't really beliefs: to have an implicit belief that

Implicit and explicit belief

P is to have the capacity to *create* the belief that *P*, in the sense of having the capacity to generate the right internal sentence under the right circumstances. In consequence, internal sentence theo-- rists make a sharp distinction between explicit and implicit beliefs: for any belief, either there is a stored sentence for it or there isn't. There can be no borderline cases: the sentence is in the belief box or it isn't. For map theorists, being an implicit belief is a matter of degree: is the amount of processing needed to produce the appro- priate belief report sufficient to put it in the implicit category or not? In consequence there will be borderline cases where it is indeterminate whether or not a belief is explicit or implicit (as, it seems to us, is independently plausible).

Water beliefs versus H₂O beliefs

There is a second, even more commonly raised objection to treating content in terms of sets of possible worlds. The belief that there is water in that cup is surely a different belief from the belief that there is H_2O in that cup; yet in view of the necessary if *a posteriori* nature of 'Water = H_2O', the worlds where there is water in that cup are the very same worlds as those where there is H_2O in that cup. And in this case, runs the objection, it seems quite far- fetched to appeal to a distinction between what is believed in some core sense and subjects' abilities to produce one or another sen- tence to capture what they believe. There is no mere difference about the right words to use here, but rather a difference about how the world itself is taken to be. After all, it was an *empirical* discovery that water is H_2O. Here, it seems to us, there is a misun- derstanding of the view under attack. The view is indeed that the content of belief can be given by sets of worlds, but not necessarily by any one set of worlds. Sometimes we need to appeal to more than one set of worlds to tell the whole story about a belief's content, and the belief that there is water in that cup is a case in point.

Two sets of worlds for content

Consider the sentence 'There is water in that cup'. There are two sets of worlds which we need to consider to tell the whole story about the content of the belief whose content is given by that sentence. One is the set of worlds where it is true that there is water in that cup, given how the actual world is – these are the worlds where there is H_2O in that cup, for H_2O is the actual watery stuff. However, there is another relevant set of worlds; these are the worlds such that *if they had been actual* the sentence 'There is water in that cup' would have been true. These are the worlds where a substance playing the water role is in that cup. Take, for instance, the *non-actual* world where XYZ plays the water role (is the watery stuff) and in which that cup contains XYZ. 'There is water in that cup' is not true at this world (given how things actually are), but if this world had been actual, the sentence would have been true. Thus, this world is a member of the second set but not of the first set. Which set is right for giving the content of the belief that there is water in that cup? According to one plausible view, neither is *the* right one; both are required.

Now consider the sentence 'There is H_2O in that cup'. The set of worlds at which this sentence is true is the first set of worlds associated with 'There is water in that cup' but not the second. So the belief that there is water in that cup has something in common with the belief that there is H_2O in that cup, and something not in common with it. So there is a difference between water beliefs and H_2O beliefs, but it is one that can be accounted for in terms of the possible worlds treatment of content. It is just that sometimes we need to appeal to more than one set of possible worlds. The issues here are tricky. What we have given is the barest sketch, and we refer you to the Annotated Reading section for a fuller picture.

We now turn to the other side of the coin, the problems for the internal sentence account.

Problems and questions for the internal sentence theory

In the previous chapter we postponed addressing the question of how proponents of a language of thought might hope to assign content to atomic representations. Suppose neuroscience has found mentalese inscribed in the brain and has identified its subject and predicate terms, its connectives and its rules of composition. Suppose, that is, that the syntactical problem has been solved for mentalese. We now turn to the question of what determines what the various subjects and predicates of mentalese stand for. What gives the words of mentalese their semantics? A major challenge for the internal sentence theory has been to find the answer to this question. We will review some proposals and their problems.

Content for atoms and the internal sentence theory of belief

Informational semantics

The most straightforward story about what might give tokens in the head their representational content is in terms of co-variation.

The idea is very simple. If something co-varies with something else, it bears or carries information about that something else. If storm clouds of a certain kind appear on the horizon if and only if there is rain soon after, then the storm clouds carry information about rain. H. P. Grice called this idea 'natural meaning', capturing the ordinary English sense of 'means' in sentences like 'Those spots mean measles', and 'The petrol gauge pointing far left means empty'. Informational semantics hopes to build a general theory of meaning from these beginnings. In recent years this idea has been used to answer the semantic question about syntactic atoms in the brain. Suppose that, having solved the syntactic problem for mentalese, we are in a position to tell that a neural symbol we will call α occurs from time to time in the head, and is a syntactic atom. What does it represent? Informational semantics at its most basic tells us to look for what the symbol α co-varies with. If α appears in the head when and only when possums appear, it bears information about possums and thus means possum. The core idea is that the syntactic atoms represent what they systematically co-vary with.

Problems for informational semantics

Objections to the view are legion; and so are attempts to answer them. For instance: (a) If the content of α is given by whatever is present just when α is tokened, then whenever α is tokened, what it stands for must be present. But then misrepresentation will be impossible; for whenever α is tokened what it stands for must be present. (b) What is in the head co-varies with what is going on in the sense-organs, with how things are at the body's periphery and so on, as well as with how things are where possums and the like are. Indeed, the local nature of causation tells us that any co-variation between head states and how things are where possums are will be underwritten by co-variations between head states and how things are *between* the head and possums. It follows that co-variance alone cannot explain why α stands for possums rather than the relevant retinal states, or indeed any other of the systematically co-varying states. This is a version of the depth problem. (c) It cannot be strictly true that α is in the head iff there is a possum present, because anything caused by perceiving a possum will also be caused by perceiving anything that impacts on the sense-organs in essentially the same way as a possum – stuffed toy possums, cats in bad light, bandicoots and so on. Thus, on a theory according to which the content of α is given by what it lawfully co-varies with, its content will be: possum or stuffed toy possum or cat in bad light or. . . . Again, it seems that misrepresentation is being made an impossibility, for the content of α becomes a disjunction covering all the possibilities (or at the least, enough of the possibilities to make misrepresentation much harder than we all know that it is).

There is an enormous literature on these problems for informational semantics. We will restrict ourselves to a discussion of two suggestions for handling the problem that informational semantics seems to make misrepresentation too hard and a discussion of Fodor's well-known attempt to avoid making content massively disjunctive – the **disjunction problem**.

Fred Dretske, one of the architects of informational semantics, has suggested that it is not co-variance in general which determines the content of tokens; it is co-variance during a special, privileged period. The idea is that there is a *learning period* during which the content of tokens is determined. If α tokens co-vary with possums during the learning period, then this fixes α as representing possums. If, after the learning period, the α token occurs in someone's belief box caused by a possum-like cat or a bandicoot, then we can safely attribute to them a false belief that there is a possum nearby since

The learning period

1   A token meaning possum (as fixed by co-variation during the learning period) has been produced.
2   No possum is nearby.

This attempt to make misrepresentation possible isn't very satisfactory.

First, it's not at all clear that there is enough co-variance in the learning period. The period when a natural language term is learned is the period when most mistakes are made. A child learning the meaning of 'dog', for example, is likely to point at any vaguely cuddly four-legged object and token 'dog'. It's only after a good deal of correction that the concept is acquired: ironically, it is the *passing* of the learning period that is typically marked by a significant increase in co-variation. It is unlikely that things are different for mentalese.

Little co-variance during learning period

A related concern is that much learning in humans is not done in the presence of the things which are being learned about. Artificial flowers will do almost as well as real ones to learn how to use the word 'flower'. Many of those who use 'Tibet' correctly have never been there. The same point applies even more obviously to terms like 'heat death' and 'nuclear explosion'.

Learning without contact with tokens that fall under the concept

How should the
learning period
be specified?

Another worry concerns the artificiality and arbitrariness of delineating a precise period to count as the learning period. If α co-varies with possums except that a cat caused an α token just before the end of the learning period, then α means 'possum or cat'. If the cat arrives just after the learning period, however, the thinker counts as having made a mistake and as falsely believing of a cat that it is a possum. So the difference between what happens during the learning period and what happen after matters a great deal. But what determines when the learning period ends? Does someone ring a bell? And anyway, don't we continue to learn throughout life?

Accidental
features of the
learning period
matter greatly

Finally, the learning period account seems to be overly concerned with *accidental* features of co-variance during the learning period. If possums co-vary with α tokens during the learning period, then it is true that α tokens would have co-varied with possums or things that impact in the way possums do during the learning period (that is what 'impact in the way possums do' means). It will be a law during the learning period itself that α tokens co-vary with possums or things that impact in the way possums do, and an accident that all the instances of this law involved examples of possums or things that impact in the way possums do that were in fact possums. This means that the content of α depends not on the lawful co-variations between head tokens and surroundings but on *accidental* features of the instances of the laws during the learning period.

Ideal conditions

A second response to the misrepresentation problem gives a central role to ideal conditions for perceiving things.

Although it is easy enough to confuse a possum with a bandicoot at dusk, most of us can tell them apart in good viewing conditions. This means that seeing them in good viewing conditions must differentially affect our brains. A natural suggestion, therefore, is that α means possum if it co-varies with possums when viewed in ideal viewing conditions. There are, nevertheless, troubles for this attractively simple suggestion. Some things are never perceived under ideal viewing conditions – planets, cities we have never been to, the abominable snowman, certain subatomic particles – but we do, surely, have thoughts about them. It might be suggested that these thoughts are all molecular, and that the atoms that make them up all stand for things perceived under ideal conditions. But this requires that all our thoughts about things that are never ideally perceived be thoughts about things that can be regarded as constructions in some sense out of materials we do ideally perceive on occasion. This may be plausible for distant cities – we do think of them as made up of kinds of things we have closer acquaintance with – but it is not very attractive when applied to the fundamental particles of plysics. Secondly, although it is harder to get things wrong in ideal conditions, it does not seem to be *impossible*. It seems possible for someone with a 'wiring diagram' error to consistently have cat thoughts when confronted with a possum, despite it being broad daylight, their eyes being open, and so on. The claim here is *not* the at least debatable one that widespread error is possible. In the discussion of intentional systems theory in chapter 9 we noted views that hold that widespread error is impossible: of necessity, most of a subject's beliefs must be true (that being part of our concept of a belief). The claim here is the surely uncontentious one that a limited amount of error on certain particular questions might survive ideal viewing conditions.

Finally, we look at a suggestion by Fodor for handling the disjunction problem – the problem that whenever someone has possum thoughts by virtue of having α in their brain, what must be true is that α co-varies with: possum or anything that impacts like a possum; so how can α, on co-variance approaches, stand for possum rather than for the disjunction? *Asymmetrical dependence*

Fodor suggests that when a brain token β, say, co-varies with D_1 or D_2 or . . . , what makes it true (if it is) that β stands for D_1, say, and not the disjunction, is an asymmetry in the relation between, on the one hand, β and D_1, and, on the other, β and each of the other D's; D_1 will have a special connection with β that the other D's lack. The special connection, roughly, is that D_1 is independently responsible for the tokening of β, whereas the other D's cause the tokening of β derivatively on the role of D_1 in causing the tokening of β. More precisely, what is required is that (a) had a D_1 not caused β, none of D_2 and so on would have caused β; but (b) had a D_2 not caused β, D_1 would still have caused β, and had a D_3 not caused β, D_1 would still have caused β, and so on. Thus, when α co-varies with possum or bandicoot, what makes it true that α stands for possum alone is the fact that had possums not caused the tokening of α, bandicoots would not have caused α, but had bandicoots not caused the tokening of α, possums would still have caused α.

This suggestion, like all proposals for assigning content to the atoms of mentalese, is the subject of much current debate. We will simply mention three objections. Suppose that we have two people,

Dum and Dee, who are very similar, both internally and in the environments they interact with. In consequence, they have the same kinds of brain states in the same kinds of circumstances. Suppose that Dum's internal tokenings include α in exactly the right circumstances for α to stand for possums according to a co-variance theory with an asymmetry condition in place – α in Dum co-varies with possums or bandicoots, but had possums not caused α in Dum, bandicoots would not have caused α in Dum, and had bandicoots not caused α in Dum, possums would still have caused α in Dum. Dee is different in only one regard. He is watched over by a brilliant brain scientist who, for whatever reason, is determined that bandicoots should sometimes cause α in Dee, and that possums should not be the only things that cause α in Dee. (Perhaps she thinks that possums have been getting too much of the glory.) As a result, the asymmetrical dependence in Dee is the reverse of that in Dum. Had possums not caused α in Dee, she would have interfered with Dee's brain wiring to make sure that bandicoots would still cause α in Dee; and had bandicoots not caused α in Dee, she would have interfered with Dee's brain wiring to ensure that possums likewise did not cause α in Dee. The theory under discussion thus delivers the result that whereas Dum is thinking about possums when he tokens α, Dee is thinking about bandicoots. But we may suppose that our brilliant brain scientist is *never* called upon to act on her resolution. Dee moves in the same environment as Dum and comes across bandicoots along with possums, and the bandicoots do quite enough causing of α in Dee to satisfy her.

It is hard to believe that Dum and Dee think about quite different things in such a case. Dum and Dee are very alike, and our scientist does *nothing* – she has a watching brief that *never* gets activated. How can a resolution that never gets implemented and does nothing to either Dum or Dee make a big difference to what they think about?

The fall-back objection

We turn now to another objection. Part of what gives the asymmetrical dependence view its plausibility is that, by and large, it does seem to give the right results in the case of natural language. It is indeed plausible that if possums were not liable to cause tokenings of the English word 'possum', then bandicoots would not have the power to cause tokenings of 'possum' in poor conditions.

However, this need not always be so. Suppose Columbus was sailing west, and planned to name the first island he encountered 'Columbia Island'. As it happens, there are two islands, *A* and *B*, in his path, and it is a very chancy matter which he will sight as he sails west, though it is very likely that he will sight one or the other. He in fact encountered island A, which is now called 'Columbia Island'. But island B is not very different from it in appearance, and is often mistaken for Columbia Island. Nevertheless 'Columbia Island' is a name for island A, not island B. But this semantic fact fails the test of asymmetrical dependence. For had island A not caused tokenings of the English phrase 'Columbia Island', then island B would still have; for had island A not done the job, it would have been because Columbus saw island B first. All the same, 'Columbia Island' is in fact a name for island A, not for A or B.

In general, this problem will arise when there is a store of names used for various things as they are encountered. For had one thing not been given that name, something else would have been. And where that something else is in the disjunction of things that sometimes cause utterances of the name, asymmetrical dependence will fail.

We have no idea, of course, if there are pre-stored syntactic tokens in the brain which are assigned to things and kinds as they are encountered. But if there are syntactic tokens in the brain, this possibility cannot be ruled out *a priori*.

Another worry about asymmetrical dependence is that it is hard to be sure that the second clause will hold. In the possum–bandicoot case, the second clause tells us that had bandicoots not caused tokening of α, possums still would have. But is this so? Maybe the nearest world where bandicoots never cause the tokening of α is one where this is because possums don't either, because some other neural state is associated with possums. It depends crucially on *why* the disposition fails, and it's anyone's guess as to which method is the natural one to use to evaluate the counterfactual 'If bandicoots didn't have the power to cause α, then possums still would'. Perhaps it would be because bandicoots looked very different from how they actually are, or because people's eyes were better, or because they cared more about the difference, and so never tokened α unless they were sure, perhaps because possums looked different or, indeed, perhaps because possums (and thus bandicoots) tokened χ rather than α. On some of these stories, though not on the last, the clause would be satisfied, but we cannot be allowed to evaluate the counterfactuals just so as to make asymmetrical dependence come out right.

The final account of content for the atoms of mentalese that we

The failure of the second clause

will consider draws its inspiration from evolutionary approaches to content.

Content, evolution and biological function

An influential approach to the problem of content in recent years has been an evolutionary approach which seeks to ground the content of mental tokens in their biological function conceived as determined by evolutionary history. Not all such accounts assume that there are syntactic tokens in the head, and so that the role of evolution in settling content is one and the same as the role of evolutionary history in settling the content of the atoms of the sentences of mentalese, but many do, and we will discuss the view in this context. However, much of what we say is independent of this context.

Function in biology The evolutionary approach to content takes off from a plausible claim about the notion of function in biology. What is the function of the heart? Hearts *do* lots of things: pump blood, make a noise that is useful for detecting life, provide food for certain kinds of carnivore, provide signals about the emotional state of their owner, and so on. In a wide sense, therefore, there are many functions they perform. But what is the heart's real biological function, what is it there *for*? The biologist says that its *biological* function is to pump blood, because that is what the heart was selected for. Natural selection favoured hearts because of the benefits conferred by pumping blood around. Among the many functions that hearts perform, the one that explains why we have them is their role in pumping blood, and so is the one that counts as their biological function. The noise they make, for instance, is a side-effect; hearts would still have been selected for had they been silent. But had they produced the noise they do but failed to pump blood, they would not have been selected for. More generally, a trait has as its biological function doing ϕ just if that trait was selected for doing ϕ.

We can think, therefore, of a trait's biological function as explaining why it exists and what it is *for*, as explaining its purpose, or *telos*. It explains the sense in which we can think of the heart as designed to pump blood. It was not brought into existence by some person's desire that blood be pumped but rather was 'designed' by nature to do so.

Content and design The next step is to ask what beliefs are for. A plausible answer is that they exist to carry information about the environment; that is why they were selected for. But then a belief's selectional history – that is, its biological function – settles which state of the world it is designed to track, and so which state of the world is its content. Suppose, for instance, that there was a state S in the head of one of our ancestors which tended to be caused by food nearby and by little else. This was a useful state to have, and there was selective pressure for this state to continue to be caused by food, and this explains why today we have S occurring in us. The biological function of S, then, is to indicate food; that is its job, and so this will be its content: S will be the belief that there is food near. Likewise, it is plausible that desires are for changing various states of the world – hunger's job is to move food from being nearby to being inside us – but then which state of the world a desire is designed to bring about will be determined by its selectional history, for that is how nature designs.

We thus arrive at an approach to content in terms of evolutionary history. The theory is sometimes called the teleological theory of content (or **teleonomy**), for it seeks to account for content in terms of a state's purpose, the theory of evolution entering the picture by virtue of being, according to teleonomists, the only biologically respectable treatment of purpose. More generally, the theory holds that the contents of the atoms of mentalese are what they were selected for in our ancestors. Also, teleonomists like to emphasize the fact that their theory is in terms of biologically respectable natural kinds: their theory explains content in terms of selectional kinds.

The teleological theory of content

Clearly, there are many questions to be asked of this theory, and the right way to elaborate it is subject to much current discussion. For instance, we have thoughts about many things that were not around when our brains were evolving – radios and presidents, for example – and theorists differ as to how to include such contents in their story. They agree, by and large, that such contents need to be built up from more basic contents that were selected for, but differ on how to spell out this idea. Further, S will most likely have first arisen as a result of a random genetic mutation. Did it only come to mean food *after* selectional pressures got to work? Teleonomists differ on how soon a structure gets to count as having the biological purpose that determines its content according to them. We will focus, though, on three well-known objections to teleonomy that apply independently of the detailed differences between various versions.

Physics tells us that there is a very small, but non-zero, probability

Swampman

of matter spontaneously rearranging itself in various ways. It is overwhelmingly unlikely, but nevertheless consistent with the laws of nature, that a slush of organic matter should rearrange itself to be a molecule-for-molecule copy of some human being. What should we say about swampman, as, following Donald Davidson, the case is commonly known? Swampman will certainly appear to have intentional states, and will behave in a manner which we find *very* natural to describe in the same kinds of psychological terms as are used for the rest of us. He will tell stories about his past that will match the past of the human being he duplicates; he will scream when red hot pokers are applied to him; he will interact in all the right ways with the environment; he will marry and have children; and so on and so forth.

Taken literally, the teleonomic theory tells us that this creature has no contentful states – no beliefs, desires, hopes, fears, apparent memories or the like. This is because it has no evolutionary history; its states have not been selected for anything. The same goes of course for his children by swampwoman. They will never have a thought in their heads until selectional pressures come into play, and their protestations to the contrary will count for nothing until some selecting happens.

Consciousness without desire

Some teleonomists bite this bullet, though they typically concede that swampman will have conscious states. But these will be strange conscious states, for these teleonomists cannot allow that swampman desires that his acute pains cease or that his sensations of pleasure continue. Others say that swampman does have contentful states, but in a *secondary* sense. His states get their content by being like those of creatures that do have the right kind of evolutionary past. But this, it seems to us, is little better than biting the bullet. If, as they hold, it is selectional history that matters for content, why should similarity in a respect which is all to do with current nature and *nothing* to do with evolutionary past count for anything? Still others argue that swampman should not be classified as a human being, since that is a biological classification reserved for creatures – *Homo sapiens sapiens* – with the right selectional history; but surely the issue is not whether swampman is happily classified as a human being, but whether swampman has intentional states.

Functions performed by accident

The second objection draws on the discussion of multiple realizability in chapter 3. We noted there that prosthetic surgery for the brain seems no more problematic *in principle* than does prosthetic surgery in general. We imagined that as they degenerate, parts of someone's brain are progressively replaced by silicon implants, and we noted that provided the implants fill the same functional roles as what they replace, the surgery would count as successful. Teleonomists have to deny this. They have to insist that the selectional history of the implant may be of vital importance when we are dealing with parts of the brain involved in the having of intentional states. The patient should be concerned not merely with whether the implant will determine the same input–output function as the organic brain structure it is to replace, but with the selectional history of the implant, for teleonomists hold that this is crucial to the thoughts that it will be possible to have with the implant. Of course, in the case of silicon implants, selectional history should be understood not in terms of natural selection, but rather in terms of the intentions of the humans who made them. The objection is that it is very counter-intuitive to hold that a patient should regard the intentions of the implant's maker as a crucial additional thing to worry about, over and above what the implant will do, how long it will last, how much it costs, and the like. Some teleonomists respond by identifying the intentions of the *surgeon* as crucial. But shouldn't patients' primary concern be directed to what will in fact happen to them, rather than to surgeons' intentions. Indeed, we can imagine a case where the implanting happens by accident. Should the patient ask for the implant to be removed and done over again with the 'right' intentions?

A reply might be that we are here moving from a point about what it would be sensible for those facing the implant operation to care about to a conclusion about what determines content. But if content is not something worth caring about, what is?

Finally, there are problems arising from our knowledge of content. Whatever sceptics may say, we get much of what people believe and desire right. How do we do it? It is clear that we do not typically use information about the selectional history of internal states. Many of us know very little about the way our internal states evolved. How then can the teleological theory explain our success?

Knowledge of content

Teleonomists have two answers. The first is that their doctrine is one about the essential nature of contentful states, and essential nature is something we typically know about *a posteriori*. Just as it is an essential but *a posteriori* known property of water that it is H_2O, so it is an essential *a posteriori* known property of contentful states that they have a certain evolutionary history. Thus, just as we can know that some stuff is water without knowing that it is H_2O – we knew that the sea was water before we knew that water was (essentially) H_2O – so we can know that some state has a certain content without knowing its evolutionary history. The problem for this response is that the contentful states, according to teleonomists (and many other philosophers, of course), are states of the brain, and it is not an essential property of states of the brain that they have a certain selectional history. (It is sometimes argued that the selectional history is needed in order to justify *describing* brain states as brain states, but that is another issue.) Their selectional history is a contingent and *a posteriori* property of them: water could not fail to be H_2O, but C fibres firing in Jones could fail to have the history it does.

Teleonomy as a kind of empirical functionalism   A better reply, or so it seems to us, holds that teleonomy should be seen as a variety of empirical functionalism. According to some empirical functionalisms (to rehearse briefly material from chapter 4) common-sense functionalism is fine as a theory of how we reference fix on mental states. Our folk theory of mind enables us to say when someone has a belief or a desire with a certain content: it is what we folk associate with believing that tigers are near that enables us to say when someone believes that tigers are near. But what we are reference fixing on, according to the empirical functionalist, is *not* having states that occupy the relevant folk roles; rather, we are fixing on a distinct functional role X that goes together with the folk roles being occupied the way things actually are. And in other worlds where they come apart, it is having the X role filled that makes for, say, believing that tigers are near, not having the folk roles filled. Teleonomists should say, it seems to us, that what we are reference fixing on via the folk roles are what the internal states were selected for, their biological purposes; they should say that the value of X is biological function. They thereby explain how it is fine to use the folk roles to arrive at opinions about what is believed and desired, yet retain their essential contention that it is the biological functions that *settle* questions of content.

Creationism   The fact that creationism is an intelligible hypothesis raises two distinct problems for this version of teleonomy. We can imagine worlds – *counterfactual* worlds, of course – where creationism is true. The teleonomist has to say that these are *all* worlds where nothing has beliefs and desires, and so that it is necessarily false that God created creatures with beliefs and desires; what creationists believe is not only mistaken, it is not even a possibility. This is because, for teleonomists, content goes with biological function, not with satisfying the folk roles, and creatures created by God have no selectional histories to give their states biological functions. Some teleonomists seek to avoid this conclusion by holding that in such a world content may be derived from God's intentions (much as the silicon brain parts we discussed above may be said to have a purpose derivatively on the intentions of their designers). But it is hard to see how they can hold this consistently. *Necessary* beings like God do not have selectional histories, for the simple reason that they are immune to selectional pressures, and so by the lights of teleonomy itself, they do not have contentful states, including intentions.

The second difficulty raised by the intelligibility of creationism concerns what the teleonomist should say if it turns out that creationism is true. Because creationism is intelligible, this is a fair question. The question is not about what to say about counterfactual worlds, but is rather about what to say about the *actual* world should it turn out, against our confident expectation but in accord with the confident expectation of many fundamentalists, that creationism is true of our world.

One answer is that this would be the discovery that there is no content, for it would be the discovery that there are no biological functions; to contemplate the possibility that our world is in fact created by God is *ipso facto* to contemplate radical scepticism about content. A more plausible answer is that this would be the discovery that 'content' names a different property from the one teleonomists think it in fact names. This is the answer most teleonomists give. They see the case as analogous to the water–H_2O case: although water is necessarily H_2O, we can intelligibly ask what should be said if it turns out that water is something else (before it was known that water is H_2O, this very question was asked); and the right answer seems to be that we should say that 'water' would name something different from what it in fact names. But if 'content' would name a different property, what property would it name? The obvious answer is functional role in the common-sense, non-biological sense. But this is to admit that there is coherent sense to be made of a common-sense functionalist account of content, and this is a significant concession. Teleonomists sometimes write as if there was some kind of incoherence in the common-sense functionalist story; moreover, it makes vivid the challenge to justify rigidifying on abstruse historical matters when there is a simpler (simpler because common-sense) account to hand.

A general objection to the internal sentence theory of the content of belief

We conclude our discussion of internal sentence theories of content by noting a problem that concerns not the specifics of the different proposals we have discussed, but rather the general shape of any internal sentence theory.

The connection
with behaviour
There is a major question that the internal sentence approach leaves unanswered. As we saw, the reason the map-system approach takes the notion of a system of belief as fundamental is to get the connection with behaviour right. Indeed, it gets that connection right in the most obvious way – by making the way states in the head cause behaviour determine the content to be given to a system of belief and desire (we, of course, have been simplifying by focusing on the belief part of the story) and letting individual beliefs drop out as properties of subjects' systems of belief. The internal sentence theory starts at the other end, so to speak, with individual beliefs. This leaves it unclear what the theory has to say concerning the connection between a rich story about belief and desire, on the one hand, and behaviour, on the other. For the story about the contents of individual beliefs and desires does not in itself tell us anything about behaviour. You will recall that functional role enters the picture on the internal sentence theory only when it comes to distinguishing belief from desire. Content is analysed not in terms of behaviour, but rather in terms of internal sentences, the representational contents of the atomic parts of those sentences, and the way the parts are fitted together.

Moreover, behaviour had better not enter into the account at the level of individual belief and desire, for the reason we have adverted to a number of times already: it is only rich systems of belief and of desire that we can plausibly see as fixing behaviour. The issue then is whether, nevertheless, the story about individual beliefs and desires is such as to guarantee that subjects with enough individual beliefs and desires, with their individually specified contents, will tend to behave in a way that satisfies their strongest desires if their beliefs are true. Can we find some kind of guarantee that the account of the contents of individual beliefs and desires offered by the internal sentence theory is such that if subjects have rich enough sets of contentful beliefs and desires, the axiom of belief–desire psychology will apply to them? This seems to us very much an open question. It is hard to see how the internal sentence

theorist could provide the needed guarantee. In consequence, we
have here an important problem for the internal sentence theory.

The problem just raised turns on two points: that the internal   *More on belief*
sentence theory assigns content to individual beliefs and desires,   *and behaviour*
combined with the point that individual beliefs and desires do not
have any intimate connection to behaviour. The puzzle is to see
how one could get the needed intimate connection to behaviour by
'addition' of items that are themselves only very distantly connected to behaviour. The problem, that is, concerns any attempt
to start with individual beliefs and desires, rather than with rich
systems of belief and desire, and so is a general point in support of
the map-system theory (just as the difficulties over (E) are a general point in favour of the internal sentence theory). However,
matters are even more difficult for the particular, standard version
of the internal sentence theory that we have been discussing. For,
according to it, connections to behaviour enter the picture only as
ways of distinguishing beliefs from desires. The contents of the
beliefs and desires are settled by quite distinct considerations – co-
variance, selectional history, asymmetrical dependencies or whatever – none of which has any *special* connection to behaviour.

In the case of the standard version of the internal sentence theory,
it seems that the only way to get the connection to behaviour right
is to *add* to the theory a requirement that the kinds of connections
between belief, desire and behaviour with which we are all familiar exist. We cannot hope that enough tenuous connections will
somehow add up to a non-tenuous connection, because we do not
have even tenuous connections to start with. Our belief regarding
where Jupiter is in the solar system governs a whole gamut of
behavioural facts. It governs, for instance, where we point our
telescopes if we want to see Jupiter in the night sky, the calculations of the rocket scientists in charge of the Voyager project, the
drawing we do on the black board of the solar system, the budget
we assign the Voyager project, and so on and so forth. We cannot
tolerate an internal sentence theory that makes these connections
and their kin a fluke; we need to add them to the theory. But to
add them to the theory is in effect to add common-sense functionalism to the internal sentence theory of belief (and desire), for
common-sense functionalism is precisely the theory of belief and
desire that reflects, among other things, our most firmly held views
about the way beliefs and desires govern our path through the
world. And now it seems that the internal sentence theory has
become, of necessity, a two-part theory of belief and desire: one

part is common-sense functionalism, the other a bold and interest-ing empirical contention about the way our brains work. Thus a theory originally offered as a superior alternative to common-sense functionalism has become a speculative addition to it.

Annotated Reading

Obviously, the items listed for the previous chapter on the language of thought are all relevant to the issue of content in general. The same is true of those listed for the next chapter on broad and narrow content. A recent demanding, but well-written, work on content is Colin McGinn, *Mental Content*. Two important sources for the possible worlds approach are Robert Stalnaker, *Inquiry*, and David Lewis, *On the Plurality of Worlds*, §1.4. Many expositions of the language of thought theory contain attacks on the possible worlds approach; see, for example, Hartry Field, 'Mental Representation'. A useful collection is Andrew Woodfield, ed., *Thought and Object*. Recent expositions of teleological content are David Papineau, *Philosophical Naturalism*; McGinn, *Mental Content*; and Ruth Millikan, *White Queen Psychology*, the last being the most detailed and demanding. An influential presentation of the informational approach to content, set in the context of the whole question of explaining behaviour, is Fred Dretske, *Explaining Behavior*. For Jerry Fodor on asymmetrical depend-ence and a discussion of teleonomy, see his *A Theory of Content and Other Essays*. For H. P. Grice's views on meaning, see his 'Meaning'.

12

Broad and Narrow Content

A configuration in the sand is a footprint by virtue of its causal history. Exactly the same configuration produced by a chance swirl of wind is not a footprint, though it might well be mistaken for one. Sunburn is a burn with a past that involves the sun. A patch of sand's bearing the imprint of a foot, a person's being sunburnt, and generally states that are possessed by objects in part by virtue of relations to the objects' environments, including their past environments, are variously called broad, contextual or wide states. The contrast is with narrow, local or individualistic states – states that objects are in in virtue of how they are in themselves, states that supervene on the current nature of the object – though we will see shortly that this characterization needs to be treated with care. The broad–
narrow
distinction

It is clear that some mental states belong in the broad category. You cannot know that the universe has existed for millions of years unless it has – knowing that P implies that it is true that P; your having the greatest idea since sliced bread depends on someone's having had the idea of sliced bread in the past. But what should we say about belief? It is obvious that Jones's having a certain belief is in part a matter of how Jones is; otherwise it would not be *Jones* who had the belief. But is it pretty much entirely a matter of how Jones is, or does her environment, and especially her causal history, play a major role in making it the case that she has one or another belief? This is an extremely controversial question. We will outline the case for the view that it is a mistake to give an across the board answer. For some P, your believing that P is a narrow matter; for some P, your believing that P is a broad matter – or, as it is often put, some content is **narrow** and some content is **broad**.

Narrow content

We start with the traditional argument for saying without qualification that belief content is narrow, that what a person believes is more or less entirely a matter of how they are, and that, in particular, how a belief came about is in no way constitutive of its content. On this view, various happenings in the past may be, and indeed often are, causally responsible for what is believed; but what is believed is not logically dependent on what caused the belief, nor is it logically dependent on the believer's surroundings. The believer's surroundings matter in general for whether the belief is true or false – if Jones believes that there is a tiger near, her belief can only be true if there is a tiger near – but they do not play a role in determining *what* she believes. This view was until relatively recently standard doctrine.

Virtual reality and brains in vats

The science fiction case for narrow content

Designers of virtual reality machines trade on the fact that the brain cannot, as we might put it, see beyond the local nature of its stimuli to the nature of their distal origins. These designers set themselves the task of producing from their machines stimuli at our peripheries exactly like those that would be produced by various external environments – the Sahara, perhaps – and to the extent that they succeed, we have an experience as of being in the Sahara. A common science fiction fantasy, exploited for instance in Verhoeven's film *Total Recall*, is to suppose that what we take to be experiences of a world and people around us are in reality a complete delusion produced in us by a suitably programmed virtual reality machine. In similar vein, science fiction stories present brain-in-a-vat fantasies in which it is supposed that we take a foetal brain, place it in a vat, subject it to exactly the same inputs – neural stimuli, nutrients and so on – as a normal brain housed in a body would be subjected to, and allow it to grow exactly as it would were it normally housed. There is a very powerful intuition that such a brain in a vat would have a rich mental life – indeed, just the mental life that a person with the same brain placed inside a normal body and moving through an environment that stimulates it exactly as it is in fact being stimulated would have.

Historically, these fantasies have played an important role in presenting the challenge of scepticism. How do you know that you are not a brain in a vat or a subject in a perfect virtual reality machine? How can anyone know that they are not a virtual reality dupe? But our interest here is different: it is simply in the implications of the contention that your mental states would be just the same were you a virtual reality dupe. If the contention is correct, and it is certainly plausible, then our mental states are narrow properties of us. What would matter for our psychology would be how we are, and our environment and history would matter only inasmuch as they have one or another effect on how we are. For if you were a virtual reality dupe, then you would have a very different environment and history from the environment and history that you in fact have. Thus, if your psychology would be the same if you were a virtual reality dupe, then it must depend most immediately on how you are, not on how your environment is. Your psychology must supervene on your current state, for that is all that you would retain of what is now true of you were you a virtual reality dupe. Your psychology must be a narrow fact about you.

Now, as we have already noted, this contention cannot be correct as it stands. What you know and remember, for instance, would not be the same were you a virtual reality dupe. This follows from the success grammar of 'know' and 'remember', from the fact that '*S* remembers (knows) that *P*' entails *P*. You remember riding a bicycle; were you a virtual reality dupe you would not, because were you a virtual reality dupe, you would never have ridden a bicycle. It is plausible, though, that you would *seem* to remember riding a bicycle. But if things would *seem* just the same, then you would presumably have exactly the same *beliefs*. Thus, the considerations arising from reflection on virtual reality machines and brains in vats strongly suggest that what a person believes is a narrow property of them (though in fact the discussion would run along much the same lines for desire, hope, fear, and in general those intentional states that do not have success grammar). Indeed, one might go further and urge that those mental states with success grammar can be analysed conjunctively in a way that reveals that the *genuinely* mental aspect of the state is narrow. Thus, many have analysed '*S* remembers *E*' along the lines of '*S* seems to remember *E* and that seeming has such and such a connection to the obtaining of *E*'. The seeming to remember is both mental and narrow, runs the idea, and the explanation of the broadness of the state of remembering is simply that it is wrong to call

Scepticism

Mental states with success grammar

a seeming to remember a memory unless it has the right kind of connection to the obtaining of E, just as it is wrong to call a coin genuine unless it has the right kind of connection to the mint.

The doppelgänger test for narrowness

One way to sharpen the issue regarding narrow content is by appeal to the notion of a doppelgänger. A **doppelgänger** of you is a duplicate of you from the skin in, a *genuinely* identical twin. If what you believe is a narrow property of you, then you and your doppelgänger believe alike. For you and your doppelgänger differ at most in history and surroundings. Is it plausible that doppelgängers believe alike? Turing test considerations suggest that the answer is yes. You and your doppelgänger will register identical scores on every behavioural test for belief. You will utter the same sentences in reply to the same questions asked in the same circumstances; the same perceptual contact with tigers will lead to the very same running away behaviour; in sum, for each and every possible input, what you and your doppelgänger would do would be exactly the same. The world's greatest behavioural psychologists and neuroscientists will not be able to tell you from your doppelgänger either in terms of behaviour and behavioural capacities, or in terms of what underlies behaviour, or indeed in any other terms, as the two of you will of course look exactly alike. You will be able to play the kinds of tricks that some sets of identical twins like to play, except that it will be *impossible* to catch you out.

There are two important things to note about the traditional case for narrow content just outlined. Both concern what is meant by narrow content. The first is that narrow content is not intrinsic – it is not like squareness. The second point concerns the sense in which **egocentric content** is narrow.

Narrow content is not intrinsic

It is sometimes objected that content cannot possibly be narrow, because we typically ascribe content using terms that pick out objects and happenings *around us* – approaching tigers, glasses of beer, and so on – and because when we investigate what goes on in the head, with a view to seeing it as representing goings-on around us, we, of necessity, address the question of how what goes on inside the head connects with those goings-on. The classic example is David Marr's theory of vision. Marr addressed the question of how two-dimensional arrays of stimuli on the retina could encode information about the location in three-dimensional space of objects around us. In order to see the happenings on the retina or, more plausibly, those downstream from the retina as visual representations of what is happening around us, we have to see them *qua* putative encodings of happenings around us. Moreover, the behavioural evidence for what we believe lies in our environmentally described responses to environmentally described stimuli. For we have very little idea about how to characterize the stimuli at our peripheries typical of tigers, glasses of beer, and so on *qua* stimuli at our peripheries; and, as we have noted several times, we characterize the behavioural responses to stimuli in environmental or distal terms, in terms most particularly of their impact on the way we are situated in an environment. Only when stimuli and behavioural responses are described in environmental terms are the patterns distinctive of what a subject believes and desires salient.

It follows that content cannot be understood in purely internal terms. We understand it, at least in part, in terms of interactions with things around us – inputs and outputs described in distal terms. In this respect, content is like being a magnet. Being a magnet is specified in terms of the interactions of magnets with things around it, not in terms of its internal nature. No amount of knowledge of the internal nature of a magnet divorced from knowing how this nature affects what happens *around* the magnet, and in particular the behaviour of any metal objects around the magnet, could reveal the fact that it was a magnet. All the same, it does *not* follow that content is not narrow in an important sense. For doppelgängers of a magnet are also magnets, and so, by the doppelgänger test, being a magnet is narrow. The reason being a magnet passes the doppelgänger test is that what matters for being a magnet is not the actual interactions undergone, but the class of possible interactions, some of which may be actual, some merely possible, that would be undergone. And though doppelgängers typically differ in their actual interactions – of two identical magnets, only one may ever be put near iron filings, say – they do not differ with respect to their possible interactions. For any situation, how they *would* interact with it is exactly the same.

The same goes for narrow content. Having a belief with narrow content is not an individualistic or narrow or local or intrinsic state in the sense in which a classic example like something's being square is. The squareness of an object is not a matter of actual and possible interactions with surroundings; it is rather a geometrical

Content and environmental interaction

property that an object could have in worlds where the interactions typical of square objects were completely different from those we associate with being square. The narrowness of narrow content is constituted not by its being independent of interactions with, and relations to, the environment, but rather by the fact that which interactions are actual and which possible does not matter. Narrow content is a matter of how internal nature governs actual and possible interactions with the environment, and is in common between doppelgängers because they are exactly alike in how their internal nature governs interactions with actual and possible environments.

Narrow content and supervenience

It follows that narrow content does not supervene in the strict sense of *globally* supervening on internal nature. Narrow content is a function of internal nature together with the laws of nature, just as being magnetic is a matter of internal nature plus laws of nature. In worlds with laws that are different from our laws of nature there are doppelgängers of you that do not share your narrow contents, and objects exactly like the magnets of this world in internal nature that are not magnetic in those worlds. This is why we spoke above of the issue about narrow content being whether what you believe is *pretty much* entirely a matter of how you are. No content can be *entirely* a matter of how a subject is.

Egocentric content

Suppose that you are here and now having an experience as of hearing a mosquito buzzing above you, and in consequence believe that there is a mosquito above you. What experience and what belief will a doppelgänger of you have? It is plausible that they will have the same experience as of hearing a mosquito buzzing above them and will hence believe that there is a mosquito above them. Is their belief the same as your belief? You might say no, on the ground that the beliefs differ in truth conditions. Their belief is true if and only if they are below a mosquito, whereas your belief is true if and only if you are below a mosquito. And as you are different people, these conditions are different. On the other hand, you might say yes, on the ground that you both believe the same thing about how things are with you: you both ascribe to yourselves the property of being below a mosquito, and you would both find the same sentence, namely, 'I am below a mosquito', the natural one to characterize your belief.

Beliefs that we naturally express in words like 'that there is a mosquito above *me*' or 'that he believes that he *himself* is below a mosquito' are called egocentric beliefs, or sometimes **beliefs** *de se* as opposed to **beliefs** *de dicto*. They are beliefs about how things are that contain an essential reference to the believer. They are very common. Beliefs to the effect that you have a beard, are over fifteen, live in Australia, like beer, and so and so forth are all egocentric beliefs, because they are beliefs about you yourself. Moreover, many beliefs that are not obviously egocentric turn out on reflection to be egocentric. For instance, the belief you express with the words 'It is sunny outside' is typically the belief that it is sunny outside the room you yourself are in; and the belief you express with the words 'The government will fall' is typically the belief that the government of the country you yourself belong to will fall. In the same way, many of the physical structures that serve as indicators give 'centred' information, information about how things are that is in some way or other centred on the structure itself. The number of rings in a tree indicates the age of the tree *itself*. The direction of a compass needle indicates the direction of magnetic north from where the compass *itself* is. The evolutionary explanation of egocentric belief is obvious. True beliefs about tigers are useful; true beliefs about where the tigers are in relation to oneself are even more useful.

There is a lively debate about whether egocentric beliefs can be reduced to beliefs that are not egocentric, or, in the alternative terminology, whether belief *de se* can be reduced to belief *de dicto*. Some hold that your belief that there is a mosquito above you is really a belief that for some set of qualities that you regard as uniquely picking you out – your name, the names of your parents, when you were born, or whatever – a person with those qualities, the unique ϕ-er, has a mosquito above them. One trouble with this suggestion is that your doppelgänger would associate with themselves exactly the same qualities as you associate with yourself. If you believe that your name is Pat, they would believe that their name is Pat; if you believe that you have red hair, they believe that they have red hair; and so on. Hence, the suggestion would make what they would believe have the same truth-value as what you in fact believe, namely, the truth-value that 'There is a mosquito above the unique ϕ-er' has, and that is wrong. As we saw, what they would believe might be true when what you believe is false, and vice versa. Moreover, you might have no opinion about what properties you alone have. Consider someone waking up in a completely

De se *belief*

The irreducibility of de se *belief*

dark room in a state of temporary amnesia and confusion. They may have no beliefs about themselves that could possibly be thought by them or anyone else to go anywhere near identifying them uniquely. They do not know their own name, how old they are, what the room they are in looks like, and so on. Yet they may well believe that there is a mosquito above them. Finally, you may have an opinion about the properties that you alone have which is quite wrong. Perhaps you think that the one property that you alone have is that of being the best chess-player in Montreal, but unknown to you there is a better player. Nevertheless, in assessing the truth-value of your belief that there is a mosquito above you, it would be absurd to visit the house of Montreal's best chess-player.

One reason some have attempted to reduce egocentric belief to non-egocentric belief despite these objections is the fear that to admit irreducible egocentric belief is to admit a curious kind of fact about the world that cannot, as a matter of principle, be captured in a naturalistic picture of the world. If your belief that you have red hair cannot be reduced to your belief that the ϕ-er has red hair, then, runs the fear, when your belief is true, there must be some fact, the fact that you yourself have red hair, that escapes any non-perspectival account of what is in the world and what it is like. We need a new category of mysterious, 'centred', facts, different in kind from those that feature in, for instance, the story science tells about the world. Others of course take comfort in this conclusion. They like mystery, especially when it suggests a failure in science. In fact, however, there is nothing particularly mysterious about centred facts. As we noted above, a compass indicates the direction of magnetic north from where it itself is, and the number of rings in a tree indicates the age of the tree itself, and these are both things science itself tells us.

Counting egocentric attitudes

We noted that there are two defensible answers to the question of whether you and your doppelgänger's beliefs that you are below a mosquito count as having the same content, and the same is true in general for whether X's egocentric belief that she herself has the property of being ϕ is the same belief or a different belief from Y's egocentric belief that she herself has the property of being ϕ. A similar point applies to desire. Suppose that Tom and Dick are doppelgängers who both aspire to be Prime Minister. Their desires are egocentric. Each desires that he himself be Prime Minister. Do they desire alike? The conditions under which their desires would be satisfied differ. Tom's desire is satisfied if Tom becomes Prime Minister, Dick's if Dick becomes Prime Minister. On the other hand, the property they desire to have is the very same in both cases, namely, that of being Prime Minister. You might say that they desire alike; or you might say that they differ in what they desire. In any case, it is clear that the phenomenon of egocentric belief and desire (and the same goes for the propositional attitudes in general) means that the traditional case for narrow content needs clarification. When it is egocentric propositional attitudes that are in question, what is in common between doppelgängers is the properties they take themselves to have, desire themselves to have, fear themselves to have, and so on, not the conditions under which their beliefs are true, their desires satisfied, or their fears realized.

It might be asked why we would want to call content that is common between doppelgängers in this sense narrow. Why not go the other way and say that egocentric content is a clear case of broad content, as in fact is often done? The answer is that we want to count as broad, content that depends on how things are *outside* the subject – that is, content that can be changed by leaving subjects unaltered while changing their history and surroundings, just as changing the history of a burn can change its status as sunburn. The phenomenon of egocentric content does not fall into this category, or, at least, does not fall into this category by virtue of being egocentric. The difference in truth conditions between doppelgängers' contents that it illustrates is entirely due to the fact that the *subjects* having the beliefs are not numerically identical. The fact that the truth conditions of your belief that you are below a mosquito are not the same as those of your doppelgänger's belief is entirely due to the fact that you are not identical to your doppelgänger. The case does not illustrate the possibility of changing the truth conditions of your belief by changing your surroundings or history. Of course, we might stipulate that broad belief is to mean belief with truth conditions not in common between doppelgängers, in which case egocentric belief would come out broad. But then we would need another term for beliefs whose truth conditions depend on a subject's surroundings. We will keep the terms 'broad' and 'wide' for the latter notion.

Why egocentric content is not automatically broad

The explanatory value of narrow content

We can now describe a distinctive explanatory role for narrow content. When we predict and explain behaviour in terms of content, we do so in environmental terms. As we have emphasized before, content explanations latch on to patterns that emerge when inputs and outputs are described in terms of typical causes of, and effects on, actual and possible environments of subjects. It thus makes sense that we should have a way of describing these patterns that abstracts away from whether these environments are actual or possible. Such a style of description will yield something shared by doppelgängers because for any possible situation they are alike in how they would interact with it. They differ only at the level of the situations they *in fact* interact or interacted with. Narrow content, because it is simultaneously given in environmental terms and is in common between doppelgängers, fills the bill. In this regard, narrow content explanations are, of course, no different from explanations in terms of the many dispositional properties shared by intrinsic duplicates: fragility, solubility, being magnetic and the like.

Explanation by what is common between doppelgängers   The essential point can be put this way. Your internal states may differ from your doppelgänger's in what actually caused them and in the actual behaviour they caused, environmentally described (but not as described in terms of raw or peripheral behaviour). But your and your doppelgänger's internal states are exactly alike in the *kinds* of situations or environments that *would* cause them and in the impact that the behaviour they give rise to *would* have on any given possible situation or environment. Explanation and prediction by narrow content is explanation and prediction in terms of this commonality between subjects and their doppelgängers.

This argument identifying an explanatory niche for narrow content should not be confused with a famous argument for the much stronger conclusion that *only* content that is narrow can causally explain behaviour. We will discuss this argument after we have outlined the case for broad content.

Broad content

We have described the case for the traditional view that belief, unlike knowledge, memory and the like, is a narrow state of subjects, and so that *all* belief content is narrow. We hope that we have made it sound plausible. It is time to observe that there are clear cases where what subjects believe depends on how things are outside them. Not all belief is narrow. There is such a thing as broad content. What is controversial, as we will see, is the ultimate significance of this fact. But first we should distinguish a more from a less radical thesis.

A footprint is a configuration in the sand. It gets to be a foot- *Strong*
print because of its connection to a foot, but it is not located where *externalism*
the foot is; it is located where the sand is. Likewise sunburn is a condition of the skin, not of the sun, despite the fact that it would not be a case of sunburn if it had not been caused by the sun. In our view, the most reasonable (and most popular) version of the doctrine that some beliefs have broad content holds that though these beliefs get to have the content they have in virtue of connections between the beliefs and matters outside the subject, the beliefs themselves are not, wholly or partly, outside the subject. The beliefs themselves are states inside the subject, being in fact states of the subject's brain. **Strong externalism** holds, on the contrary, that some, or in some versions all, beliefs are states partly outside the head.

One motivation for this view is the conviction that if we locate beliefs inside the head, we make it impossible to capture adequately the way a belief may be about particular things outside us. The contention is that the common approach to the problem of intentionality (underlying, for instance, the discussion of content in the previous chapter) which sees it as the problem of how a state inside a subject may be about something outside the subject is an approach to the problem that makes it insoluble. Rather, we have to view your belief that there a particular tree in front of you as literally including the tree itself. It is hard to see how this helps with the basic problem, however. Obviously your belief about the tree is not located in its entirety where the tree is. For in that case it would not be a state of *yours* at all. That is, when you have a belief about a particular tree, you yourself must be in some distinctive state. But then the issue remains of what links this state of yours – whether it is a belief or not – with the tree, and that *is* the basic problem of intentionality.

However, the main reason for rejecting strong externalism is the fact that belief is typically a *response* to the environment. Just as sunburn is not a state of the sun but rather a state caused by the sun, so your belief that there is some particular tree in front of you will typically be a causal response to the tree and hence distinct from it. In what follows we will be concerned only with the more moderate thesis that certain internal states of subjects get to be beliefs with a certain content because of how things are outside the subject, not with the more extreme thesis that the belief state itself is partially or wholly outside the subject.

There a number of cases that show that some content is broad. We will describe three. The first involves our old friend Twin Earth and the way in which how things are outside the head can affect reference.

Twin Earth and broad content
We saw in chapter 4 that the word 'water' in the mouths of Earthians denotes H_2O and in the mouths of Twin Earthians denotes XYZ, and that the explanation of the difference lies in the difference in the causal history of the use of 'water' on the two planets. What about the *beliefs* of Earthians and Twin Earthians that they express using the word 'water'. You believe that rivers contain water, and use the sentence 'Rivers contain water' to express what you believe. But you cannot use this sentence to capture what Twin Earthians believe. Although they, speaking Twin Earth English, will use the sentence 'Rivers contain water' to express what they believe, you, an Earthian, cannot use it to express what they believe. For the sentence in your mouth is true if and only if rivers contain H_2O, and this is *not* the condition under which what they believe is true. The condition under which what they believe is true is the condition under which the sentence 'Rivers contain water' in their mouths is true: namely, that rivers contain XYZ. Your belief is about water, their belief is not about water at all. It follows that your belief is different from your Twin Earth doppelgänger's belief. You believe that rivers contain water. You have a belief that is true if and only if rivers contain water, that is, H_2O. Your Twin Earth doppelgängers believe that rivers contain retaw, our word for what they call 'water', and has a belief that is true if and only if rivers contain retaw, that is, XYZ.

The general point is that once we allow that the truth conditions of some of the sentences we use to report belief (and equally desire and the propositional or intentional attitudes in general) may depend on matters outside the head, we must also allow that the conditions under which the beliefs we so report are true may likewise depend on matters outside the head. But then part of what makes it true that you believe that rivers contain water is the fact that certain states in your head have a certain causal connection to water; this is part of what makes it the case that your belief really is *about* water. Had your head states been the same but causally connected to XYZ and not water, then your belief would have been about XYZ, not water, and accordingly your belief would have been a different belief. But if the identity of your belief that rivers contain water depends on how things are outside the head, then your belief is broad. And the same goes quite generally for beliefs we express using natural kind terms. The same line of argument can be developed for any natural kind term to which the Twin Earth thought-experiment applies. The Twin Earth thought-experiment does more than show that the reference of natural kind terms depends on how things are outside the head. It also shows that the conditions under which a belief reported by a sentence containing a natural kind term is true depends on how things are outside the head.

Our second and third examples of broad belief content are provided by beliefs we report with subject–predicate sentences constructed using names and demonstratives as subject terms. The role of proper names and demonstratives is essentially that of picking out particular things, and in consequence the truth conditions of beliefs with contents given using them depends on the identity of the particular things in question, and that concerns how things are outside the head. Here is a simple illustration of the point for the case of demonstratives. Suppose that you form a belief about a particular filing cabinet – say, that it contains essential office supplies. You might naturally express what you believe in some such words as 'That filing cabinet contains the essential supplies'. Now suppose that you doze off for a moment, and the filing cabinet in question, cabinet$_1$, is silently replaced by a second one, cabinet$_2$, that looks exactly like the first one. On awaking, unaware of the change and looking at what you take to be the same cabinet, you again utter the words 'That filing cabinet contains the essential supplies' to express what you believe. Although the words are the same, what you believe has changed. The first belief is true if and only if cabinet$_1$ contains the essential supplies; the second belief is true if and only if cabinet$_2$ contains the essential supplies. The contrast is with your belief that, say, there is a cabinet of a grey colour with three drawers in a room with '2207' on its door, which contains the essential supplies. That belief is the same before and after. Because it is not a demonstrative belief, its identity is not tied to the identity of the filing cabinet.

A similar point applies to belief contents expressed using proper names. In order to have beliefs whose content can be given using the name 'London' in subject position, that is, beliefs about London, you have to be in some way connected to or acquainted with London itself: perhaps you have been there, perhaps you have spoken to people who have been there, perhaps you have read

Demonstrative content

Beliefs expressed using proper names

books by people who have been there, or whatever. It is not enough to have a raft of true beliefs of the kind: there is a city called 'London', it is important, it is in a country called 'England', it contains over six million people, and so on. For suppose that all these latter beliefs come from a work of fiction. Someone sat down and simply made up a story about a city they called 'London', and in the story this city is said to have over six million inhabitants, to be in a country called 'England', to be important, and so on. By accident, the claims about the fictional city tally with the facts about London. You believed it all because you mistakenly thought that the book was a work of history. In consequence, you accept as true such sentences as 'London is important' and 'London contains over six million people'. Nevertheless, you do not simply by virtue of accepting the story have beliefs about London, and you do not believe that *London* is important. Hence, how your head is, is not enough for having London beliefs. Your head must have the right kind of causal connections – possibly highly complex and indirect ones, but enough to constitute an information channel – to London.

The common theme in all these examples is that many beliefs are essentially about *particular* objects and features of the world around us, and get to be about these objects and features in part in virtue of a causal link, possibly highly indirect via books, the reports of others or whatever, to them. The identity of such beliefs depends on the causal links outside the head as well as on what goes on inside the head, and this is why they are broad.

The explanatory value of broad content

We are now in a position to address the famous argument mentioned earlier to the conclusion that only a narrow notion of content can play the needed role in the causal explanation of behaviour. The examples of broad content discussed above were seen to be examples of broad content by reference to semantic considerations, considerations to do with the conditions under which the beliefs were true, and how these were in part a function of external facts. But, it has been argued, when we turn to content's causal-explanatory role, we see that only a narrow notion of content will serve. The argument appears most particularly in the writings of Fodor, and varies somewhat in its various manifestations. What follows is what we take to be the essential thrust of the argument from **methodological solipsism**.

We have just seen that defenders of broad content hold that the *Methodological solipsism* very same internal state S may differ in its content according to its causal origin – according, for instance, to whether water or some other substance with much the same causal powers causes it, or to whether or not it lies at the end of a causal chain that has London at the other end. However, the effects which the state has on other internal processes and on the behaviour that in due course arises from it will not be directly influenced by which causal origin the state has. The local nature of causation tells us this. S's causal origin will be 'blind' to the states and behaviour downstream from it. The point here is the same as the point made earlier about virtual reality machines. Hence, concludes the argument, the properties of S that are causally efficacious in the production of behaviour (and other mental states) cannot include highly relational ones like having one rather than another causal origin, and so cannot include what makes content broad. The same point can be made by noting that what makes your arm rise and what makes the arm of your doppelgänger rise will be exactly the same internal state; hence, it must be properties in common between you and your doppelgänger that do the causing. The moral drawn is that causal explanations of behaviour in psychology should be in terms of features local to subjects, properties in common between subjects and their doppelgänger, and this rules out broad content. This principle is sometimes called the principle of autonomy, and sometimes the principle of methodological solipsism. The core idea is that causal explanations of behaviour in psychology should be in terms of properties that supervene on the current nature of the subject.

There are two different ways of replying to this argument. One is to note the many cases in which highly relational properties feature in perfectly respectable causal explanations. The tracking behaviour of a predator may be explained by its perceptual contact with its prey, and perceptual *contact* is defined in part in terms of causal origin. Causal explanations in economics are often relational in character: such notions as *competition* for resources and poverty *traps* are clearly relational in character. And in astronomy the movements of the planets are explained in terms of their being planets – that is, bodies having the relational property of being under the influence of a sun.

This reply is only half an answer to the concern that lies behind *Causal relevance and causal efficacy* the argument, or so it seems to us. There is no doubt that knowledge of relational properties, and in particular of matters of causal origin, can provide useful information about how things come about, and are thereby part of good causal explanations. If information about causal origin is not causally explanatory, what is? Moreover, the explanatory value of knowing the causal origin of the information-sensitive states inside a subject is clear. You then know which *thing*'s properties are being encoded inside the subject, even if you do not know which properties of that thing are being encoded. But there is a problem about causal efficacy or productivity, as opposed to causal relevance in some wide sense, that is left unaddressed by these observations. It concerns which properties of my internal states here and now are making my arm move; and surely the answer to that question must advert to local properties of my internal states. From this perspective, the example of the planets heightens the worry, rather than laying it to rest. True, we explain the movement of the planets in terms of the effects of the sun on them. But what is operating on any planet at any particular time is the gravitational field *at the point where the planet is*. Although the relation of a planet to the sun is causally relevant to how it moves, it does not actually produce the movement on any particular occasion. The strength of the force field at the point where the planet is located does that. How then, runs the worry, can the broad content of my belief that there is water in that glass be part of what brings about or produces the movement of my arm towards the water? The history of a state may be causally relevant to what it causes, for it may explain why the state has the properties required to do the causing, but, runs the worry, the properties required to do the causing are local and not historical.

You might respond by challenging the coherence of the distinction between causal relevance in a wide sense, and causal efficacy or productivity. There is, you might argue, no coherent distinction that stands up to scrutiny between properties that are causally relevant to some effect and those among them that actually do the causing. Or you might respond by holding that it is enough to have broad content come out causally relevant; we can live with the dissonance with intuition involved in denying it causal efficacy, with denying that the content of your belief that rivers contain water is among the properties that actually cause you to drink from a river. We respond, however, by appealing to the central idea in the type–type identity theory, the idea that psychological properties are neurophysiological properties.

The identity theory and the causal efficacy of content

Suppose that you believe on some given occasion that rivers contain water. As we have noted, what makes the belief broad is the fact that you could not have a belief with this content unless there were certain causal links between your belief and water.

Nevertheless, the content may *be* a neurophysiological property of your belief. This neurophysiological property itself is not a broad property. It is a local property of a certain internal state. It gets to be the broad content of my belief in virtue of its causal history. Your belief will have that neurophysiological nature because of interactions between your head and water, and that is essential for that nature to be the content of a water belief. But now there is no puzzle about how the content can be causally efficacious with respect to behaviour or other internal states. Local properties, and in particular neurophysiological properties, are causally efficacious.

The basic idea behind our response to the question about the causal-explanatory role of broad content can be put in terms of a simple example. Suppose we tag the chemical structure that has killed more people than any other 'the killer structure'. Its being the killer structure is a very broad matter involving all the other poisons that there are and its own dubious causal past. Nevertheless, the killer structure is a narrow, or local, property, a property in common between doppelgängers of any substance that has it, a property that supervenes on a substance's nature. This is important when we consider the nature of an explanation of someone's dying in terms of their having ingested a substance with the killer structure. Although it is a good (though of course incomplete) answer to why someone died that they ingested something with the killer structure, we know that were we to trace out the causal path from ingesting the substance with the killer structure to someone's death, the nature of other poisons and the deaths caused in the past by substances with the same structure will not appear. What will matter for each step in the chain will be local properties of what is happening inside the victim. But this does not mean that the killer structure did not actually cause or produce the death. It did, because it *is* one of those local properties.

Deflationism about broad content *versus* scepticism about narrow content

We have noted the strength of the traditional case for narrow content. We have also noted the clear exceptions – some beliefs have broad content. A major debate in this area is between the deflationists about broad content, those who seek to downplay the significance of beliefs with broad content and to understand them in terms of the allegedly more fundamental beliefs with narrow content, and those who urge that *all* belief content is broad – that, in effect, we should simply talk of belief itself as a broad state of subjects, and dismiss, for one reason or another, the traditional case for beliefs with narrow content. (Sometimes the dismissal of narrow content is qualified. What is dismissed is narrow *truth-conditional* content. It is allowed that there is narrow non-truth-conditional content. We argued earlier though that being truth-conditional is an essential property of content. A non-truth-conditional notion cannot play the distinctive role of content in explaining and predicting behaviour. In any case, 'content' in this work means 'truth-conditional content'.)

Deflationism about broad content

Deflationists about broad content latch on to the sunburn example. Sunburn is simply a burn with a certain causal history; we can think of sunburn conjunctively, as the conjunction of a burn and its history. Likewise, runs the deflationary approach to broad content, beliefs with broad content are beliefs with narrow content plus a certain history. Take the example of broad content afforded by the belief that London is important. We saw that it is not enough for having this belief that you believe that there is a city called 'London', that the city called 'London' has over six million inhabitants, . . . which is important. You need also to be acquainted with London in the sense of being at the end of an information chain that reaches from your head to London. Thus, say the deflationists, the belief that London is important is the conjunction of (a) believing that there is a city called 'London' . . . which is important – this belief is a narrow state of the believer, something any doppelgänger of the believer would share with the believer, with (b) having a certain causal-informational link to London, something that is not really a matter of belief at all. (a) is the inside-the-head part of the story, (b) the outside-the-head part of the story. Again, your belief that that filing cabinet contains the essential supplies is the conjunction of (a) some such belief as that there is in perceptual contact with you a cabinet of a grey colour with three drawers in a room with '2207' on its door, which contains the essential supplies – the narrow belief that remains unchanged when the cabinets are exchanged, with (b) a causal link between *that* cabinet and your head. Finally, the belief that rivers contain water is the conjunction of (a) the narrow belief that rivers contain the odourless, colourless liquid that fills the oceans and is called 'water' by experts (the watery stuff) with (b) the fact that it is water – that is, H_2O – that has the right causal link to the believer's head via the baptismal chain that played a role in settling the reference of 'water'.

Sometimes deflationism about broad content is expressed in a special notation. Special angle brackets are placed around the sentence that ascribes the broad content to S's belief in order to capture the narrow content. The deflationist story about broad content can be expressed in general form thus:

S believes that P (a broad belief) if and only if

   (a)   S believes that <P> (a narrow belief)

and

   (b)   S's head is connected in such and such a way to . . . (story about causal link to London, H_2O or whatever).

It is important to appreciate though that the narrow belief that <P> for some given broad content may vary from case to case. There is no single narrow belief that constitutes the in-the-head part of a given broad belief. As we might put it, according to deflationism, broad belief is multiply realized by narrow belief plus environmental embedding. Your narrow beliefs true of London which, combined with the right connection to London itself, make it true that you believe that London is important may be very different from Fred's narrow beliefs true of London which, combined with the right connection to London, make it true that Fred believes that London is important. For the descriptions you associate with London may be different from the descriptions Fred associates with London.

Indeed, as Saul Kripke shows in a famous example, *one and the same* person, Pierre, may associate very different descriptions with London, provided that Pierre is acquainted with London via two distinct information channels. Perhaps Pierre has visited the uglier parts of London and as a result believes that London is ugly. Perhaps he has also been told about London by French friends who have been to the prettier parts of London. They told him about it under the name 'Londres'. As a result, he believes, and says in so many words: 'Londres est jolie'. He says, that is, that he believes that London is pretty, for this is what the French words mean in English. Obviously, the narrow beliefs of his that constitute the (according to deflationism) in-the-head part of his broad belief that London is ugly will be very different from the narrow beliefs of his that constitute the in-the-head part of his

Pierre and London

belief that London is pretty. The first will be beliefs that Pierre expresses in words (let's suppose that he settles on English as the language to use) like 'There is a city called "London" that I visited in the past which is ugly'; the second will be beliefs that he expresses in words like 'There is a city called "Londres" that my friends know well which is pretty'. How does he end up with inconsistent beliefs – after all, he does not appear to have made any logical errors or to have been guilty of any failure to put things together aright, the usual sources of inconsistency in belief? The deflationist has a simple answer. The narrow beliefs that constitute Pierre's belief that London is pretty are distinct from and *not* inconsistent with the narrow beliefs that constitute his belief that London is ugly. He is, as we might put it, consistent in his head.

The arthritis A similar point can be made about an example due to Tyler
example Burge. Kripke's example involved one person having two inconsistent beliefs. In Burge's example one person has a single inconsistent belief. Arthritis is by definition a disease of the joints. It is conceptually impossible to have arthritis in one's thigh. Nevertheless, as Burge points out, there are cases where we might well describe someone as believing that she has arthritis in her thigh, without our having to suppose that she is conceptually confused. Perhaps Mary has had arthritis in her hands for some time, and has been worrying about where it will strike next. One day she wakes up with a pain in her thigh rather like the one she is only too familiar with in her hands. Ignorant of the fact that arthritis is by definition a disease of the joints alone, she says 'I have arthritis in my thigh'. Couldn't we properly say that she believes that she has arthritis in her thigh? This raises the puzzle as to how a simple mistake about word usage could mean that she has an inconsistent belief. Here the deflationist will insist that the in-the-head part of what Mary believes is to the effect that she now has the disease called 'arthritis' in her language community, the disease she has had for some years in her hands, in her thigh. This belief is false, and false because of a mistake about word usage, but it is not inconsistent. So the deflationist makes Mary consistent in her head. What, on this view, makes it correct for us to report her belief simply as the belief that she has arthritis in her thigh is that the disease that we call 'arthritis' is indeed the one she falsely believes she has in her thigh. Her thought and talk really is about arthritis, by virtue of the way it is causally linked with arthritis through her membership of a certain linguistic community, despite her mistake about the defining conditions for arthritis.

Essential to deflationism is the contention that there is such a thing as narrow belief content. The opposition to deflationism espouses scepticism about narrow content, arguing that all content is broad. You cannot, runs the argument, find the needed narrow beliefs to form the (a) clauses, the 'in-the-head' clauses, in the sketches just given. Of course, you can take '*S* believes that London is important' and write down '*S* believes that <London is important>', but the latter does not pick out any *belief* state of *S*'s; the narrow part of the belief that London is important is not a belief. *Scepticism about narrow content*

Why is there no such thing as narrow content? One line of argument urges that belief can be thought of as a special kind of putative information state, and we know that the information carried by physical structures is broad, for it is a function of how they are connected to their surroundings. To take an example from the previous chapter, a petrol gauge's pointing to the far right indicates that the tank is full only if it is wired up to the tank in the appropriate way. Wired up differently, or to some other device altogether, it will carry quite different information. That is, which states of the gauge co-vary systematically with which states of the tank depends on the way the gauge and the tank are connected one to the other, and this is very obviously a matter of how things are outside the gauge. Hence the information carried is broad, and, therefore, concludes the argument, by analogy so is belief content. *The argument from information*

This argument is not, it seems to us, of any real force. It is perfectly possible to think of the information carried by a physical structure as narrow. The state of the petrol gauge co-varies systematically with how things are around it quite generally, including the level of petrol in the tank *and* the nature of the connection between tank and gauge. That is to say, the gauge's pointing to the far right can be thought of as carrying information of the form: if the gauge is wired up in such-and-such a fashion, the tank is full; if the gauge is wired up in so-and-so a (different) fashion, the tank is empty; if the gauge is not wired up to the tank, the tank may be in any state; . . . . This way of thinking about information carried by gauges becomes salient when we are in situations where it is not clear what sort of connection, if any, the gauge has to what (we hope) it is giving us information about. It is a way of thinking about the information that is carried which is only too familiar to operators of workshops that make and repair gauges. On this second way of thinking, information carried is narrow. A physical structure *S* simply carries the information that things around it *Information as narrow* are in any one of the enormously many states that are nomologically compatible with S. We then extract more useful information by adding in collateral knowledge that rules out some of these enormously many states.

The argument from charity   Another line of argument appeals to the principle of charity that we discussed in the chapter 9. Interpreting the thoughts of another – that is, assigning them content – requires that we suppose that the subject's thoughts are largely true, or largely true by our lights, and that requires that we allow the subject's actual environment, or what it is by our lights, a major role in settling content. This is because the subject's thoughts will be largely about their environment, and so to get them mostly true we need to assign them content that pretty much fits with the nature of their environment. In particular, your virtual reality duplicates cannot be assigned thoughts with contents very like yours, for then their thoughts would be almost entirely false – both in fact and by your lights – and that would violate the principle of charity.

We saw, however, that the principle of charity has a powerful competitor: namely, the principle of humanity. According to the principle of humanity, we are guided by the maxim: assign the thoughts that we would have were we in the same position as the subject we are interpreting, rather than by a maxim of truth or truth by our own lights. And the traditional case for narrow content just is an argument that were you in the same position as your doppelgänger, virtual reality dupe, then you would have exactly the thoughts you in fact have. The traditional case for narrow content is fully consistent with the principle of humanity.

Twin Earth extended   A third line of argument claims that we can do a 'Twin Earth job' on language generally. The Twin Earth case shows that the conditions under which 'water' denotes something depend on how the actual world is outside speakers' heads. Had the actual world been one where XYZ fills the water role, 'water' would have denoted XYZ in all worlds; in fact, H_2O fills the water role, and this is why 'water' denotes H_2O in all worlds. In the same way, runs the extension of the Twin Earth argument, we can describe a Twin Earth case for just about any term you care to name; for any term we can show that the conditions under which it applies to something depend on how the actual world is outside speakers' heads. But this means that we cannot give the allegedly narrow truth-conditional content in language. If S has a belief with narrow content, we will not be able to capture it using a sentence of the form 'S believes that P'. Any 'P' we choose to give the content will have truth conditions that depend on how the actual world is outside speakers' heads, and so will fail to capture the narrow content. But this makes narrow content a strange and elusive beast – a content whereof we cannot speak!

We doubt the claim that a Twin Earth job can be done on language generally. We know of no convincing Twin Earth stories for 'square', 'flat', 'bald', 'happy' and the like. The force of the Twin Earth story for 'water' rests on the fact that the very same behaviour can, depending on context, be viewed as the production of 'water' as a word for H_2O or as a word for XYZ. But the behaviour distinctive of using the word 'square' for square things cannot be turned into behaviour distinctive of using the word for round things merely by changing the environmental context. For instance, 'tracing the shape in the air' is very different in the case of square and the case of round, as is moving in such a way as to assemble something made from square blocks as opposed to assembling something made from round blocks.

Context sensitivity and pseudo-Twin Earth arguments

We *do* know of what might be mistaken for Twin Earth stories if one forgot about the implicitly contextual nature of everyday descriptive language. What is flat for a sports field is not flat for a table top. What is accurate for a wrist watch is not accurate for an atomic clock. What is hot in England is not hot in Florida. For a great many descriptive terms, what counts as satisfying them depends explicitly or implicitly on context. This means that whenever you are asked of some object in some counterfactual possible world whether or not it is, say, flat, you need to distinguish two questions: Is it flat by the standards of *its* world? and Is it flat by the standards of the *actual* world? The answer to the second question will, of course, depend on how the actual world is, but the answer to the first question is independent of how the actual world is. If the fact that there are really two questions here is overlooked, and the answer to the second question is thought of as the answer to the simple, undifferentiated question 'Is it flat?', it is easy to slip into thinking that what counts as flat *simpliciter* depends on how the actual world is. It is easy, that is, to think that a Twin Earth job can be done on 'flat', and indeed on all of the very many terms that are context-sensitive.

Speaking more generally, it would be very strange if the content of all language depended on how the actual world is. We can, it seems, discuss among ourselves various hypotheses about which of the various possible worlds might be the actual world, and we do this using language. The history of science is the history of the canvassing and progressive discarding of various hypotheses about which of the various possibilities is actual, all conducted in language. When we do this, we trust that the device of language that we are using to identify the various possibilities to one another, identifies them independently of how things actually are. We need to know *what* we are talking about independently of whether it is actual or not. We need, and seem to have, a stationary target, not one that unavoidably shifts as we consider whether it is or is not in fact the case.

Argument from teleology   A fourth line of argument is via the teleological theory of content. According to most versions of this theory, what a subject believes depends on how things were millions of years ago, and you cannot get much broader than that. Not only is there is no content that supervenes on how the head is; there is no content that supervenes on how things are now, inside or outside the head. We gave our reasons for rejecting the teleological theory in the previous chapter. The swampman objection we considered there draws, of course, on the same kinds of considerations as those that underpin the traditional case for narrow content described earlier in this chapter.

Argument from the internal sentence theory of belief   A final line of argument combines the internal sentence view of belief with a causal theory for the contents of the representational atoms of mentalese. If the reference conditions of the words in the language of thought are in part a function of the actual causal links between the words and the subject's surroundings, then the truth conditions of any belief on the internal sentence view will depend essentially and centrally on causal connections between subjects and their surroundings; hence the content will be in large part a function of how things are outside the head. We gave our reasons for rejecting the causal theory for the contents of the representational atoms of mentalese in the previous chapter. And, of course, to the extent that you find the argument from virtual reality for narrow content convincing, you have an argument against an internal sentence theory of belief coupled with a causal theory of reference for the atoms of representation.

The last two arguments for scepticism about narrow content are the two that seem to us to have the most force. Hence, the choice between deflationism about broad content and scepticism about narrow content turns largely on how you feel about swampman, virtual reality and like examples, and more generally about the traditional case for narrow content as against the case for an internal sentence theory of belief combined with a teleological or causal theory of the contents of the atoms of mentalese. We find the traditional case for narrow content persuasive, and are thus deflationists about broad content. Many go exactly the other way. But remember that, however you go yourself, the choice is not that between dubious intuition and hard science. We are not backing intuitions about swampman, virtual reality dupes and the like against the solid science that supports causal or teleological accounts of atomic content. As we have said before, the causal and teleological accounts of content draw heavily on intuitions about possible cases.

Annotated Reading

Obviously, the items listed for the previous two chapters on the language of thought hypothesis and on content are relevant. In particular Colin McGinn, *Mental Content*, has a lot of highly relevant material. Two useful collections are P. Pettit and J. McDowell, eds, *Subject, Thought, and Context,* and Andrew Pessin, ed., *The Twin Earth Chronicles.* A demanding but important exchange is that between Tyler Burge, 'Individualism and Psychology', and Gabriel Segal, 'Seeing What Isn't There'. For an easier way into the issues see Kim Sterelny, *The Representational Theory of Mind,* chapter 5. The most detailed expositions of a deflationary approach to broad content are to be found in the writings of David Lewis; see, for instance, 'Reduction of Mind', and *On the Plurality of Worlds,* §1.4. The issues surrounding whether broad content is good for the explanation of behaviour are canvassed in Jerry Fodor, 'Methodological Solipsism Considered as a Research Strategy in Cognitive Psychology'; Stephen Stich, *From Folk Psychology to Cognitive Science*; Paul and Patricia Churchland, 'Stalking the Wild Epistemic Engine'; and Frank Jackson and Philip Pettit, 'Functionalism and Broad Content'. The Pierre example is in Saul Kripke, 'A Puzzle about Belief'. The arthritis example is in Tyler Burge, 'Individualism and the Mental'.

Part IV
Explaining Behaviour: Eliminativism and Realism

13

Eliminative Materialism

We now turn to a radical version of physicalism. Instead of upholding physicalism by identifying mental states in some way or other with physical features of the world – behavioural dispositions understood as supervening on the physical, purely physical states of the brain or whatever – it upholds it by denying that there are any mental states. Typically, the view is restricted to intentional states or propositional attitudes. It is that beliefs and desires, for instance, are not a problem for the physicalist world-view for the same reason that witches, fairies and phlogiston are not problems – science has shown that there are no such things. This view is usually known as eliminative materialism or **eliminativism**. Eliminativists are usually identity theorists of one kind or another about the more sensational side of psychology: they admit bodily sensations and perceptual experiences into their ontology by identifying them with physical brain states. We will in any case be concerned only with their views about the propositional attitudes, and will in fact conduct the discussion in terms of beliefs and desires.

The view is certainly radical – it says that no one ever believes or desires anything. And it is easy to mock eliminativists – they *believe* that there are no beliefs, and *desire* to tell us that there are no desires! We will see, however, that the theory deserves careful attention, and that it cannot be dismissed so easily.

The case for eliminativism

Although the view is radical, the argument for it is fairly straightforward. It turns on two main claims: one is about how we should conceive or think of the propositional attitudes (and beliefs and desires especially); the other concerns the history of science.

Propositional
attitudes as
posits

Eliminative materialists argue that we should think of beliefs and desires as the posits of a theory of the causes of behaviour, a theory which is part of common sense, as opposed to the kind of theories to be found in advanced scientific texts, but a theory nevertheless. When we say that Jones crossed the road because she desired an ice-cream, we are hypothesizing that Jones's behaviour has certain inner causes – the desire for an ice-cream together with (presumably) the belief that crossing the road is a good way to get one. More generally, when we predict and explain behaviour in terms of beliefs, desires, hopes and the various other propositional attitudes, we are predicting and explaining behaviour on the hypothesis that subjects have inside them as inner causes of behaviour these propositional attitudes. It is here that eliminativists differ from instrumentalists: eliminativists think that we should understand talk about beliefs and desires as talk about posited inner causes of behaviour, whereas instrumentalists hold that we should understand talk 'about' beliefs and desires purely instrumentally.

role of the
propositional
objects

On the eliminativists' view, the role of the propositional objects of the attitudes is to describe the way the posited inner causes work; we use them to express the laws of our theory about these inner causes. What does the desire for ice-cream do? It combines with beliefs about the behaviour that will lead to ice-cream so as to cause that behaviour. The beliefs and desires get their propositional objects by virtue of what they do, and the assignment of these propositional objects thereby serves to describe what they do. Or consider the fact that the belief that if P then Q, when combined with the belief that P, typically causes the belief that Q. Again, the assignment of propositional objects reflects what certain beliefs and desires do. This account of the role of propositional objects is, of course, essentially the same as the one we described in more detail when giving the map-system theory of belief in chapter 11.

Eliminativists are fond of calling our everyday talk of beliefs and desires a folk theory – **folk psychology** – to emphasize that it is a set of pre-scientific, and so in their view dubious, opinions held by the folk, and point out that we have many folk theories: folk physics which encapsulates common opinion about how bodies move (unsupported bodies fall, etc.); folk nutrition, which encapsulates common opinion about diet (if you don't eat, you die, etc.), and so on.

Eliminativists combine this view that the propositional attitudes are theoretical posits with some morals they draw from the observation that the history of science is full of examples of theories whose posits turned out not to exist: witches, demons, caloric fluid, phlogiston, the aether, abhorrence of vacua, and vital spirits are just some examples of entities, states and properties posited to explain and predict various phenomena, which turned out not to exist. For instance, as we noted in discussing the flight from dualism in the first chapter, growth turned out to be explained by cell division and not a vital spirit; the operation of pumps turned out to be explained by air pressure and not nature's abhorrence of a vacuum; combustion turned out to be explained by oxidation and not phlogiston; and epilepsy turned out to be explained by certain disturbances in the brain and not by demonic possession. Perhaps, suggest the eliminativists, beliefs and desires will go the way of vital spirits, phlogiston and the like. *The lesson of the history of science*

The suggestion is not that we have as of now replacements for the posits of folk psychology. We have here and now no alternative but to use beliefs and desires to explain and predict the behaviour of complex organisms like ourselves. The instrumentalists are right that we cannot do without the intentional stance, and eliminativists are careful to say that their view is put forward as one that may well be true, not as one that has been shown to be true. But they argue that folk psychology has a number of disturbing similarities to the famously discredited theories. It has been around for a very long time – the Homeric legends make it clear that the ancient Greeks used folk psychology to predict and explain behaviour. It has changed little since antiquity – perhaps its only significant innovation has been the incorporation of unconscious desires under the influence of Freud. There are a lot of things about behaviour it cannot handle – why we dream, why we sweat, why we shiver when cold, and so on. It notoriously delivers wrong predictions on occasion. And, finally, in neuroscience we have the glimmerings of an alternative way of explaining behaviour that promises to handle everything about behaviour and never to make a wrong prediction.

Folk psychology has, in short, all the signs of what Imre Lakatos called a degenerating research programme: it is an old theory that has hardly changed since it was first developed; there are many facts about its chosen field – namely, behaviour – that it cannot handle, either in the sense of having nothing to say or in the sense of having something to say that is wrong; it does not seem to have the resources needed to remedy these deficiencies; and there is a *Degenerating research programmes* new theory that promises to do all that it does, and more besides. Just as Aristotelian physics was replaced by Newtonian physics, which in turn was replaced by relativity theory and quantum theory, and just as Ptolemaic astronomy was replaced by Copernican and Keplerian astronomy, precisely because the older theories were exposed as degenerating research programmes by the newer ones, so the eliminativist urges that all the evidence points to folk psychology being replaced in the future by a neuroscience that provides us with new, superior categories for explaining and predicting behaviour.

The quick dismissal   We can now say why the quick dismissal ('They believe we have no beliefs and desires, and desire to tell us about this!') of eliminativism fails. Eliminativists must concede that until we have to hand the new categories that will, they hold, eventually come to replace belief and desire in the project of explaining behaviour, we perforce must talk in the old way. But, they can argue, when the category that comes to replace belief – say, belief* – is to hand, and the category that comes to replace desire – say, desire* – is to hand, they can say, without paradox, what their eliminativist view is: they believe* that there are no beliefs and desires, and desire* to tell us this.

The functionalist reply to eliminativism

One way to reply to the argument for eliminativism is to deny the premiss that beliefs and desires are posits of a causal-explanatory theory of behaviour. This way is open to behaviourists and instrumentalists, but not to us. We have already indicated our sympathy for some form or other of common-sense functionalism, and common-sense functionalism is of course another name (a less tendentious one!) for folk psychology. Our reply is that the posits of certain sorts of theories are peculiarly immune from elimination by new information, and that common-sense functionalism falls into this category. The crucial property of these theories is that their posits are characterized only in terms of functional properties that it is particularly obvious must be possessed. They say nothing, or nothing particularly controversial, about what relatively intrinsic properties the posits may have, and nothing open to serious doubt about the causal roles the posits play. The core idea is best given with a simple example, that of filial imprinting.

Chickens (and ducklings) are disposed to keep company with *Imprinting*
the first thing of a suitable sort that they see after hatching. Usually it is the mother hen that they see first, but sometimes it is a
small dog, the experimenter or whatever. They are said to imprint
on the first thing they see, and their behaviour is explained in
terms of their having imprinted on the mother hen, the experimenter or whatever.

Although we ascribe imprinting on the basis of observation of
behaviour in circumstances, what we ascribe, or are in a position
to ascribe, goes well beyond facts about behavioural patterns. We
know, for instance, that: the chicken's initial sighting lays down a
persisting trace inside the chicken, otherwise its 'following' behaviour would fade away quickly; that the nature of the internal trace
that is laid down depends on the nature of the thing first seen,
otherwise it would not be able to discriminate between the thing
first seen and things seen subsequently (we also know that had it
seen something different, it would have followed it instead); and
that the trace laid down is causally connected to the ways the legs
and the head of the chicken operate, otherwise the information
being carried by the trace inside the chicken would be irrelevant
to the observed operation of its head and legs in sustaining the
accompanying behaviour.

Now it would clearly be a mistake to argue as follows about
imprinting: 'The imprinting story is a little theory about the causation of the chicken's behaviour. The predictions it yields are
much better than guessing, but much worse than those that would
be yielded by a comprehensive neuroscientific story about the
chicken's internal workings combined with an account of the relations of these internal workings to its environment. Moreover,
imprinting makes some wrong predictions, and is silent about a
whole range of behaviours that chickens manifest. Accordingly,
we should regard it as a live possibility that the theory of imprinting will turn out to be radically mistaken, and so that its posit of
an internal state of imprinting on the thing it first sees may well
turn out not to exist.'

The situation with the theory of imprinting is, rather, that although in principle it could be overthrown by the discoveries of
neuroscience, we know perfectly well that it won't be. The behavioural evidence is too strong for that to be more than abstractly
possible. Neuroscience will reveal not that imprinting does not
occur, but how it occurs: how the traces are stored, how they
manage to be informationally sensitive to diverse initial sightings

and to the difference between initial sightings and subsequent ones, and how the traces link to the muscles that control the head and legs of the chicken.

Modesty in explanation

Our view is that, as it is for the theory of imprinting, so it is for the theory of belief and desire. The theory of belief and desire as captured in common-sense functionalism does involve substantial commitments about how things are inside subjects, but the commitments are like those that feature in the theory of imprinting, ones that are *very* plausible given what we know concerning how subjects behave in various circumstances. We can put the point by distinguishing modest from immodest explanatory theories. Both traffic in explanatory posits to explain observed phenomena – the behaviour of bodies of one kind or another, let us say. But the modest ones say little about the intrinsic nature of the posits. They focus on the roles the posits must play in order to explain the observed behaviour, but say little about how it is that these posits play these roles. The immodest ones speculate about how it is that the needed roles get to be occupied.

A simple illustration is the difference between explaining the way a refrigerator turns on and off in terms of its having a thermostat – a modest theory – and explaining the way it turns on and off in terms of its having a bimetal strip that bends as the temperature changes, so throwing a switch – an immodest theory. A short period of observation makes it virtually certain that a refrigerator has a thermostat, for it quickly becomes beyond belief that the mains power is failing and coming back on at just the right times to keep the temperature in the refrigerator inside the desired range. But it might well remain unresolved whether the device that turns the refrigerator on and off contains a bimetal strip or works electronically; internal investigation is needed to settle that question. Our claim is that common-sense functionalism is a modest theory, and that this is why it is so secure. It is logically possible that we are Blockheads or robots controlled from Mars, in which case we do not have beliefs and desires, but it is no more than merely logically possible.

Is common-sense functionalism modest?

Why is common-sense functionalism a modest theory? First, because it says almost nothing about intrinsic nature, and, second, because the core of the common-sense, or folk, theory of belief and desire is the role of belief and desire in the prediction and explanation of behaviour in circumstances over time. In sum, common-sense functionalism has the two hallmarks of a modest theory: silence about the intrinsic nature of its posits, and the limitation of the functional and causal roles ascribed to its posits to those needed to explain behaviour.

The claim that common-sense functionalism is a modest theory can be challenged. Indeed, a good deal of recent discussion has been directed to the question of whether there are central folk convictions about the operation of the mind, convictions that are central enough to demand inclusion in the clauses definitive of common-sense functionalism, that involve controversial assumptions about how we are inside. Thus, it has been pointed out that it is a tenet of common-sense theory that in a subject who believes both that P and that Q, some bit of behaviour may be explained by one belief, not the other, and it has been inferred from this that common sense functionalism is committed to the view that the belief that P and the belief that Q are distinct, relatively localized states – maybe relations to different internal sentences. We discussed this question in chapter 11, and argued that the explanatory distinctness of the belief that P from the belief that Q does not imply their distinctness *qua* internal states. Again, the earlier discussion of content affords a reply to the following argument:

Explanation by discrete beliefs

1 It is part of common sense that beliefs are truth-evaluable.
2 The only way beliefs could be truth-evaluable is if they are relations to semantically evaluable internal sentences.
But,
3 it is a matter ultimately for neuroscience, and in any case a matter open to doubt, whether or not there is a language of thought.

The discussion of content showed us how to resist (2), though, of course, language of thought theorists will insist that there is no need to bother, since they regard the empirical evidence for the language of thought theory as overwhelming.

We think that the argument for the immodesty of functionalism sometimes equivocates between two possibilities which it is important to distinguish.

We can divide the implicit and explicit common-sense platitudes about the mind into two groups. One group is neutral about the detail of what goes on inside the brain except to the extent revealed by the behavioural regularities. The other group is concerned with the nature of the internal processes themselves that underlie our predictive success in using folk psychology. The Blockhead example in chapter 7 told us that, at the very least, common

Immodesty and what goes on inside

sense insists that there are ways a being's brain might be which would disqualify it from having a mind.

How might functionalism be immodest? That is, how might functionalism be committed to claims about how the brain works which are vulnerable to empirical refutation?

One possibility is that the immodesty might be in that second group of the platitudes. Perhaps the folk are more or less directly committed to the language of thought or some other empirical hypothesis that is a great deal more risky than the assumption that we are not Blockheads or robots controlled from Mars. We simply don't think this is so: though if it were, eliminativism would be a worry.

The other possibility is that the apparently contentious empirical hypothesis is entailed by the first group of platitudes. The principles that govern our predictive success might, on reflection, entail a more detailed story about internal architecture than we might have expected. So if the folk roles are occupied, then it would follow that the brain states that realize them have a certain detailed architecture. But this view is not hostage to empirical fortune, for we know that the folk roles – those given by the first groups of platitudes – *are* occupied. This much follows from our predictive success using folk psychology. If this entails some detailed story about the brain, then the moral would have to be that we can know more about the brain than we might have thought by observing behaviour.

So neither of these possibilities is one which will lead to eliminativism. The second explains how common-sense functionalism could be (though we think it is not) committed to a view about the details of brain architecture, though not one that is empirically risky. The first gives an empirically risky doctrine, but one to which functionalism would need to be committed to in a transparent way, which it clearly isn't.

A successful argument for eliminativism along these lines would have to mix illicitly aspects of both: a story about how the immodest commitments are to be found in functionalism, given that they cannot be read off from the platitudes, and a story about how the immodest commitments are empirically risky. We think that some of the plausibility of eliminativism may come from equivocation between the two possibilities we have described. You may be able to tell a consistent story about how immodest commitments are to be found in functionalism, and you may be able to tell a story about empirically risky hypotheses about the brain, but you cannot combine them in the required way.

The remainder of this chapter will be concerned with three questions: the eliminativists' response to our 'reply from functionalism' to their position; how the *empirical* functionalist can draw on the common-sense functionalist's response to eliminativism; and, finally, the question of whether psychological kinds have to be natural kinds in order to be kosher parts of what there is.

Does functionalism make it too easy to save folk psychology?

Eliminativists see the reply from functionalism as part of a general attitude that seeks to resist scientific eliminations. It is, so to speak, *too good* a reply. Paul Churchland, for instance, sees 'the functionalist stratagem' as potentially 'reactionary, obfuscatory, retrograde, and wrong'. His objection is that functionalism can always be invoked to save old theories from more than deserved elimination by giving a functionalist account of the posits of the old theory. He argues, for example, that a 'cracking good defence of the phlogiston theory of combustion can . . . be constructed along [functionalist] lines' by construing 'being highly phlogisticated and being dephlogisticated as functional states defined by certain syndromes of causal dispositions' ('Eliminative Materialism and the Propositional Attitudes', §4).

Is functionalism too cheap a way of avoiding elimination?

To evaluate this objection, we need a minimum of history before us. Phlogiston was hypothesized to explain certain facts about combustion. The reason some substances were more combustible than others was said to be that they contained more phlogiston, were more phlogisticated; and the reason why burning something reduced its mass and volume was that phlogiston was given off during combustion. We now know that combustion is essentially a matter of oxidation, and that it leads to an increase in mass due to the taking in of oxygen, the appearance to the contrary being due to fact that combustion often causes a partial dispersal of the burnt material.

How could functionalism about phlogiston save it from elimination? Phlogiston was a functionally understood notion in the phlogiston theory: it was specified roughly as the X such that both the more of it there is in something, other things being equal, the more combustible that thing is, and it is given off during combustion. However, this functional account of phlogiston did *not* save phlogiston from elimination when it turned out that combustion is not a process in which something is given off, but rather one in which something, oxygen, is taken into chemical combination. Far

Functionalism and phlogiston

from trivializing the debate by making phlogiston beyond elimination, it makes it transparent why the development of the oxidation theory showed that there is no phlogiston: namely, by showing that nothing plays the hypothesized 'given off' role.

Avoiding elimination by redefinition

The only way you could save phlogiston from elimination by the oxidation theory would be by *redefining* phlogiston to mean, say, whatever is crucial to combustion. On this redefinition, what happened when the oxidation theory came along should be described as the discovery that phlogiston is oxygen. But this is not a point against functionalism but a point against radical redefinition. You can always save the hypothesis that K exists by suitable redefinition of what is to count as K (if in doubt, say that K is raspberry jam – we know that exists), but this is a phoney 'saving', of course. Really what is happening is a changing of the subject. You do not save what you *did* mean by K, only what you *now* mean by K.

What we have here is an illustration of the trivializing evils of radical redefinition, not of functionalism. A certain amount of moderate redefinition is fine; indeed, it is often more a matter of making precise what was vague before, or of identifying more precisely the really important property or properties. Take as examples the terms 'atom' and 'solid'. Has science shown that there are no atoms and that nothing is solid? Historically, atoms were taken to be absolutely indivisible, and solids to be pure matter with no empty space. But the atom has been split, and solids are gappy. So arguably nothing satisfies definitions based on these understandings; but plenty of things come quite close enough to count. The common-sense functionalist holds that plenty of things come quite close enough to count as believers and desirers, because we can be confident that plenty of things satisfy the really central clauses of common-sense functionalism.

Empirical functionalism: how to have strong internal constraints without inviting scepticism

The crucial difference between common-sense functionalism and empirical functionalism is, as we noted earlier in chapter 5, that empirical functionalists believe that beliefs and desires have essences that are distinct from their common-sense functional roles. As we saw, the most plausible versions of empirical functionalism see the common-sense, or folk, roles as serving to pick out beliefs and desires by reference fixing on the internal functional roles that make something a belief or desire; but once we have discovered the states that fill these roles, we will have discovered the *essences* of beliefs and desires. The key idea is that empirical research on the brain will reveal what beliefs and desires really are by revealing the internal functional organization or internal flow chart that an organism *must* have in order to have beliefs and desires (and other mental states, but our interest here is restricted to belief and desire). What is revealed is a necessary *a posteriori* fact about belief and desire.

Empirical functionalism thus places strong internal constraints on being a creature with beliefs and desires. Creatures must be internally a *lot* like the exemplars of believers and desirers – us – to count as believers and desirers. Such a position opens the door to a limited extent to eliminativism. Martians that interact with the environment much as we do, that are perhaps *very* like us externally, that are normal inside in the sense of not being Blockheads or being under external control and so on, may nevertheless fail to be believers and desirers through differing in how they process the information internally (even if they do so more effectively than we do; this was one reason we resisted empirical functionalism). Eliminativism would then be true for them. Nevertheless, the door would not be opened to scepticism about beliefs and desires across the board. For, according to empirical functionalism, something is only an internal necessary condition for the existence of beliefs and desires *if in fact we already meet the condition*. Because *we* determine the essential nature of belief and desire, we at least are believers and desirers.

Eliminativism for Martians

Natural kinds and scientific reductions

The eliminativist points out that we have every reason to think that completed neuroscience can explain everything about behaviour that folk psychology can, and more besides. How then can we be confident that the posits of folk psychology, beliefs and desires, really exist? The instrumental value of positing them is not in question, but that is consistent with their being mere convenient fictions for the prediction of behaviour, as in fictionalism. Our reply was to point to the ontological security of the posits of modest theories and to argue that folk psychology (and thus common-sense functionalism) is a modest theory in the relevant sense. A very different, much discussed, but it seems to us misguided, approach to the challenge draws its inspiration from certain well-known **reductions in science**. We will start by giving the briefest of descriptions of two cases of such reductions.

Two famous reductions

The first is the reduction of genetics to molecular biology. Genes were postulated to explain the patterns of inheritance articulated by Mendel (and, of course, also the patterns known to the folk, for example, that tall parents tend to have tall children). The reduction of genetics to molecular biology occurred when it was established that these inheritance patterns could be explained in terms of strings of DNA. This, however, did not show that genes were mere convenient fictions. It showed that genes *were* strings of DNA, by showing that strings of DNA played the causal-functional roles definitive of genes.

Likewise, the thermodynamic theory of gases was reduced to the kinetic theory of gases by showing that the known laws relating the temperature, pressure and volume of a gas could be derived on the assumption that gases were collections of widely separated, comparatively small, freely moving particles (molecules) whose temperature was a function of their molecular kinetic energy, and whose pressure was a function of their molecular impacts. What was discovered, that is, was that everything that could be explained in terms of temperature and pressure could be explained in terms of molecular kinetic energy and molecular impacts, respectively. This, though, did not show that temperature and pressure were mere convenient fictions; it showed rather what they *were*, namely, certain molecular motion properties, by virtue of showing that these molecular motion properties played the roles definitive of temperature and pressure.

Smooth reductions

These two examples illustrate the point that the explanatory success of a new theory – molecular biology and the kinetic theory of gases, say – may leave the posits of an older theory – Mendelian genetics and the thermodynamic theory of gases, say – intact by virtue of identifying the posits of the older theory in terms of the new theory. Thus, the anticipated explanatory success of complete neuroscience is consistent with realism about beliefs and desires. The two examples have led, however, to what seems to us to be an important misreading of what they teach us. An accidental feature of the two examples, as far as the issue of elimination of the old by the new is concerned, has been mistaken for an essential one.

A feature of both the reduction of the thermodynamic theory of gases to the kinetic theory and of Mendelian genetics to molecular biology is that there are *relatively* simple linkages between the explanatory categories of the new theory and those of the old. There are relatively simple biconditionals with forms like these: gas X is at such-and-such a temperature if and only if X has so-and-so a mean molecular kinetic energy; plant Y has such-and-such a genetic resistance to sooty mould if and only if its DNA contains a strand of so-and-so a kind at a certain locus; and so on. We had, it seemed, relatively simple **bridge laws**, as they are often called, connecting the terms of the reduced theory with those of the reducing theory; accordingly, we have what is called a smooth reduction from the reduced theory to the reducing one. (In fact, as we will mention later, the smoothness in the case of genes was somewhat overestimated, perhaps because of a prevailing belief that there is no reduction without smooth reduction.)

The misreading is to suppose that this feature of the two examples is essential to their being new theories that leave the posits of old theories intact: to their being reductions that are not also eliminations.

Smoothness and elimination

The point is important because if being a smooth reduction were essential to being a non-eliminative reduction, eliminativism about the propositional attitudes would be a live possibility; for it may turn out that the explanatory categories of completed neuroscience fail to match at all smoothly the folk categories of belief and desire. Take the example of imprinting again. It is likely that the neurological explanation of imprinting is much the same in ducklings and chickens, that there is some common structure in both that carries the trace induced by sighting the mother hen or duck, or the experimenter, or the small dog or whatever. But it is far from certain. It might even turn out that the way the trick is turned differs from one species of duck to another, or indeed from one duck of the same species to another, depending on, say, happenings during hatching (though this is harder to believe). In such cases there would be no smooth reduction of imprinting theory to neuroscience, no reasonably simple and encompassing biconditionals of the form: a bird has imprinted on A_i if and only if it is in neurological state N_i. Rather, there would be only messy, highly restricted biconditionals, which vary from one bird species to another, or even from one bird of a given species to another.

But this would not mean that we had discovered that imprinting did not occur. The hypothesized fact that the trick is turned differently in different birds does not imply that it is not turned at all! For each bird that imprints on its mother, there will be, we can be sure, a neurological state which is *its* so imprinting and which explains the behaviour that manifests the imprinting. Imprinting will be reducible to neurophysiology. The fact that we have to give a significantly different story for, say, ducklings and chickens does not alter this fact. Hence, the example of imprinting tells us that a reduction can fail to be smooth without thereby eliminating the posits of the reduced theory.

Failures of smooth reduction without elimination

Moreover, the relationship between genes and DNA is far more complex than is sometimes realized. There are at least four different accounts of what genes might be in molecular terms, and the version which is closest to the common-sense idea of a gene – Dawkins's optimon or Mayr's selecton – allows reduction, but certainly not smooth reduction. There are no straightforward biconditionals linking gene talk and molecular talk, but this does not mean that genes should be eliminated, only that their connection with molecular structure is not as simple as might have been wished. Or consider the relatively smooth reduction of thermodynamics to the kinetic theory. We know that the kinetic theory can in principle be further reduced to the laws of individual molecular motion. Gases are collections of widely spaced, very loosely bound molecules. Hence any particular instance of gas behaviour that can be explained in terms of the averaged-out kinetic energy of its molecules can in principle be fully explained in terms of the motions, locations, velocities and masses of its individual molecules. But there are no interesting biconditionals linking mean molecular properties with individual molecular properties; there is nothing worth saying of the form: a volume of gas has a mean molecular kinetic energy of so-and-so if and only if an individual gas molecule has such-and-such a position, mass and velocity. But obviously the failure of smooth reduction from the kinetic theory to the individualistic molecular theory does not imply scepticism about mean molecular kinetic energy or about its explanatory value.

Our final example is meteorology. We predict and explain the weather with a fair bit of success (whatever the general public may think of their local met service), in terms of tornadoes, cool changes, wind patterns, thermal inversions and the like. Yet there is not the slightest prospect of a smoothly reductive account of the kinds of meteorology to the kinds of some basic, preferred science. Nevertheless, tornadoes, cool changes and thermal inversions are real parts of our world – they are not mere fictions of a convenient scheme of prediction.

There is a different way of arriving at the view that to avoid eliminativism, psychological kinds must be shown to be natural kinds, to be kinds that match smoothly and so are identifiable with the kinds of some established explanatory science: the view that, contrary to our argument, it is not enough that we have states which play common-sense functional roles; they must in addition be natural kinds. The crude version starts from the premiss that only natural kinds exist: but terminal illnesses, famines, vitamins, typhoons and ways of getting to Paris exist but are not natural kinds on the usual understanding. There is, for instance, nothing interesting in common between vitamins other than their causal role with respect to health; hence explanations of ill health in terms of lack of vitamins cannot be smoothly reduced to explanations in terms of body chemistry.

Psychological kinds, natural kinds and serious science

The interesting position grants that plenty of things exist which do not form natural kinds, but insists that the kinds worth incorporating into serious science, including psychology, must be natural kinds. On this view it may be granted that beliefs and desires as common-sense functionalism understands them exist, but argued that unless they are natural kinds, they have no place in serious psychology. An example helps make the idea clear. Since Greek times we have grouped together stars in the night sky, and given these groups names: the Big Dipper, the Southern Cross, the Bear, Orion and so on. It was once thought that these constellations had some special explanatory significance. We now know that although they certainly exist, they have no significance for astronomy or science in general. According to the position under discussion, beliefs and desires might be like constellations. We can, that is, distinguish two kinds of eliminativism: the first sees beliefs and desires as analogous to phlogiston, the second as analogous to the Big Dipper or Orion.

The demand that psychology traffic only in natural kinds

However, the trouble with the Big Dipper and Orion is that they do not play any significant functional roles that make them useful in predicting or explaining the movements of the planets and the stars. *If* by a natural kind is meant simply a kind that plays an important role in a predictive and explanatory science, then many functional kinds – vitamins, thunderstorms and terminal illnesses – will count as natural kinds. And so will beliefs and desires, because the functional roles they play are important for predicting and explaining behaviour. But constellations won't count. Of course, if, as is usual, 'natural kind' is taken to mean something more demanding: intrinsic similarity, common aetiology or

Why beliefs and desires are better than constellations

whatever, beliefs and desires may not count. But then the view that only natural kinds are a proper part of science is mistaken. The science of nutrition is heavily involved in highly relational and functional properties – witness our earlier example of being a vitamin. Likewise, the concept of a terminal illness is important in medicine, and that is essentially a functional classification – the important commonality between strokes, cancer and heart disease is their end result. Functional nature of the right kind is enough for mattering and for being part of serious science: it is not enough, perhaps, for being part of fundamental physics, but who said that beliefs and desires were part of fundamental physics?

Annotated Reading

Early versions of eliminativism are W. V. Quine, 'On Mental Entities', and Richard Rorty, 'Mind–Body Identity, Privacy and Categories'. Recent discussions of eliminativism have been driven largely by Paul Churchland, 'Eliminative Materialism and the Propositional Attitudes'. A good idea of the various possible positions can be gleaned from *Mind and Language*, vol. 8, no. 2, which is devoted to eliminativism. One place to consult for the idea of a degenerating research programme is Imre Lakatos and Elie Zhahar, 'Why Copernicus's Programme Superseded Ptolemy's'.

14

Psychological Explanation and Common-sense Functionalism

At a number of places in this book we have explored the adequacy of common-sense functionalism as an account of the mind. Although our primary concern has been to provide a reasonably comprehensive discussion of the views of the mind that dominate the current debate, we have not hesitated to indicate our predilection for common-sense functionalism. We hope this book will win some converts to this view of the mind, or at least to this view of the intentional aspects of the mind if qualia and consciousness belong in the 'too hard' basket. We now turn to a final worry for common-sense functionalism. It is a realist theory of the mind, according to which psychological states exist, are internal, and serve to give causal explanations of behaviour. The worry is whether this strongly realist attitude to psychological explanation is compatible with what we earlier called the common-sense theory's *modesty*: the fact that common-sense functionalism attributes these internal states to a being more or less without recourse to empirical investigations as to the internal causal mechanisms of the mind. We can approach the issue by reminding ourselves of how instrumentalists understand psychological explanation.

If the ascription of psychological states were nothing more than the ascription of patterns in behaviour in circumstances, if some form of instrumentalism about the mind were true, then the explanations we offer of behaviour in circumstances in terms of psychological states would be explanations in name only. We would be describing not the causes of the behaviour, but rather the behaviour itself. But at least the rationale for psychological (pseudo-) explanation would be transparent on the instrumentalist proposal. We predict the future by noting patterns in the past and projecting them. Often the patterns in the behaviour of something as complex as a human being are not at all obvious. But, as detailed in

Instrumentalism and explanation

chapter 9, we appeal to the intentional stance to make the patterns salient. We capture the patterns in the behaviour of a human being by describing them in terms of psychology. We make sense of the various movements of a golfer on a golf course in terms of her beliefs about how to get a small ball to drop into eighteen different holes and her desire that it do so after the smallest possible number of contacts between the ball and one of fourteen clubs in her bag. Without the regimenting effect of the hypothesized beliefs and desires, we would not see the patterns that are there in her behaviour, and consequently, would not be able to predict her future behaviour. The rationale for the ascription of psychological states is thus transparent, given instrumentalism. It makes transparent behavioural patterns that would otherwise be opaque, and so aids in predicting behaviour.

Three questions for common-sense functionalism

If, on the other hand, psychological explanations are genuine causal explanations in terms of intentional states, they must do more than just make patterns salient. Thus the common-sense functionalist who holds that psychological explanations are genuinely empirical, causal explanations of behaviour owes us an answer as to the rationale and interest of psychological explanation. In particular, the common-sense functionalist owes us an answer to the three questions we discuss below.

The triviality question   First, according to common-sense functionalism itself (or indeed any genuinely functionalist doctrine), to ascribe a psychological property to someone is to ascribe a highly relational, causal-functional nature to an internal state in them, and one, moreover, that is in part defined by what it causes. But if it is in part *defined* by what it causes, how can it *explain* in any significant sense what it causes?

The connection question   Second, we know that a complete explanation of each and everything a person does is in principle giveable in terms of the neurophysiological nature of what goes on inside them, combined with physical information about how this interacts with their surroundings. We noted this in discussing the causal problem for dualism. By contrast, the explanations afforded by psychology are limited and partial. What purpose, then, do the psychological explanations serve? And how are the explanations offered by psychology related to the, in principle, complete ones offered by neuroscience?

The puzzle is not how neurophysiological states and psychological states can both cause behaviour. As 'they' are one and the same, nothing is easier. The puzzle is to understand the relationship or connection between the two ways of describing one and the same set of states in such a manner that both ways of describing the same set of states can be seen as causal-explanatory, especially in light of the fact that only one way is in principle complete.

Finally, there is the intuition that psychological properties are causally efficacious. My belief's being that there is a tiger nearby, its having that content, is in part what makes my legs move. But where in the complex sequence of neurophysiological states that runs from the sensory input triggered by the light rays from the tiger to the contracting of the muscles that move my body away from the tiger does the content property figure? Each and every transition from one neurological state to the next will be governed by the relatively intrinsic, neurological features of the various states, not by the highly relational features that figure in the most plausible approaches to content. As it is sometimes put, the mind is a syntactic (neurophysiological) engine, so how can semantic (content) properties be doing any driving? This is, of course, much the same problem as one we discussed in chapter 12.

The causal question

The triviality question

It is often suggested that to explain the breaking of a glass on dropping in terms of its fragility is worthless – that is what it is to be fragile, and what we want from an explanation is empirical information about how something came about, not a reminder about a definition. In *Le Maladre Imaginaire*, Molière famously mocks explanations of sleeping draughts that are given in terms of a *virtus dormitiva* – which is just Latin for 'power to cause sleep'. The same question can be raised about the role of explanation in terms of psychological states. If such states are defined by a functional role specified in part in terms of how they mediate between certain inputs and certain outputs, how can we explain the outputs consequent on the inputs in terms of them?

The answer to this challenge comes in two parts. First, it is not trivial to explain a glass's breaking in terms of its being fragile; and secondly, there is an important difference between simple dispositions like fragility and dormitive power, on the one hand, and the functional roles definitive of psychological states, on the other.

How dispositions explain

There is something about fragile things that explains their breaking on being dropped. Perhaps it is the nature of the bonding between the molecules; perhaps it is the kind of lattice structure in which the molecules are embedded; perhaps it is the thinness of the material; perhaps it is some combination of these factors; or perhaps the answer varies from case to case. This (possibly variable) nature is called the 'categorical' basis of the disposition. It is a live issue in metaphysics, sometimes described as the issue between realism and phenomenalism about dispositions, whether or not it is some sort of necessary or conceptual truth that for every disposition there is a categorical basis. But it is close to common ground that dispositions like fragility, elasticity and dormitive virtue have categorical bases, be this a matter of necessity or not (though there is debate about how apt the term 'categorical' is). Hence, to explain the breaking of a glass in terms of its fragility is not a trivial exercise. It is to say that the nature of the glass was an important factor in the breaking, that something about the glass that differentiates it from the many things that are not fragile was important. Likewise, if it is dormitive virtue that explains a substance sending you to sleep, what is important is something about the substance itself and accordingly we would expect that it will send you to sleep next time you take it, that it will probably send Jones to sleep, that any other sample enough like it in intrinsic nature will be equally effective, and so on and so forth.

Explanations by multi-track dispositions
Secondly, dispositions like fragility are single-track in the following sense. There is a more or less homogeneous class of inputs and outputs. The relevant inputs are droppings and like events that are associated with impact on the object, and the relevant outputs are disintegrations to a greater or lesser extent. That is why the key idea can be given with a single conditional like 'x is fragile iff x has a nature responsible for it being such that on being dropped, it will break'. By contrast, the functional roles definitive of distinct psychological states can share particular inputs and outputs. There is substantial overlap in the definitive inputs and outputs for distinct psychological states. The desire for nourishment is different from the desire for gustatory pleasure, but often they mediate between exactly the same inputs and outputs. Both result in the sight of Brie being followed by the consumption of Brie. Again, believing that tigers are dangerous while desiring to die is a very different combination of psychological states from believing that tigers are nice while desiring to be near what is nice, and yet both combinations may lead to the same behaviour on

seeing a tiger. This means that a psychological explanation of a given piece of behaviour in a given circumstance tells us not only that the explanation of the behaviour lies in part in the nature of the person – the kind of information we get from an explanation of breaking in terms of fragility – but in addition tells us important information about the *other* inputs and outputs that the state typically mediates between. To illustrate: suppose you want to save the life of the person whose behaviour is explained by the belief that tigers are nice together with the desire to be near what is nice. You will tell him that tigers are not nice. By contrast, suppose you want to save the life of the person whose behaviour is explained by the belief that tigers are dangerous together with the desire to die. You will remind him of all that there is to live for. Your very different responses in the two cases are explained by the very different information about inputs and outputs you get from the two different psychological explanations.

The relationship question: partial and complete explanations

The relation between the partial, exception-filled explanations of behaviour afforded by psychology and the, in principle, complete explanations of behaviour afforded by brain science plus physical information about the brain's interconnections to the subject's environment is a special case of a general phenomenon: the relation between limited explanations and one or another underlying complete explanation.

Suppose an electron is acted on by a force of value ten acting due north, and a force of value seven acting due south, and no other forces. Then we can predict and explain the subsequent motion of the particle in some detail. But in order to predict and explain the electron moving northwards, it would be enough to know that the force acting due north is greater than that acting due south. Part of the story about the situation is enough for the more limited purpose. Although a detailed story about how things are at one time may be needed to explain in detail how things are at a later time, a partial story about the earlier time is nevertheless enough to explain part of the story about the later time. Or suppose that by some incredible piece of scientific measurement you know the exact position and velocity of each and every molecule of a gas in a glass container, and in consequence can predict and explain the exact way in which the container breaks when the gas

Two simple examples

is heated. (This would require a theoretical breakthrough, since we would need to solve the n-body problem.) You identify the exact molecules whose increase in velocity triggers the breaking, identify exactly where and when they hit, and as a result can give a highly detailed story about the breaking of the glass – where it starts, how rapidly each fragment disintegrates, the precise molecules responsible, and so on. But if all you want is to explain the container breaking – somehow or other, at some more or less closely delineated time or other, as a result of some molecules or other hitting the sides of the container – it is enough to appeal to the increase in temperature of the gas. That information is only a fragment of what there is to say about how the container came to fracture, for it concerns only the increase in the average kinetic energy, not the detailed changes in energy of the crucial molecules; but it is enough to explain the fact of fracture, though not the details of fracture.

The general picture   In both cases we have the following picture. There is a rich, detailed story, S, about how things are at one time that causally explains how things are, L, in some detail at a later time. We have also something we can think of as part of the story S tells about how things are, something that follows from S, or follows from S given accepted background facts, but which says much less than S. It does not explain L but does explain something that follows from L, or follows from L given accepted background facts, something we can think of as part of the story L tells about how things are. S explains L; and a certain part of S, S^-, explains a certain part of L, L^-, in the sense that had S^- not obtained, L^- would not have obtained (roughly, we set aside problems of pre-emption and overdetermination). Had the force north not been greater than the force south, the electron would not have moved north. Had the temperature not increased, the container would not have fractured. Pictorially, the situation is as shown:

S^- causally explains L^- (partial story)

S causally explains L (detailed story)

It is important that the dots do *not* represent causal connections. Otherwise the diagram would represent S^- and L^- as epiphenomena, with the real causal work being done by S and L. S neither causally explains nor is causally explained by S^-, for the latter is part of the former; likewise, L^- is part of L. To put the matter in terms of one of our illustrations, the force of value ten due north, together with the force of value seven due south, does not cause the resultant force due north – there is no energy transfer, and no time lag (so if the case were causal, we would have a quick refutation of the special theory of relativity). Rather, the former state of affairs includes in some sense or other the latter.

The relationship between the explanation of behaviour offered by psychology and the explanation of behaviour offered by neuroscience is essentially another example of this kind of situation. Consider the full neuroscience story about Jones supplemented by the relevant environmental information. It will explain Jones's behaviour in full detail. This neuroscience story will automatically include the full story about the interconnections between her internal states, between them and peripheral stimulations and motor responses, and between these stimuli and responses and the environment. Hence it will include the full story about the functional roles occupied by those states. But that is to include the full story about Jones's psychology on the functionalist picture. (If you were unconvinced by our objections to including selectional facts in the psychological story, you could add here the story about how our neurophysiological nature evolved.) Facts about Jones's psychology are, that is, part of the full neuroscience story about her – they are included in the full neuroscience story about her. Equally, the facts about behaviour explained by psychology are part of the full story about her behaviour. The situation can be diagrammed as in figure 7. *Application to psychological explanation*

On this picture of the relationship between psychological and neuroscientific explanations of human (and animal) behaviour, it is clear why it is a mistake to worry about whether we have a case of explanatory *exclusion*. We noted in our discussion of the problems for dualism in chapter 1 that distinct explanations of a given phenomenon are typically in competition. The air pressure explanation of the operation of pumps displaced the abhorrence of a vacuum explanation. But the explanation of behaviour offered (in principle) by neuroscience is not by appeal to something distinct from what is appealed to in the explanation offered by psychology. The latter appeals to something which is part of what is appealed to in the former.

The picture also makes it clear how psychological explanations can make a distinctive contribution to the explanation of behaviour. One advantage of such explanations, of course, is that they *The value of psychological explanations*

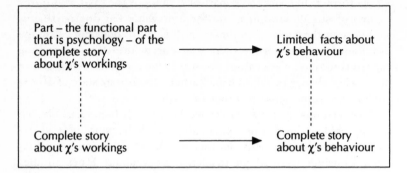

Figure 7 Complete and partial explanations of behaviour. The '→' stands for the kind of counterfactual and temporal relations that make it true that we have a causal explanation; the dots stand for inclusion, not causation.

are actually available. We do not as of now know anything like enough of the neuroscience to explain even elementary facts about how people get to be near glasses of beer. We can say very general things, such as that the sight of beer lays down some sort of trace in the brain that somehow guides the movements of bodies towards the beer, but we cannot give the fine detail. But psychological explanations make a contribution over and above that which results from the fact that they traffic in what we know, as opposed to what we might come to know a long way down the track. The simplest way to see the nature of the contribution is to note a feature of our forces example. There is a certain kind of loss of explanatory information when you go from the story in terms of the precise nature of the forces to the story in terms of the force to the north being the greater.

The detailed story says that the movement north is explained by a force of ten due north and a force of seven due south, but it does not say that provided the force to the north is greater, the electron will move north. It does not say that the particular values of the two forces do not matter provided the one to the north is the greater. Of course, we can say in detailed terms things like 'The explanation of the movement to the north is that the force north takes the value ten and the force to the south takes the value seven, and had the respective values been eleven and five, or seventy and sixty, or two and one, or . . . , the electron still would have moved north'. But this conveys the information that what matters is the fact that the force north is the greater *only if* it is understood that the right way of going on, indicated by the dots, is precisely that the force to the north is the *greater*. This piece of explanatory information requires either an explicit or implicit understanding of what was said in the less detailed explanation.

The same is true of the relation between the explanations of behaviour offered by psychology and those offered by neuroscience. The full neuroscience story will explain why a certain body moved exactly as it did – at such-and-such a time, at such-and-such a rate, with such-and-such a trajectory, and so on – towards a certain precisely located glass of beer. Or, to take a famous example of Dennett's, the neuroscience story will explain why after a phone call a certain body moved in such a way that it travelled from one location via a wine shop to a location where there is food on a table and a number of other bodies – the process we normally describe as accepting and acting on an invitation to dinner and picking up a bottle of wine on the way.

Dennett suggests that the neuroscientist will have to view this result as a fantastic fluke. The probabilities of the various neurological interactions running just the way they did and the various external stimuli having just the effect they did will be *fantastically* small. But this is not quite right. The *full* neuroscience story will include all sorts of counterfactual information, and when that is taken into account, the appearance of fluke will disappear. True, it will come out as a fantastic fluke that things happened *just* the way they did – and that is right: it is a fantastic fluke that things came out *just* the way they did. However, the counterfactual information will make it clear that, despite all sorts of things going rather differently from the way they actually did, the body in question would still have ended up near the food and the other bodies around the table. The body ending up near the food and near the table will be no more a fluke than a heat-seeking rocket's ending up near a heat source. What is true, though, is that the language of psychology gives us a way of describing in a non-trivial manner the various perturbations that would in all probability not prevent the body ending up near the food. Just as a language with 'is greater than', as well as 'seven', 'ten' and so on, gives us the resources to describe the variations on how things actually went that would still mean that the electron moves northwards, so the language of psychology gives us the resources to describe the variations on how things actually went that would still mean that the body ended up near the food. In this sense, the laws of psychology might be described as autonomous, though we suspect that some advocates of the autonomy of psychology have had something stronger (and more dubious) in mind.

The causal question

Dispositions do not cause their manifestations

We noted that it is causally explanatory to say that something is fragile. This does not mean, though, that it is right to say that an object's fragility causes it to break when it is dropped. We distinguished fragility from the categorical basis of fragility. The former is the same property in all fragile objects, being roughly the property of being such that were it to be dropped, it would break. The latter is the property that varies, or may vary, from fragile object to fragile object, and which causally explains the fragility of an object: perhaps it will be a certain sort of molecular structure in some objects and a certain sort of molecular bonding in other objects. We can think of the first property as a second-order property, the property of having a property that does or would do a certain causal job, and the second as the first-order property that actually does the job in some particular fragile object. Now, when a fragile object is dropped, it is the categorical basis of the object's fragility that gets together with the dropping and the various surrounding factors to cause the breaking, not the fragility itself. There are not two properties of the object that do the causing. Rather, there is one, the categorical basis, and the other, the disposition itself, is possessed by virtue of the fact that the categorical basis does the appropriate causing in the appropriate way. Hence, there is a distinction between a property's being causally explanatory and its being causally efficacious; in particular, second-order properties of having a property that plays a certain causal role are typically causally explanatory, but are not themselves causal. The causing is done by the first-order property that plays the role.

The point is important in discussions of the dispositional theory of colour. We can agree that something like 'x is red iff x is such as to look red in normal circumstances' is a conceptual truth, but this leaves open the metaphysical question of what property redness is. Perhaps it is the second-order property of having a nature such as to look red in normal circumstances, or perhaps it is the first-order nature, the basis of the disposition. The case against opting for the second-order property is that it goes against the intuition that redness is what *makes* objects look red in normal circumstances, that looking red is typically a causal response to redness. For it is the basis that does the causing.

Similar considerations bear on psychological properties in general and content properties in particular. Functional properties do not cause behaviour. Thus, as we noted in our discussion of the identity theory in chapter 6, the problem for functionalists who identify psychological properties with functional properties is that they cannot allow that the itchiness of an itch causes the scratching or that the content of the belief that a tiger is near causes the running. This is the causal problem for psychological explanation.

One response is to point out that we can still insist that properties intimately connected with the itchiness or the 'tiger nearby' content cause behaviour, just as a property intimately connected with fragility causes the breaking. The categorical bases of the functional and dispositional properties do plenty of causing, and that is good enough. We do not have to go down that path, however. If we are right that the type–type identity theory is compatible with functionalism – indeed, is the obvious position for a functionalist to hold – then psychological properties are *not* functional properties. As we put it in the discussion of the identity theory, psychological properties are realizer states, not role states. They are the kinds of states that satisfy the conditions functionalism tells us determine which psychological state a subject is in. The mind is indeed a syntactic engine. But that is consistent with its also being a semantic engine.

There remains an issue to address, however. Suppose that in Jones here and now, the kind of state that is her belief that a tiger is near is neurological state of kind N. N itself will simultaneously satisfy many descriptions, including 'N', 'is belief that a tiger is nearby in Jones here and now', 'is one kind of state that Jones is in here and now', and so on. What makes it true that it is N *qua* belief with this content that explains Jones's running, rather than, say, N *qua* N? Here the answer must be that it is because in causing the running, N is doing the kind of thing that makes it true that it fills the functional role definitive of the belief. When we causally explain Jones's running in terms of her believing that there is a tiger nearby, two conditions must be satisfied: the property that is her believing must do (some of) the causing, and it must do so as part of its functional brief as the property that is her believing. After all, if N did the causing of the running, but in some freakish way that had nothing to do with its belief role, it would be wrong to explain Jones's running away in terms of her belief. Perhaps N (a) played the right role to be the belief that a tiger is nearby but, because Jones desired to be *near* a tiger, *that* role was irrelevant to how her legs moved him away, but (b) by chance, in a way that

Functional properties are not causal

A qua *problem*

had nothing to do with its normal function in Jones, N triggered a series of muscle spasms that made her run to get relief from them. In this case the explanation of her running away is not her having the belief that there is a tiger nearby, but rather her desire for relief from a muscle spasm.

Annotated Reading

A full-scale discussion of psychological explanation set in the context of various philosophies of mind is Jerry Fodor, *Psychological Explanation*. An influential paper defending the autonomy of psychological explanation in particular and the special sciences in general (roughly, those other than physics and physical chemistry) is his 'Special Sciences'. The *virtus dormitiva* question for psychological explanation has centre stage in Daniel Dennett, 'Skinner Skinned'. The story about neuroscientific explanation (by a Martian in his version) of the bottle of wine is told, with a different moral from ours, by Dennett in 'True Believers'. A radical version of an autonomy of psychology thesis which we do not discuss can be found in various writings of Donald Davidson. 'Mental Events' would be a good place to start. Some of the issues raised by the question of whether functional properties are causes are discussed in more detail in Frank Jackson, 'Mental Properties, Essentialism and Causation'.

Glossary

accidental properties
A property of something is accidental if that thing (or kind) could have failed to possess it. A red triangle could have been some other colour, and, therefore, being red is an accidental property of red triangles. However, no triangle could have failed to have at least one side, and so having at least one side is not an accidental property of triangles.

action
Actions are things we do, like signalling a taxi. The contrast is with mere bodily movement. You should be aware that the term 'behaviour' in the philosophy of mind sometimes slides between action and movement.

analytical behaviourism
The view that the meaning of the various mental state terms can be given by specifying the relevant behaviours or dispositions to behave for each. The concept of a mental state is the concept of behavioural disposition.

analytical functionalism
The view that the meaning of mental state terms can be analysed in terms of functional roles. Because the most plausible candidates to be the meaning-giving functional roles are the folk roles – the roles that common sense most centrally associates with the various mental states. In practice, analytical functionalism is usually identified with common-sense functionalism.

attribute dualism
The view of the mind that holds mental states to be material or physical states with special immaterial or non-physical attributes (properties). Sometimes called property dualism.

behaviourism
The view that mental states are behaviours or dispositions to behave.

belief–desire psychology
Psychology according to the principle that the behaviour of subjects with beliefs and desires typically leads to the satisfaction of their desires if their beliefs are true.

beliefs *de dicto*
See: beliefs *de se*.

beliefs *de se*
Some beliefs are about the way the world is: examples are the belief that there are 18 million people living in a country called Australia, and the belief that neutrinos exist. Their contents are typically given by sentences that do not contain phrases like 'me myself' or 'her herself'. They are beliefs *de dicto*. Other beliefs are not so much about how the world is, but rather about where the believer is located in the world, or more generally about how things are with the believer. The contents of these beliefs *de se* are typically given by sentences that refer back to the believer, as in 'He believes that he himself has a tiger behind him'. Similarly, there are desires *de se*, such as Mary's desire that she herself learns what it is like to see red.

Blockhead
A creature, famously imagined by Ned Block, which behaves in a way which seems intelligent by virtue of 'following' a huge, internally inscribed look-up tree.

bridge laws
Laws which link states of affairs described at one level with states of affairs described at another, typically lower, level. A classic example is the set of laws linking the thermodynamic properties of gases with their statistical-mechanical ones.

broad content
Content which depends on environmental and historical factors. In consequence, it need not be in common between doppelgängers. The contrast is with narrow content, which is in common between doppelgängers. Also called wide content.

categorical
The term is used to mark a contrast with dispositional properties like elasticity and fragility whose possession is essentially tied to

what *would* happen in various circumstances. Squareness is a classic example.

causally closed
The physical world is causally closed if and only if every physical event has a purely physical cause and a purely physical effect. The term comes from the idea that causal relations never take you from the physical to the non-physical.

causal theory of mind
An improvement on behaviourism according to which mental states are not behaviours or dispositions to behave, but are typical causes of behaviour and dispositions to behaviour. Led to analytical functionalism.

chauvinism
Derived from a term for a kind of narrow and bigoted nationalism (and recently used to mean a narrow and bigoted sexism). Chauvinism in the philosophy of mind is the holding of unduly narrow views on the kinds of things that can have mental states.

cluster concepts
Concepts associated with a number of properties. Something falls under a cluster concept if it possesses a goodly number of the properties. Often it is vague just how many of the properties need to be possessed. There is no unique set of properties which is sufficient.

cluster terms
Terms for cluster concepts.

combinatorial explosion
A relatively small number of possibilities each with its own relatively small number of possibilities quickly leads to an enormous number of different combinations of possibilities.

common-sense functionalism
A species of analytical functionalism in which the roles that common sense most centrally associates with the various mental states give the meaning of the mental state terms.

content
The content of the belief that P is variously thought of as its propositional object, as the meaning of 'that P', as how it represents the world as being, and as what individuates it (makes it the belief that it is). The content of the desire that P is variously

thought of as its propositional object, as the meaning of 'that P', as
how the world is desired to be according to it, and as what
individuates it (makes it the desire that it is). The relations between these various conceptions, and the corresponding conceptions for the other intentional states, are highly controversial.

contingent

A contingent sentence or proposition is one that is neither necessarily true nor necessarily false: it is true at some worlds and false at
some worlds. A property is possessed contingently (i.e. is accidental
or not essential) if it is possessed by the thing or kind in question
in the actual world, but not in every world where it exists. Sometimes 'contingent' is used as shorthand for 'contingently true' (i.e.
true in the actual world, but false in some worlds). This should be
apparent from context.

core belief

Language of thought theorists typically do not assign a sentence
of mentalese for every belief in an inclusive sense of belief: there
would not be enough room in the head. Core beliefs are the ones
for which the subject has sentences of mentalese in the belief box
at the time. The other beliefs, the derived ones, in some way
(details vary) derive from these core beliefs. The idea that there is
a distinction between the beliefs most 'before' a person's mind and
ones that are more dispositional in character has also been found
attractive by theorists not wedded to the language of thought and
the core/derived (or similar) terminology.

depth problem

What we are seeing depends in part on what we are causally
responding to. The depth problem is to say which element in the
causal chain that ends with our perception should be designated as
what we are seeing. A similar problem arises for words, in public
language or the language of thought, whose reference depends in
part on a causal chain that ends with a token of the word.

derived belief

See: core belief.

disjunction problem

A problem for co-variance approaches to content. States in us that
typically co-vary with the presence of flowers will also co-vary
with the presence of flowers or very lifelike artificial flowers. The
problem for the co-variance theorist is then to explain how states
can have the content *flower* and not *flower or artificial flower*.

doppelgänger
Usage derived from German mythology by philosophers to mean an intrinsic duplicate. If physicalism is true, a molecule-for-molecule duplicate of you from the skin in would be a doppelgänger of you.

dualism
The view that there is a fundamental, irreducible difference in kind between the physical and material on the one hand and the mental on the other.

egocentric content
Content which is essentially self-involving. Thus, beliefs and desires *de se* have egocentric content.

eliminativism
The view that there are no beliefs and desires, and in general no intentional states or propositional attitudes as conceived in folk psychology.

empirical functionalism
A form of functionalism according to which it is an empirical, a posteriori matter, which roles count as crucial for the possession of mental states.

entailment
A entails *B* iff *B* follows necessarily from *A* . One understanding of entailment in possible worlds terms is that *A* entails *B* iff every world where *A* is true is a world where *B* is true.

epiphenomenalism
Epiphenomenalism about some feature or other of mind is the doctrine that the feature has no causal impact on the material world, while being itself causally influenced by the material world.

essential property
A property that an individual or kind has in every possible world in which it exists is an essential (or non-contingent) property of that individual. It is a property that the individual or kind could not fail to have.

fictionalism
See: instrumentalism.

folk psychology
Our everyday 'folk' theory of mind. Just as folk physics contains commonplaces like that unsupported bodies fall, so folk psychology

contains commonplaces like that people tend to do that which satisfies their desires. So understood, the existence of folk psychology is uncontroversial. However, sometimes the term is used almost as a synonym for some version or other of common-sense functionalism.

full overdetermination

An effect E is fully overdetermined if there are distinct, sufficient, independent causes of E such that E would have been the same in every respect had any one of the causes acted alone.

global supervenience

The kind of supervenience we express in terms of relations between possible worlds rather than between parts of worlds or things in worlds. So A properties globally supervene on B properties just if all the worlds that are alike in the B respect are alike in the A respect.

idealism

The view that everything is at bottom mental.

implication

As we are using the term, logical implication is another term for (logical) entailment. There are important issues in philosophical logic involved here which we steer clear of.

indeterminism

The view that there are some irreducibly chancy events; the laws of nature do not determine whether or not they occur, but rather determine their chance of occurring.

input–output or stimulus–response functionalism

The kind of functionalism which defines mental states solely in terms of the kind of actual and counterfactual behaviour (in circumstances) they produce.

instrumentalism

As a doctrine about beliefs and desires, it is the view that we should see them as instruments for the prediction of behaviour in circumstances. It comes in two varieties: one claims that belief–desire ascriptions are true just if they have the right sort of predictive utility. The other, best called fictionalism, is a version of eliminativism which holds that belief–desire ascriptions are false, but that it is nevertheless predictively useful to pretend that they are true: beliefs and desires are convenient fictions.

intentional stance
Dennett's term for a predictive or explanatory strategy that treats persons, machines or whatever, as more or less rational believers and desirers in order to predict their behaviour.

intentional states
See: propositional attitudes.

interactionism
As applied to dualism it is the doctrine that mental states thought of as non-physical have a causal impact on physical states, and vice versa. Usual versions of the view have the causal interface between mental and physical located somewhere in the brain.

interpretation
In the case of language, the assigning of things, properties and relations to parts of language; in the case of the mind it is usually used for the assigning of intentional states – beliefs, desires and so on – to agents on the basis of what they do.

interpretationism
The view that part of what makes it true that a subject has certain intentional states is the fact that they would be interpreted as having them by a suitably placed expert interpreter of their behaviour.

inter-world supervenience
The kind of supervenience that concerns relations between things of some specified kind possibly located in different possible worlds.

intra-world supervenience
Intra-world supervenience theses concern how things are within all possible worlds, or all possible worlds of some specified sort. Thus the claim that for any world it is true that any two people alike in height in that world are alike in whether they are tall in that world is an intra-world supervenience thesis. But note that the inter-world claim that any two people alike in height in their respective worlds are alike in whether they are tall in their respective worlds is false, for worlds differ in what counts as being tall in them.

intrinsic
Intrinsic features of things concern how the things are in themselves rather than how they interconnect with their surroundings. Squareness is a common illustration. The contrast is with relational or extrinsic properties like being taller than the person next to you.

introspection
A term for the way we are aware of what is going on in our own minds. Introspection is sometimes characterized as a kind of inner sense, though this is itself a debated view in the philosophy of mind.

logical necessity
The broadest, strictest kind of necessity. A sentence or proposition which is logically necessary could not fail to be true in the most inclusive sense: it is true in all possible worlds, not just in all worlds of some restricted kind. A sentence or proposition is logically possible if it is true in at least one possible world in the most inclusive sense.

logical possibility
See: logical necessity.

machine functionalism
A style of functionalism about the mind that draws its inspiration from the fact that input-output devices can be characterized in terms of machine tables. According to machine functionalism, the crucial similarity among psychologically alike beings is in the machine table they implement.

materialism
Used by us and in the more recent literature pretty much as a synonym for physicalism: the doctrine that the universe contains nothing over and above the substances and properties acknowledged in the physical sciences, or some natural extension of them. The term goes back to the idea that matter is the fundamental kind, a view made implausible by recent developments in physics.

mentalese
A term for the language in which thoughts – intentional states or propositional attitudes – are encoded in the brain according to the language of thought hypothesis. Sometimes called 'brain writing'.

mental objects
A traditional view is that mental states like pain and experiencing a red after-image should be understood as relations to mental objects. The usual view today is that we should think of having a pain and experiencing a red after-image as like having a limp. Just as there are no limps, and consequently no relations to them – to have a limp is simply to limp – so there are no things called pains and after-images to which we are related when we are in pain or 'after-imaging'.

metaphysical necessity

We treat metaphysical necessity as necessity in the strictest or widest sense, as truth in all worlds. But, as we noted, sometimes it is suggested that 'water = H_2O' has a different kind of necessity from that possessed by '$2 + 2 = 4$', in which case the term 'metaphysical necessity' is reserved for the first, and the second is called 'logical' or 'conceptual'. Metaphysical possibility is truth in at least one world.

metaphysical possibility

See: metaphysical necessity.

methodological behaviourism

The view that the way to study the mind is via the study of behaviour. No claim is made as such about how to analyse mental language or about the metaphysics of mind. We suggested that many methodological behaviourists are also revisionary behaviourists.

methodological solipsism

As it appears in modern philosophy of mind, the doctrine that in explaining human behaviour we must confine ourselves to how agents are from the skin in, because it is their internal nature which determines how they behave: two internally identical agents will behave in exactly the same way in any given situation. Also known as the principle of autonomy.

modal realism

Sometimes this term is used simply for the view that claims about possibility and necessity are on occasion true, perhaps allied with the view that their truth is to be sharply distinguished from our opinions about their truth. But sometimes what is meant is the view also called extreme modal realism. On this view, the possible worlds' elucidations of the modal notions – for example, that to be necessarily true is to be true in all possible worlds – are to be understood literally in the sense that the possible worlds referred to in the elucidations exist and are as concrete as our world.

multiple realizability

The view, particularly associated with functionalist views of mind, that gross differences in the way various functional roles are realized are compatible with similarities in psychological nature. If 'Martians' are enough like us functionally, then regardless of the very considerable differences in what may realize the relevant functional roles in them and us, they are psychologically exactly like us.

narrow content
Content that is not broad.

necessarily false
A sentence or proposition is necessarily false (impossible) iff it is false at every possible world.

necessarily true
A sentence or proposition is necessarily true iff it is true at every possible world.

nomologically possible
Something is nomologically possible if it is consistent with the laws of nature. This can be spelt out roughly in terms of truth at some world with the same laws as our world. Some things are logically possible which are not nomologically possible (for example, a perpetual motion machine), but of course everything which is nomologically possible is logically possible.

occurrent beliefs
A term used by holders of the view that there is an important distinction between the beliefs of which one is consciously aware, or which are currently guiding behaviour, or some such – these are the occurrent ones – as opposed to those which one would have if such and such happened.

overdetermination
An event is overdetermined if it has multiple sufficient causes.

overdetermination by the non-distinct
An overdetermination that is less than the real McCoy. There are two causes, but one is in some sense not distinct from or is included somehow in the other.

partial overdetermination
An event E is partially overdetermined by C and C' if C and C' both cause E and either by itself would have caused E, but in that case E would have been different in nature.

phenomenal feel
See: qualia.

physicalism
The doctrine that the universe contains nothing over and above the substances and properties acknowledged in the physical sciences, or some natural extension of them. In much current writing, the term 'physicalism' is pretty much interchangeable with

'materialism'; it is used to avoid suggesting a commitment to the superseded view that the universe is entirely composed of matter, and to highlight the role of the physical sciences in settling the doctrine's content.

physical stance

Dennett's term for a predictive or explanatory strategy that focuses on the physical internal nature and surroundings of persons, machines or whatever, in order to predict their behaviour.

possible worlds

Complete (in the sense that every detail is settled) ways that things might be. The actual world is the way things in fact are; it is the universe we live in. Non-actual possible worlds are alternative complete ways things might be.

possibly true

A sentence or proposition is possibly true iff it is true in at least one possible world. Everything which is (actually) true is of course automatically possibly true.

practical rationality

Behaviour is practically rational to the extent that it serves the desires of agents according to their beliefs; or in other words obeys the axiom of belief–desire psychology.

pre-emptive overdetermination

Sometimes a cause as well as bringing about an effect prevents something else from bringing about that same effect. The effect is overdetermined in that had what actually did the causing not happened, the stand-by 'cause' would have stepped in and done the job. The actual cause is said to pre-empt the stand-by one, and the situation is described as one of pre-emptive overdetermination.

principle of charity

The principle that in interpreting another we must start from the presumption that their beliefs are largely true, or in some versions, that their beliefs are largely the same as ours, that is, true by our lights.

principle of humanity

The principle that in interpreting others we must start from the presumption that their beliefs are largely the ones we would have in their circumstances, even if this means that they would be interpreted as having largely false beliefs due to their unfortunate circumstances.

productivity
Productivity is the feature of many languages whereby they can
generate indefinitely many new sentences from old ones. For example, we can insert 'the daughter of' into 'Jane is the daughter of
Mary' to produce 'Jane is the daughter of the daughter of Mary',
and we can conjoin any two sentences to form a new sentence,
their conjunction. Thought is also productive – we can think quite
new thoughts – and some take this as evidence for a language of
thought.

proposition
Propositions are variously said to be what sentences express, the
meanings of sentences, the objects of the propositional attitudes,
and to be sets of possible worlds or sets of truth conditions. The
relations between these conceptions are matters of controversy.
We mainly used the term in the 'sets of worlds' sense.

propositional attitudes
Those mental states that can be viewed as attitudes taken to
propositions and which we describe using indicative sentences in
'that' constructions. If you take the attitude of acceptance to the
proposition that it is hot here, then you believe that it is hot here.
If you take the attitude of wanting the proposition that it is hot in
here to be true, then you desire that it is hot in here. Also known
as intentional states.

qualia (sing. quale)
The properties (allegedly) distinctive of those psychological states
known as raw feels, or as experiences with a phenomenal character
for which there is something it is like to be in them. Examples are
colour perceptions and bodily sensations. Sometimes the term is
given a more restricted use to mean these distinctive properties
conceived of as properties that refute physicalism.

Ramsey sentence
A technical device for making it explicit that certain definitions of
theoretical terms in terms of their interconnections are not viciously circular.

reductions in science
Some of the most dramatic advances in science involve showing
how a theory about how things are at one level can be recovered
from a theory about how things are at some lower level. The
theory at the higher level is said to be reduced to the theory at the

lower level. The two famous examples we give in the text are the reduction of the thermodynamic theory of gases to the kinetic theory via statistical mechanics, and the reduction of genetics to molecular biology via the identification of genes with sequences of DNA.

reference
Traditionally, the relation between words in a language on the one hand, and things and features in the world on the other, which allows us to use the words to make claims in sentences about the things and features. A theory of reference is a theory about what makes it true that the words refer to what they do in fact refer to. Language of thought theorists also talk of reference as the relation between the words of mentalese and things and features, and philosophers of mind often now talk of reference more generally as the relation between representational units, be they in a public language or in the head, and what they represent.

revisionary behaviourism
A behaviourism which admits that mental concepts and terms as they now stand cannot be analysed behaviouristically, but advocates revising them along behaviourist lines. In other words, it is granted that analytical behaviourism is false, but we are urged to refine our terms and concepts so as to make it true.

rigid designators
Terms which pick out the very same individual or kind in every possible world in which the individual occurs.

rigidification
The process of making a descriptive term rigid by fixing on what satisfies the description in the actual world. In consequence the term refers in every world to that which satisfies the description in the actual world. For example, 'the tallest woman' picks out different women in different worlds, but 'the actually tallest woman' picks out in every world w in which she exists the person who is the tallest woman in the actual world whether or not that person is the tallest in w.

semantics
Semantics is to do with the interpretations or meanings that attach to words and sentences in the case of language, and to intentional states in the case of the mind. It is in virtue of having a semantics that words and sentences in a language can make claims about how

things are, and it is in virtue of having mental states with a semantics that subjects represent how the world is, or how they would like it to be. Semantics is contrasted with syntax. In the case of language, syntax concerns questions of grammar, sentence structure and so on. As applied to mental items, supporters of the language of thought often use 'syntax' for the syntax of that language, but the term is also used more generally for the non-representational properties – shape, structure, neurological properties and so on – of internal representations.

sequential overdetermination
What happens today is the causal outcome of what happened yesterday, which in turn is the outcome of what happened the day before. In this sense what happens today is overdetermined, but obviously this is not an interesting sense of overdetermination; it simply reflects the familiar fact that there are causal chains.

strong externalism
The view that some intentional states are in part located outside the head. It goes beyond the view that external factors are essentially involved in determining the contents of intentional states like belief and desire by holding in addition that beliefs and desires themselves are located in part outside the head.

substance dualism
The kind of dualism according to which there are two fundamentally different kinds of substances in the world: physical substances and non-physical substances. As a theory of mind, the view is that the non-physical substance is 'where' the mind is (the quote-marks are because usually it is also claimed that the mind is in time but not in space).

supervenient behaviourism
A close cousin to input–output functionalism. It holds that mental states supervene on behavioural dispositions – subjects exactly alike in behavioural dispositions are exactly alike in psychology.

systematicity
Most languages that can express that Mary is Jane's employer can also express that Jane is Mary's employer; similarly, if they can express that someone is Mary's emloyer, they can express that someone is Jane's employer. They have the property of systematicity. Thought also has systematicity – for example, if you can think that

Mary is taller than Jane, you can think that Jane is taller than
Mary – and some take this as evidence for a language of thought.

tacit
Silent or unspoken.

teleonomy
The enterprise of finding purposes in the natural world via the
theory of natural selection. Something's purpose is what it was
selected for. Some current philosophers of mind give this notion
of purpose an important role in the determination of the content of
mental states.

theory of reference
See: reference.

Turing test
Alan Turing proposed that if competent human experimenters
communicating with a computer through a teletype terminal for
an extended period are unable to tell whether they are typing to a
machine or a human, then the machine is intelligent. In current
discussions it is common to say that something is Turing-test
intelligent, or passes the Turing test, when its performance on a
suitable quiz compares with ours.

verificationism
The view that the meaning of a sentence is given by the circumstances which would verify it.

virtual machine
When the workings of a computer of one kind are emulated in
detail by a computer of another physical kind, the emulation is
said to be a virtual machine. Thus the programs which allow you
to run Microsoft™ Windows™ on an Apple™ computer create a
virtual Windows™ machine.

Bibliography

Armstrong, D. M., *A Materialist Theory of the Mind*, Routledge and Kegan Paul, London, 1968.

Armstrong, D. M., *Belief, Truth and Knowledge*, Cambridge University Press, Cambridge, 1973.

Armstrong, D. M., and Norman Malcolm, *Consciousness and Causality*, Basil Blackwell, Oxford, 1984.

Bigelow, John, and Robert Pargetter, *Science and Necessity*, Cambridge University Press, Cambridge, 1990.

Block, Ned, 'Psychologism and Behaviourism', *Philosophical Review*, 90 (1981), pp. 5–43.

Block, Ned, 'Troubles with Functionalism', in Block, ed., *Readings in the Philosophy of Psychology*, vol. 1, pp. 268–305.

Block, Ned, 'What is Functionalism?', in Block, ed., *Readings in the Philosophy of Psychology*, vol. 1, pp. 171–84.

Block, Ned, ed., *Readings in the Philosophy of Psychology*, vol. 1, Methuen, London, 1980.

Block, Ned, ed., *Readings in the Philosophy of Psychology*, vol. 2, Harvard University Press, Cambridge, Mass., 1981.

Block, Ned, and Jerry Fodor, 'What Psychological States are Not', *Philosophical Review*, 81 (1972), pp. 159–81. Reprinted in Block, ed., *Readings in the Philosophy of Psychology*, vol. 1.

Braddon-Mitchell, David, and John Fitzpatrick, 'Explanation and the Language of Thought', *Synthese*, 81 (1990), pp. 373–89.

Burge, Tyler, 'Individualism and Psychology', *Philosophical Review*, 95 (1986), pp. 3–46.

Burge, Tyler, 'Individualism and the Mental', *Midwest Studies in Philosophy*, 5 (1979), pp. 73–122. Reprinted in Rosenthal, ed., *The Nature of Mind*.

Campbell, Keith, *Body and Mind*, Macmillan, London, 1970.

Chalmers, David, *The Conscious Mind*, Oxford University Press, Oxford, 1996.

Child, William, *Causality, Interpretation, and the Mind*, Clarendon Press, Oxford, 1994.

Churchland, Paul, 'Eliminative Materialism and the Propositional Attitudes', *Journal of Philosophy*, 78 (1981), pp. 67–90. Reprinted in Lycan, ed., *Mind and Cognition*.

Churchland, Paul, *Matter and Consciousness*, 2nd edn, MIT Press, Cambridge, Mass., 1988.

Churchland, Paul, and Patricia Churchland, 'Stalking the Wild Epistemic Engine', *Noûs*, 17 (1983), pp. 5–18.

Copeland, Jack, *Artificial Intelligence*, Basil Blackwell, Oxford, 1993.

Davidson, Donald, *Essays on Actions and Events*, Clarendon Press, Oxford, 1980.

Davidson, Donald, *Inquiries into Truth and Interpretation*, Clarendon Press, Oxford, 1984.

Davidson, Donald, 'Mental Events', in L. Foster and J. Swanson, eds, *Experience and Theory*, University of Massachusetts Press, Amherst, 1970, pp. 79–101. Reprinted in Rosenthal, ed., *The Nature of Mind*, and Davidson, *Essays on Actions and Events*.

Davies, Martin, and I. L. Humberstone, 'Two Notions of Necessity', *Philosophical Studies*, 38 (1980), pp. 1–30.

Davies, Martin, and Glyn W. Humphreys, eds, *Consciousness*, Basil Blackwell, Oxford, 1993.

Dennett, Daniel, *Consciousness Explained*, Little, Brown and Company, Boston, 1991.

Dennett, Daniel, *The Intentional Stance,* MIT Press, Cambridge, Mass., 1987.

Dennett, Daniel, 'Skinner Skinned', in *Brainstorms*, Harvester Press, Brighton, 1979, pp. 53–70.

Dennett, Daniel, 'True Believers', in Rosenthal, ed., *The Nature of Mind*, pp. 339–53.

Devitt, Michael, and Kim Sterelny, *Language and Reality*, Basil Blackwell, Oxford, 1987.

Dretske, Fred, *Explaining Behaviour*, MIT Press, Cambridge, Mass., 1988.

Evans, Gareth, *The Varieties of Reference*, Clarendon Press, Oxford, 1982.

Field, Hartry, 'Mental Representation', in Block, ed., *Readings in the Philosophy of Psychology*, vol. 2, pp. 78–114.

Flanagan, Owen, *Consciousness Reconsidered,* MIT Press, Cambridge, Mass., 1992.

Fodor, Jerry, *The Language of Thought*, Thomas Crowell, New York, 1975.

Fodor, Jerry, 'Methodological Solipsism Considered as a Research Strategy in Cognitive Psychology', *Behavioral and Brain Sciences*, 3 (1980), pp. 63–110. Reprinted in Rosenthal, ed., *The Nature of Mind*.

Fodor, Jerry, *Psychological Explanation*, Random House, New York, 1968.

Fodor, Jerry, *Psychosemantics,* MIT Press, Cambridge, Mass., 1988.

Fodor, Jerry, *A Theory of Content and Other Essays*, MIT Press, Cambridge, Mass., 1990.

Fodor, Jerry, 'Special Sciences', *Synthese*, 28 (1974), pp. 97–115. Reprinted in Block, ed., *Readings in the Philosophy of Psychology*, vol. 1.

Gettier, Edmund, 'Is Justified True Belief Knowledge?', *Analysis*, 23 (1963), pp. 121–3.

Grandy, Richard, 'Reference, Meaning and Belief', *Journal of Philosophy*, 70 (1973), pp. 439–52.

Grice, H. P., 'Meaning', *Philosophical Review*, 66 (1957), pp. 377–88.

Harman, Gilbert, *Thought*, Princeton University Press, Princeton, NJ, 1973.

Horgan, Terence, 'From Supervenience to Superdupervenience: Meeting the Demands of a Material World', *Mind*, 102 (1993), pp. 555–86.

Jackson, Frank, 'Epiphenomenal Qualia', *Philosophical Quarterly*, 32 (1982), pp. 127–36. Reprinted in Lycan, ed., *Mind and Cognition*.

Jackson, Frank, 'Mental Properties, Essentialism and Causation', *Proceedings of the Aristotelian Society*, 95 (1995), pp. 253–68.

Jackson, Frank, 'What Mary Didn't Know', *Journal of Philosophy*, 83 (1986), pp. 291–5. Reprinted in Rosenthal, ed., *The Nature of Mind*.

Jackson, Frank, and Philip Pettit, 'Functionalism and Broad Content', *Mind*, 107 (1988), pp. 381–400.

Jackson, Frank, Robert Pargetter, and Elizabeth Prior, 'Functionalism and Type–Type Identity Theories', *Philosophical Studies*, 42 (1982), pp. 209–25.

Kahneman, Daniel, Paul Slovic, and Amos Tversky, *Judgment under Uncertainty: Heuristics and Biases*, Cambridge University Press, Cambridge, 1982.

Kripke, Saul, *Naming and Necessity*, Basil Blackwell, Oxford, 1980.

Kripke, Saul, 'A Puzzle about Belief', in A. Margalit, ed., *Meaning and Use*, Reidel, Boston, 1979.

Lakatos, I., and E. Zahar, 'Why Copernicus's Programme Superseded Ptolemy's', in J. Worrall and G. Currie, eds, *The Methodology of Scientific Research Programmes*, Cambridge University Press, Cambridge, 1978, pp. 168–92.

Lewis, David, 'An Argument for the Identity Theory', *Journal of Philosophy*, 63 (1966), pp. 17–25.

Lewis, David, *On the Plurality of Worlds*, Basil Blackwell, Oxford, 1986.

Lewis, David, 'Psychophysical and Theoretical Identifications', *Australasian Journal of Philosophy*, 50 (1972), pp. 249–58. Reprinted in Rosenthal, ed., *The Nature of Mind*.

Lewis, David, 'Reduction of Mind', in Samuel Guttenplan, ed., *A Companion to Philosophy of Mind*, Basil Blackwell, Oxford, 1994.

Lewis, David, 'What Experience Teaches', in Lycan, ed., *Mind and Cognition*, pp. 499–519.

Lycan, W. G., ed., *Mind and Cognition: A Reader*, Basil Blackwell, Oxford, 1990.

McGinn, Colin, 'Charity, Interpretation, and Belief', *Journal of Philosophy*, 74 (1977), pp. 521–35.

McGinn, Colin, *Mental Content*, Basil Blackwell, Oxford, 1989.

McGinn, Colin, *The Problem of Consciousness*, Basil Blackwell, Oxford, 1990.

Millikan, Ruth, *White Queen Psychology*, MIT Press, Cambridge, Mass., 1993.

Moore, A. W., ed., *Meaning and Reference*, Oxford University Press, Oxford, 1993.

Nagel, Thomas, 'What is it Like to be a Bat?', *Philosophical Review*, 83 (1974), pp. 435–50.

Nisbet, R., and L. Ross, *Human Inference: Strategies and Shortcomings of Social Judgment*, Prentice-Hall, Englewood Cliffs, NJ, 1980.

Papineau, David, *Philosophical Naturalism*, Basil Blackwell, Oxford, 1993.

Peacocke, Christopher, *Sense and Content*, Oxford University Press, Oxford, 1983.

Pessin, Andrew, ed., *The Twin Earth Chronicles*, Paragon House, New York, 1995.

Pettit, Philip, and John McDowell, eds, *Subject, Thought, and Context*, Clarendon Press, Oxford, 1986.

Putnam, Hilary, 'The Meaning of "Meaning"', in *Mind, Language and Reality*, Cambridge University Press, Cambridge, 1975, pp. 215–71.

Putnam, Hilary, 'The Nature of Mental States', in *Mind, Language and Reality*, Cambridge University Press, Cambridge, 1975, pp. 429–40. Reprinted in Lycan, ed., *Mind and Cognition*, and in Block, ed., *Readings in the Philosophy of Psychology*, vol. 1.

Putnam, Hilary, *Representation and Reality*, MIT Press, Cambridge, Mass., 1988.

Quine, W. V., 'On Mental Entities', in *The Ways of Paradox*, Random House, New York, 1966, pp. 208–14.

Ramsey, F. P., 'General Propositions and Causality', in *The Foundations of Mathematics*, Harcourt Brace, New York, 1931, pp. 237–55.

Rorty, Richard, 'Mind–Body Identity, Privacy and Categories', *Review of Metaphysics*, 19 (1965), pp. 24–54.

Rosenthal, David, ed., *The Nature of Mind*, Oxford University Press, Oxford, 1991.

Ryle, Gilbert, *The Concept of Mind*, Hutchinson, London, 1949.

Searle, John, 'Is the Brain's Mind a Computer Program?', *Scientific American*, 262 (1990), pp. 20–5.

Searle, John, 'Minds, Brains, and Programs', *Behavioral and Brain Sciences*, 3 (1980), pp. 417–24. Reprinted in Rosenthal, ed., *The Nature of Mind*.

Searle, John, *Intentionality*, Cambridge University Press, Cambridge, 1983.

Searle, John, *The Rediscovery of the Mind*, MIT Press, Cambridge, Mass., 1992.

Segal, Gabriel, 'Seeing What is Not There', *Philosophical Review*, 98 (1989), pp. 189–214.

Shoemaker, Sydney, 'Functionalism and Qualia', *Philosopical Studies*, 27 (1975), pp. 292–315. Reprinted in Rosenthal, ed., *The Nature of Mind*.

Shoemaker, Sydney, *Identity, Cause and Mind*, Cambridge University Press, Cambridge, 1984.

Skinner, B. F., *About Behaviourism*, Jonathan Cape, London, 1974.

Smart, J. J. C., 'Sensations and Brain Processes', *Philosophical Review*, 68 (1959), pp. 141–56. Reprinted in Rosenthal, ed., *The Nature of Mind*.

Smith, Peter, and O. R. Jones, *Philosophy of Mind*, Cambridge University Press, Cambridge, 1986.

Stalnaker, Robert, 'Assertion', in P. Cole, ed., *Syntax and Semantics*, vol. 9, Academic Press, New York, 1978, pp. 315–32.

Stalnaker, Robert, *Inquiry*, MIT Press, Cambridge, Mass., 1984.

Sterelny, Kim, *The Representational Theory of Mind*, Basil Blackwell, Oxford, 1990.

Stich, Stephen, *From Folk Psychology to Cognitive Science*, MIT Press, Cambridge, Mass., 1983.

Stich, Stephen, *The Fragmentation of Reason*, MIT Press, Cambridge, Mass., 1990.

Tye, Michael, *The Imagery Debate*, MIT Press, Cambridge, Mass., 1991.

Wittgenstein, Ludwig, *Philosophical Investigations*, trans. G. E. M. Anscombe, Basil Blackwell, Oxford, 1953.

Woodfield, Andrew, ed., *Thought and Object*, Clarendon Press, Oxford, 1982.

Index